# BEING RAISED UP

BY

**Christine G. Roberts**

PublishAmerica
Baltimore

First printing

Photos done by Alecia Alexander, Alexander Photocraft in Rome, GA

Scriptures quoted from The Holy Bible, New Century Version, copyright 1987, 1988, 1991 by Word Publishing, Dallas Texas 75039. Used by permission

PublishAmerica has allowed this work to remain exactly as the author intended, verbatim, without editorial input.

Hardcover 978-1-4626-0952-9
Softcover 978-1-4626-0951-2
PUBLISHED BY PUBLISHAMERICA, LLLP
www.publishamerica.com
Baltimore

Printed in the United States of America

# Table of Contents

# FOREWORD

This is a book about a girl being abused. Not just physical, but emotional, sexual, verbal and spiritual. I was literally getting abused twenty-four hours a day, seven days a week. Even at church where everyone says is a sanctuary, immunity afforded by refuge, in such a place and nothing bad ever happens there. Believe me even not being in some kind of cult, like you see in the news, a "normal" church can no longer be a safe haven. But one that people is abused so bad that they are shunned out and end up having post traumatic stress disorder or what is known as PTSD. I even ended up trying to kill myself two times. This made me to be listed as a suicide potential when I was only twenty years old. I've had to get counseling for my rape thirty years later. The physical and emotional abuse I didn't get till I was forty-six years old. The spiritual abuse I just started last year and I am still working getting over it thanks to the new home (church) I go to now. This is why 10% of every sale of this book goes to the church I belong to that has helped me in so many ways through all of this and encouraged me to get counseling. Because of this the names in this book have been changed.

They were the ones who encouraged me to get counseling for the physical and emotional abuse I was keeping hidden. Now that I found out that I was spiritually abused I am working on that. There really is a family for someone out there. Sometimes it might just be a spiritual one since your physical one isn't there anymore. Believe me you can be a survivor from all of this.

# BEING RAISED UP

It seems like places I go to or people I talk to always tell me the same thing. "Family comes first."

"I would do anything for my relatives."

"Family is sacred." It isn't just where I live now that I hear it, but I have lived in other places where they say those types of things and different religions and people who talk to me who are from other backgrounds. They all agree on the same thing. Me? I have never heard of that, nor have I even seen that as an example. For me I guess my life has been one of an outcast or in some places like a bomb that has been dropped into the lives of others. I have this weird look on my face when I hear this expression. When I tell people about my life they almost have a heart attack or cannot even comprehend that something like this can even happen to someone.

If you think this cannot happen or you feel like someone on a TV episode that is rated PG14 and is too hard for you to handle I recommend you put this book down and do not even read further than this page. Because believe me this will get worse. Between the stories I'll be posting on here, flashbacks that I have had it will probably give someone else a flashback and I've seen some people who say they are experts and are not be able to handle hearing some of these things that I've gone through. Even writing this I have to stop what I am doing and quit writing this down, leave the room and go cry, vent or even worse go throw up, because I am literally reliving what I just wrote down and have to "get it out of my system" before I come back and finish where I left off.

You have been warned before reading further…

Thank you for coming back or deciding to continue from the previous page. It took a lot of guts to continue on and be brave to decide to read on, but believe me it will be worth it. Not only can you see what or traumatic one person's life can be you will learn a lot from it. No there won't be any quizzes later, but it will be worth your time to read this. Thanks again.

One of the things I've noticed is that my dad was told that girls don't cry. He was an only child so he was being a boy, but was taught that kids don't cry either. So when he had five girls, a wife and later his mom living with us when she had cancer. So one of the rules in the house was nobody cries in this house. He didn't have to so he wasn't going to deal with it in this house. If someone cried in this house you were told not to. If that didn't work you got smacked in the face. If that didn't work there were other options to quickly "train" you not to. Almost makes you think we were animals instead of people. We had a dog and a bird. Sometimes looking at them I felt like they were freer than we were. I wanted to trade places with them or wish I was an animal since they got treated better than we did. During my lifetime we had pet birds, dogs, cat and even a chicken while living in Texas so you can see why I felt they were treated better than the family. It has been proven over and over again that people who abuse children usually are abusing the pets first, then the kids and then the adults. In this case the kids, wife were abused and not the pets. Doing this book has brought out a lot of things I didn't even know was repressed memory until now. One of the earliest things I remembered was…

# NEVADA

Swearing

My dad would swear all the time. Even when he would just tell a story about what happened at work and laugh about it. Use the Lord's name in vain every day. It would be amazing if he went a day without doing that. I could tell my mom wanted to leave the room, but wasn't able to and had to stay there with her hand supporting her like she was getting bored to death. He would ask her if she was getting bored. She would say "No." and he would end up yelling at her. As soon as he found out she was lying he would get furious and hit her. He didn't just swear once a day, but several times a day. It didn't matter if he was at work or it was his day off.

He would even use it in a conversation with friends. The more frustrated he got about anything the more swearing we heard from him. The more he drank the more swearing we heard. Like I said it didn't take much of anything to get him started. The question is when he was going to stop.

One time I remember him using a vintage reel to reel player and was listening to their wedding on it. My mom wanted to hear it again since she hadn't heard it in ages. What happened? He got drunk again, angry and started yelling at everyone while swearing every word in the book. He took the player with their wedding on it and beginning heading toward the door. My mom frantically yelling at him. "No!"

"Don't do it!" hoping and praying he wouldn't do what she thought he was planning on doing. He went outside and threw the machine on the ground and busted it so bad that not even he could fix it.

My mom ran out of the room crying and devastated that she will never be able to hear it again. My dad came back in yelling. "Are you happy now?" Waiting for my mom to say something and she wasn't there. He looked at me and yelled. "What do you want?"

I knew what that meant after hearing it twenty times already. I ran out of the room in a hurry. My dad was in the room all by himself. That happened a lot. I don't know if he enjoyed it like that or if he just got used to it being like that. Where he was alone and no one was around to bother him.

Sometimes I think that is another reason he drank. He was raised up like that where everyone in the family drank. Both of his parents were heavy drinkers. During their time they didn't associate medical problems with drinking and if you didn't drink you were considered an outcast for not socializing. His mother took it to an extreme.

Living Here

Keep in mind that Las Vegas is like a fast paced world. The city that never sleeps. Everything is going on twenty-four hours a day seven days a week. Every time a new celebrity was performing a hotel or someplace doing something. There would be two search lights that you can see for miles. Where you live I bet you never see those unless something big is going on.

I remember one time hearing that a store called seven eleven were now going to be open twenty-four hours for your convenience. I couldn't understand why they were saying that. The seven eleven that we would go to was already opened twenty-fours a day. My mom had to explain to me that some other places had seven eleven stores that weren't open then. They first started only being open from seven in the morning to eleven at night. This is why it is called seven eleven.

They would do things to even get the local people to come to their hotels. For example the hotel would give you coupons to use their slot machines. Like a roll of coins free to use play the slot machines. Then you were glued to the machines that you would buy more rolls and play more. Plus souvenirs for the kids. Like a plastic slot machine where the handle moves. A deck of cards with a hole punched in so they know you weren't sneaking in a new deck to cheat with and ash trays with their logo on it. A coupon could be used to get a free drink.

My mom would tell me about how they used to have a program where you would get a roll of coins and a couple of free drinks if you have your paycheck cashed at the hotel. Another way to get local people in. My mom enjoyed it. She would take the coins and play the slot machines. My dad would go to the bar and get the free drinks. She missed it when they stopped it.

Over in Vegas you see them so much that you can sleep through them. Billboards wouldn't advertise for cigarettes or other merchandise, but just who is performing at what hotel. Things are so different here. Please keep that in mind while you are reading this chapter.

## Lip Reading

My Dad had to repeat things over and over again since I had trouble hearing. I would only hear part of what he was saying so I didn't know what to say. He got mad at me for not listening to him. After he had to repeat things a few times he would be mad at me to the point where he would hit me with the belt he wore on his pants. To make sure I got the message he would make sure the buckle would hit me, causing the most pain. I wanted to get away from him hitting me so I backed up. He hit me, when I was backing up so he didn't hit me where he was planning on doing it at.

He wouldn't hit me on the rear end like other parents would do to discipline their kids. I saw him getting ready to take his belt off and began running. He quickly grabbed me and made me sit down. I was terrified from the fear of what would happen. He was aiming for my knees to make a clean straight line going over my knees to teach me a lesson. I moved and he ended up hitting me on the area below the knees on the front of the legs. This in turn made him very angry. He yelled at me, grabbed my left leg. To make sure I didn't go anywhere. I panicked and tried to back up again. He yelled "Stop it!" I was so scared all I could think of was to run off. When he pulled me back since he was getting ready to hit me again.

He would yell at me demanding I repeat what he said to me. I never did hear what he said so I guessed it. I was wrong at my guessing. He got ready to hit me again. Again I pulled away. It all happened again so he did it again. I guessed wrong and so I got hit again. This happened over and over and each time he was getting angrier and angrier from the frustration of me not getting it right. He thought I wasn't paying attention to him. Plus trying to get away and all this drinking he was doing.

This kept going on and on. I kept watching how he was taking. Getting to the point where got closer and closer to figure out what he was saying. Even though I couldn't hear him I did it till I finally guessed it right. I don't know if I passed out from all of it or not. There was bleeding during and after it stopped. Now I have scars to prove it. The left leg that he was grabbing is closer to my knee than the right.

I ended up being a good lip reader from this. So next time when he said Something, I couldn't hear him and I would be able to lip read what he said. This way I would not get hit again. Just like when I wasn't able to hear him. (when I was four) Today, every time I would go to a doctor's office they would enquire about it since the scars are so unusual for anyone to have. Even today it hurts when I get on my knees from all of this. People would hear cracking noises and wonder where it is coming from.

I can see why God wanted me to be so good at this. It came especially handy when I was in seventh grade. But even today I use lip reading so much. Like if the orchestra director says something to me and I can't hear him, I can lip read what he is saying. I use it almost everyday so God was definitely teaching me something I needed to know all through my life. Again he knows what we need. Even if you don't.

Swing

I would have these seizures that are called, complex partial seizures, where you would just stare. I was on a swing. Swinging upward and you are up in the air. Then I had a complex partial seizure and ended up letting go of the swing. I remember falling backwards toward the ground. It was like watching a show in slow motion. Doctors refer to this as dissociation. It is God's way of protecting people through a dramatic event. Especially at a young age. I remember my hands letting go of the swing and falling toward the ground. Looking back now I can Jesus' hands grabbing me as I release the swing, grabbing me and gently laying me on the ground to protect me. I was knocked out for a bit and I woke up. Afterwards I was crying from getting hurt. My mom ran out and I ended up going to the doctor.

Apparently I had a broken leg. My right one was broken to the point to where they had to put a cast on it. I knew how to walk, but I hadn't started kindergarten yet so I ended up getting around the house by crawling like a toddler while wearing the cast till my leg was better and I could walk on it again.

Because of what happened with the belt on my knees and this, sometimes I feel like my right leg was not properly developed. I can even see where my leg is turned in some compared to my left one. Plus today it hurts if I do certain things. It definitely shows where God is in control. I could have died from a head injury. Considering what happened to my legs it is amazing I ended up being as good as a runner that you will see later in this chapter. God certainly knows how to get us out bad circumstances and saves us in times of trouble.

Basketball

There was a street on the other side of where I lived. It had a used alley with a basketball hoop at the end. Of course the neighborhood kids would use it. Plus the other ones that were on the other street like me. We became good friends and play in teams. I was usually last to get picked because of my size.

After they saw me play they ended up picking me a lot to be on their team. I didn't realize I was good at this. Usually the guys would play and the girls didn't play much.

As soon as my dad was home from work everyone was expected to be back. I would rather stay there and play. It didn't matter to me if it got dark or not. I wanted to stay there have fun and avoid going home. My mom understood this. She would tell me. "I know, but we have to be here for dinner when your dad gets home." I dreaded that.

Finally more and more houses were being built on the street so the basketball got moved out and they made that into a through street. So

I ended up finding other things to do. Like having friends who would have me to do things I was good at for example pick pocketing. One of the reasons I didn't like being at the dinner table was…

Dinner Table

All of us would sit around the dinner table. My dad sat at the head of the table. Across from me seated from left to right was my oldest sister Cynthia. Next to her was the second oldest Debbie. Directly across from me was the middle sister Liz. I sat next to my dad. My mom would sit between my older sister Mary and me. So I was sitting closest to dad and Mary was sitting closer to my grandmother. After my grandmother passed away I ended up sitting on the other side of my mom. My dad always had his beer or mixed drinks at the table with him like a kid with their teddy bear. If he was finished it was my mom's job to go get him another one. He wasn't supposed to run out.

While I was sitting between my mom and dad, my dad would pay attention to not what I was eating. My sisters who sat across from me were older and were already "trained" on how to eat. Since I was the youngest I didn't know how to eat the way he wanted it done.

One example was eating spaghetti and meatballs. Some people would twirl their spaghetti. Others would cut them up. I saw my dad twirling his so I would copy it. Apparently I didn't do it right. So of course he yelled at me. He would tell me how to twirl it, if I didn't get it right he would demonstrate it to me.

Of course I still didn't get it right. I don't know if it was my vision or hearing, but I never did get it right. So finally he gave it up and twirled it for me and shoved it in my mouth. I got upset and he took the bottom part of his knife and slammed it on my right hand in the center area with it. I got upset more and he told me to stay there, not leave even if I was going to cry all night. My sisters, who were sitting across from me, all had a worried look on their face. I could see fear in them as if they wanted to leave, but couldn't. After dinner Debbie and Liz came up to my room. They were yelling at me for causing trouble at the dinner table. Plus I almost got them in trouble.

He then ordered my mom to take care of me so he wouldn't have to deal with all the crying. My mom went ahead and cut up the spaghetti for me so I wouldn't get in trouble. She told me that is how she has been eating it since she got married. So she wouldn't get in trouble with him on her eating.

She would rather twirl it the way she wanted to and eat it that way, but we were all trained that it wasn't that way. The sisters who didn't get yelled at or had it right twirled their spaghetti and ate it. The others cut it up so they wouldn't get yelled at. Again showing what is more important in this house.

Even in my teenage years I still didn't get it right and got yelled at again. Spaghetti was just one example. Other foods were supposed to be done right also. I really lost track with which way things were supposed to be eaten which way and how things were supposed to be done at the dinner table. All I know is that I never got it right.

Grocery Store

There was a store near us; of course I didn't know where it was from home since I was only five years old. My mom would take all five of us kids into the store. We would get groceries and come home. I don't know what happened, but no one was around. I couldn't have someone pronounce mom's name since we just called her mom. I went to the parking lot and couldn't find the station wagon.

I didn't see it anywhere. So I didn't know what to do and started walking home. If I was at the school I knew my way home, but this was farther. As far as I knew you could only get there by car. Nobody from my house walked to that place or rode a bike.

Since I was walking home by myself I had to walk across busy intersections where there were traffic lights. I never knew how they worked or what the different colors stood for. Several times I would be walking against the traffic and almost got hit. All I would do is try to get out of their way. All they did was yelling at me just like my dad did at home. So I just got scared.

Apparently what happened was my mom and sisters went home and left me at the store. I was crying trying to figure out a way to get home. No one at that time had cell phones or 911 systems. Back then no one bothered to help you in Las Vegas. I learned early on here, that everyone is for themselves. No one helps the other person. Almost like it was a law in this city, every man for himself.

To this day I still don't know how I got home. All I saw were a lot of cars and intersections. God must have been watching out for me that day. There is no way I could even draw you a map and tell you how to get from the grocery store to my home. It took over thirty minutes for me to finally get home. (If I timed that right) It seemed longer to me. As soon as I got home, I could hear my mom saying lets go get her. As soon as she opened up the door there I was crying. She grabbed me and told me they just figured out I was left at the store. She asked me. "How did you home?" While I was crying I told her "I don't know." She kept apologizing. My sisters, Debbie and Liz, kept saying stuff like "She is just trying to get attention."

"I told you she knew how to get home." Just like usual no one believed me. My question is what took them so long to even notice I wasn't even at home? One answer I know for sure is that good Lord was definitely guiding me home.

I know today I still don't remember what streets I was one. I can visualize the way I went home, but I can't tell you how I got home. So there had to be a higher power involved in this.

Santa Ana Winds

When I was living in Las Vegas, we would have what is known as Santa Ana winds. According to a local meteorologist, this is how he explains the Santa Ana winds. "I know about the conditions that set up Santa Ana winds is that high pressure builds up and centers itself over the upper plateau of northern Nevada and Western Utah. This then results in strong and dry northeast to easterly winds over southern Nevada and southern California. So the barometric pressure is usually higher than usual."

This would affect my seizures the same way a musical sound on a radio would trigger the auras. Because the atmosphere is changing in the room. They would come by between three and four o'clock pm. Pretty much every day like clockwork for certain parts of the year. They would be like a high pitch sound that would trigger my seizures. I learned quickly that my seizures were caused by sound. Now days they think a lot of epileptics are triggered by light so there are signs posted everywhere.

"Warning: If you have epilepsy these lights might trigger a seizure." No one thinks to look for sound or any other reason that triggers seizures. Apparently these winds form when the atmosphere in the air changes. I would play outside in the backyard when the weather was hot. A lot of my relatives would be indoors where the air conditioner was going. It would get up to 120 degrees or higher in the summer. Even the dog would go inside rather than be outdoors with me. So I usually would play by myself. I remember one day when one of these Santa Ana winds came by and was triggering what is now called an aura. My body felt weird. It was hard to describe. I would get a weird feeling in my stomach that would move up to my head.

Sometimes it would move slowly and other times it would move fast. I didn't know what to do or what to even say. I was like a frozen statue. Didn't know if I should go inside and tell someone. At times I was afraid to after all the abuse I got. If I stayed outside what was going to happen. I heard voice, looked around and no one was around in the yard except for me, told me to put my hands up to my face. Since I didn't see anyone I just kept playing. Again I heard the same voice saying the same thing. Finally I knew it had to be someone else. I figured out that it had to be God since there is no way any four year old would know what to do. He told me to put my hands up to my face. I put them up to cheeks and I hear the voice saying "your ears". I put them in my ears.

Then I heard the voice say "Go away" I ended up saying "Go away" out loud. I heard "again" so I said "Go away" again. I ended up pushing myself against the wall of the fence in the backyard and saying "Go away" again and pressing harder on my ears. Finally the weird feeling went away. Doctors today refer to that as biofeedback. There is no way a four year old can learn to do that by themselves. Someone else had to be helping me through that.

My mom would always laugh when she told a story about how I would come into the house, just stare and then run outside again. She loved telling that story to everyone and got a laugh. I had repressed memory from it, that when I heard it over and over I got my memory back when I was in my twenties.

When I got my memory back this is what I told her. What happened was I was having an aura and trying to do the biofeedback. I was loosing on controlling it and I went to see her and tell her what was going on. By the time I got into the kitchen the aura stopped and I ended up having a seizure. (Complex partial where I just stared) Then when it stopped I forgot what I was there for and went back outside. After I told her the story she felt guilty and quit telling people the story.

I've talked to several neurologists about it. It is common to have repressed memory from seizures and then your memory come back later and you remember incidents before and after the seizure, but not during. Hearing the story over and over can cause you to remember things also. Your body is so traumatized from it that you forget things till later. I believe God is using it, because you can't handle it at the time and lets you remember it later when you can handle it.

Today I am on medication. So I don't even get auras when I am sick. I was sick with two different things going on at the same time. I should have had auras and seizures, but I never did. Now I didn't even have the auras. Praise the Lord for helping me on that.

Mother, May I?

When I was a little kid being raised up on Las Vegas, all five of us girls would play a game called "Mother May I". For those of you who aren't familiar with the game. The mother would sit in a chair. The kids would be standing up, in the farthest part of the back yard or a certain distance from the mother. The object of the game is to get to your mother as close as you can by the time ran out. She would say to you for example: "Mary you can move five big steps forward". If you didn't ask "Mother May I?" she would remind you "You didn't say Mother May I" and you were stuck where you are. If you asked "Mother May I?" she would reply "yes". Then you got to move five big steps forward. If she replied "no" then you had to stay where you were. Everyone liked that game. It didn't cost anything to play the game. It gave the mother attention, which she liked and control over the situation. I dreaded playing it myself. I already felt like I was nobody and being the youngest always picked on in the family. Getting picked on at school and home was not good.

Then she would always make sure either Cynthia, Debbie or Liz would win. Thinking back maybe it was because she knew they would leave the house sooner so she wanted to please them since they wouldn't be around much longer, especially since them were already teenagers.

Dust Storm

I was in the backyard playing by myself and the family dog. After being outside for a while, the dog ran inside. I didn't think anything of it and kept playing outdoors. This was during the late 1960's. In Vegas we would have dust storms that showed up at the last minute. They came by without warning like a tornado. Some people would refer to them as black blizzards. Sometimes the dirt would be all over the place that the only thing you can see is the street lights. These street lights were on at the time because it had gotten so dark in a hurry. It reminded me of more of night time than thunderstorm darkness. This one was definitely a severe one. The winds were more than forty- five miles per hour. My mom and neighbors could see it coming from out front. My mom came to get me into the house. You had to get out of there ASAP. Otherwise you could get hurt. Being a kid at the time, I just wanted to stay outside and play.

My mom made sure everything and everyone was in the house. I didn't understand it being so young. My room was on the second floor so I just stayed in my room and watch the cars go by on the road where the intersection was. I was so mad at God for making me stay in my room when I wanted to be outside and play. I wasn't bothering anybody. I kept an eye on the storm.

My mom came in and checked on me. She told me to watch the storm and see what happens. "Nothing is happening."

"I just want to go back outside."

"You can't." She answered. "I have to go downstairs and do some housework."

"Keep an eye on it."

"It is going to be bad." She told me and then left the room.

Sure enough she was right. It got worse. Cars were going up and down the road. The sky got to an unusual shade of brown. I've never seen it before. Tumbleweeds were flying all over the place. Cars were stopping off the side of the road. Fewer and fewer cars were on the road. The ones I could see parked were not moving, but were like blending in with the dirt and everything that was in the air. All the same color. I could see an elcamino going up the road and pulling a u-haul trailer behind it. In case you don't know your cars, an elcamino looks like a half car and half truck. About five minutes later the u-haul trailer was coming down the road with the hitch undone from the elcamino. It looked like it was driving itself.

More likely God was driving it down the road. Every time the hitch would get near the ground and try to stop, the winds from the dust storm would raise the hitch again and it would move on. It came down the intersection, make a right, and again like someone was driving it. I know it sounds so weird, but thinking back it was like God was entertaining me. I wish I had a video camera I would have won ten thousand dollars easily. Ah sorry people they weren't invented yet. At least for personal use.

After it went down the new street for a few feet, the trailer's hitch went up again, turns left and ends up coming down my street. I started panicking, jump out of my chair and have the most shocked look on my face. "Is it coming near my house?" I said getting paranoid.

The hitch did come down a couple of times as it did come near my house. My heart rate was going up and up from all of this. I thought for sure, this was some kind of a sign from God. Like what is this he is trying to tell me. I don't know what I would have done if it did park next to my house. Sure enough the trailer went past my house. I began to feel relieved when it passed my house. It kept going till it passed a few more houses on the same side that my house was on stopped and parked next to the house.

My mom was so excited and came up to the room and asked me if I saw it. I said. "Oh yea."

"I saw it."

"There was no way I could have missed that one." We talked about it some. She went back downstairs. The storm lasted for another half hour and then passed. About an hour after it stopped the guy in his elcamino found his trailer and was surprised that it had gone this far away from him and was totally surprised there wasn't any damage to his stuff. I know a higher power was in complete control of it. No doubt about that one. I never saw another dust storm since then.

Dad's Driving

When we were living in Las Vegas my dad did so much drinking that when he came home from work he would be carrying a six pack of his beer or if he needed too he would bring a big bottle of Jim Beam home. If he already had been drinking the beer the six packs would be down to two cans by now. So if he was doing that he would bring two six packs home instead of one.

My mom would be worried at first depending on how he acted. Since he did so much drinking his body was used to it. He wouldn't appear or act like a drunk because of the absorption rate of the liquor. He could have drank a whole six pack and no one could tell the difference. You would think he didn't have any liquor.

This is before they did breath analyzer tests on people. Not many people were being caught drinking and driving especially here since everyone drank, gamble, prostitution and do other things here that would be illegal in every other state. Sometimes I would hear my mom yelling "Everyone go to your room!" We didn't ask questions and knew that mom saw dad coming toward the house from the kitchen window. She could see him stumbling or doing something else before he got to the door. So we knew we were safer to listen to her and head to our rooms. Once he got to the door mom would open up the door, grab him and kind of help him to a chair and let him fall into the chair since he was so drunk. He would act like some of the guys on TV who would want sex because he was so drunk.

Other times when he was so drunk like that he would be in a mad rage to where we could hear him slapping mom on the face or somewhere else. When we went up the stairs there was a landing area and then you had to go up some more stairs to get to the bedroom area. There was a few bars at the landing spot so we could sit there and watch things. It took quite a while before someone noticed we were there.

One time I was at the landing spot and dad came home drunk. He was slapping mom hard and I didn't say anything, but watched. He finally saw me and ran up the stairs. I ran as fast as I could up the stairs to the bedroom. Dad of course was running faster and caught me. He yelled at me for watching instead of being in bed. It was only five o'clock pm, but since he was drunk and in a bad mood we were supposed to lying in our beds and not causing any trouble.

Of course what happened? I got slapped and beaten up for it. "Don't you do that again!"

"You are not supposed to be watching from that landing!" He yelled. I would be so scared of his yelling and slapping that I wouldn't say anything. Again that isn't what he wanted so he slapped me again thinking I wasn't paying attention or trying to cause trouble. "No wonder you get into trouble so much at school!"

"You do nothing but cause trouble at home too!" He yelled while slapping me several times.

Of course after this I just went to bed crying myself to sleep like I usually did. Still not knowing why I was in trouble and couldn't figure out why I was in this family. Again blaming God for what was happing and I didn't want to go to heaven thinking that if he is my father that he would do nothing, but hit me or abuse me even worse than what my earthly dad was doing.

If we were in the car or a truck that dad was driving he had it all figured it out. He would be drinking and driving. If a cop decided to pull him over he would hand the beer can over to me and I was supposed to hand it to mom. That way the cops would think she was drinking and there was no proof he was. I was the youngest so he would pass it to me since I was sitting in the middle of the pick up.

One time I didn't know what was going on so when he handed the beer to me I took it like I always do. Except this time I tried to drink it. The cop saw me holding the drink. He asked if I was drinking it. My dad said no and he told my mom to hold the beer. She did. When the cop left, my dad hit me for holding the beer. He tried hitting my mom and missed. Of course I got hit again since I was in the middle and he missed my mom. He decided I needed it anyway.

I dreaded sitting there at times when he was drunk. This would happen more than once. We didn't have to be stopped. It would also happen while he was driving. He would want me to do something to her since he couldn't reach her. She told me to pretend I hit her and she would say something to have him think I did hit her when I didn't. He was too plastered by then to even know the difference. If you think about it she was protecting me. By having me not deal with the burden and pretending that she got hit. This was better for her that way, physically, emotionally. It was better for me physically, emotionally and spiritually.

Since my other sisters were older they were in the back of the car or somewhere else in the truck. I was usually in the front since I was they youngest. If they were lucky they were at home and didn't have to ride in the car. But since no one wanted to baby-sit me I was forced to go with the parents. Sometimes I think my mom wanted to use me as a shield from dad in case he didn't handle his booze.

## Grey Area

There have been a few times that I would literally turn "grey". It wouldn't be just one area like a hand or a leg, but all over my body. My mom told me about one incident when I was three.

My mom and I were walking down the street on the sidewalk when we were living in Vegas. She was holding my left hand at the time when I was on her right side. She could feel her right hand going down. "You were getting heavier and heavier." She told me. She could feel her arm going down to the ground. She looked at me and saw that I was grey from my head to my toe.

Immediately she didn't know what to do and carried me back to the house. My dad was inside the house in the kitchen. My mom yelled for him and he rushed over to grab me. He was about to perform mouth to mouth resuscitation on me to get me to breathe again. Just when he got ready to start the process, I gasped for air and began breathing again. My breathing went back to normal again and my color came back to normal.

One reason for the body becoming grey like that is from a lack of oxygen to the brain. They loose consciousness, the heart and circulation is cut off and they literally turn grey and end up dying if not necessitated in time.

Another time was when I was five years old. My mom, sisters and I went to see the circus when it came to Vegas. So there were six of us who went. She didn't realize I wasn't breathing until I was very dark grey. She rushed me to the emergency room and they were able to get me breathing again. Because of this she became paranoid about a circus performance and wouldn't take any of us to see one for fear that I would not breathe again.

A reason for not breathing could be from the drugs. I was taking them for my seizures and they were interacting while I was growing. The dosage on the meds should have been changed when I was growing. I remember the meds always being the same. Even my mom would mention it to me. Nowadays they know about different meds interacting with each other. Back then they didn't. I don't know if I would classify as being dead each time this happened or not.

## Gambling

Since we lived in Las Vegas there were slot machines where ever you went. Grocery stores, airports, convenience stores, parks, pretty much everywhere you go. Of course the law is that you have to be twenty-one to use the machines. I would see people using the machines and the kids would be standing around watching the parents using the machines. If the mother had to go inside the liquor store to go get beer for someone, the kids were left alone where the slot machines were at and those would be our babysitters.

I was left in a store where the slot machines were lined up. Four on each side while my mom went into the liquor part of the store to get what my dad needed for his mixed drinks. She would be gone for a while. So I ended up playing the slot machines. By the time I was ten years old I had it all figured out. You put a coin in, depending on what was on the machine pull the handle maybe halfway down and let go. Then the machine would roll and you get more than your money back. If something else was on the machines pull maybe three fourths of the way or just a quarter of the way down and watch you get more money back than what you put in. If you just got a machine that paid you back quickly go to another one or you will loose what money you just put in. If someone was standing at a machine for a while and they left, take their machine because the odds were in your favor that it will pay off quickly and you will get a cupful or more of the money they just lost. If we didn't have any money to use, there were these new things on newspaper machines and pay phones that would give you your money back. Called coin returns. I had gotten so good at it, that I would get a coin from somewhere and check the machines out. After I examined them all I would go back to the ones that were more likely to give me a return. Eighty percent of the time I got money back. Pretty good for a ten year old?

People didn't know that when the coin returns first came out so I could easily find change when no one would remember. So instead of trying to figure out who lost their money or trying to save it in a piggy bank type of place we would use it for ourselves or gamble it away. Keep in mind this is the same city that would give you tokens for free drinks at the bar and a roll of coins to play the slot machines if you cashed your paychecks at the hotel you gambled at.

Counting cards would work the same way. People use it even today to try and win money from the house. Hotels even have two way mirrors or people "watching" you to see if you are the type of person who would count cards. By the time I was twelve years old I was pretty good at counting cards. Of course I couldn't sneak in to these places, because you had to be at least twenty-one to get in. I would be obvious to someone I was under age, but I could show someone who was and explain them what to do. Then they would pay me for teaching them.

Hyperactivity

As soon as the doctors figured out I had epilepsy. They put me on two types of anti-convulsive medications. One of them made me hyperactive. My sisters would always complain that I would never sit down. I was running in and out of the house. I'm sure some of it was the medication, but I'm sure my dad's abuse was another reason.

So many times it was an automatic reaction for me to leave the room or wherever I was just because my father was in the same room as I was. One of the meds I was on causes hyperactivity in kids. Usually when the kid is growing it is hard to figure out the correct dosage so this can be a problem also.

One time when I was in fourth grade my teacher was abusing me so much that it was even causing me to have more seizures than normally I would have. She wouldn't believe anyone that it wasn't my fault and assumed it was. Between the meds making me hyperactive and the seizures where I would just stare she couldn't handle it anymore and took it out on me. Of course this gave me more stress than I could handle also.

One day I was sitting on the couch in the living room. Between the stress and the medication making me hyperactive I ended up just leaving the couch in a hurry and ran clear into whatever was in front of me. My mom said I was like a freight train that couldn't be stopped. If I had gone into the sliding glass door I would have been cut up, but she doubts that it would have stopped me. I ended up running straight into the brick fireplace that was in the living room. I was knocked out and woke up a few hours later.

My mom always asked me why I did that. I always replied: "Don't look at me."

"I don't even remember it." Today I still have a scar on my left face to remind me of it. She said she was screaming at me to stop, but of course being in a seizure type state and hyperactive from the meds. There was no way I would have heard her or stopped. Sometimes when I think about it, God was protecting me then. If I had gone through the glass door, kept going I would have hit the volleyball net outside, got tangled and kept going to the brick wall outside the house. By then more things would have happened to me.

This is the only account I have from doing something like this my whole life. So the stress from the fourth grade teacher must have had something to do with it. Like it was getting too much for me to handle and keeping it bottled it. Years later I ended up remembering the incident from fourth grade.

Relatives Visiting

Since we lived in Las Vegas all of our relatives who we didn't know existed or hardly ever see came out of the woodworks to visit us. I never saw so many relatives before. Every year there would be some distant relative who was visiting us. This way they could stay at our house so they wouldn't have to stay at a hotel. They would go gamble, see the celebrities and then come home late at night and crash. We even kept a spare key next to the front door. When I asked about it, my mom replied. "It is for when a relative comes and visits".

Every time a relative come to visit they would want to see me. I thought of them as strangers. I guess they wanted to see me since I was the youngest. My mom would push me up to one of them and go "Here is your youngest (how I was related to them) her name is Betty." Then they would say something to me and I had the weirdest look on my face. Thinking are you sure we are related? When I looked at my mom and she would tell them about me. Here is a list of a few of them I remember and what they did for a living:

One relative of ours was Gene Roemer, my second cousin. He came and visited us in 1972 shortly after retiring from showbiz in 1970. He was a make up artist for Filmways Television and worked on shows such as: Beverly Hillbillies, Petticoat Junction, The Bob Cummings Show, George Burns and Gracie Allen Show, Something for the Birds Movie and The Window movie. Since a lot of shows he worked on involved animals maybe that is why I like being around animals myself.

Another relative who visited us was my grandfather. (my mom's dad) After his wife died he was a successful newspaper reporter/ editor and did some writing for the Mack Sennett Movies such as the Keystone Cops rather than Charlie Chaplin movies. He told me that they were easy to write for compared to how they write scripts now days. Back then you just wrote down the words that go on the screen and what was supposed to be done. Since these were silent movies and not talkies back then. He won an award in Gary, Indiana for coming up with the safety slogan *Watch Out for the Other Guy* he would spend the winters with us and the summers with his other grandkids in Milwaukee, Wisconsin where it was cooler. This makes me the third generation of my family to work in showbiz.

The third one I remember was Lloyd Lincoln who was working for General Foods Corporation at the time. He invented Jell-O and converted cakes into powdered mixes that we use today. He lived in an apartment complex and would work on the projects for the company at home. He would feel like he messed up and then give them to the neighbors instead of throwing them away. They thought they were good when he didn't think so and the neighbors' ended gaining weight from his work. Since he was working for the company they did the work of patenting it so he never got credit for his work. He was named Lincoln since we born on February 12, 1909. One hundred years later on Lincoln's birthday. We just called him "Link" for short.

Whenever the relatives would come by we would give them a tour. I would be sitting in the back, since to me this was a repeat. I would see the same things over and over again that I could give you a tour of this. We would go to Hoover Dam. It was outside of Las Vegas and named after the guy who was President of United States when it was built.

They would take a tour of the dam, drive past Red Foxx's house, and show them the strip. Explain the history of each gambling place, hotel, etc. Explaining why each hotel and other spots got their name. There would be a mechanical sign outside with a cowboy moving his right hand. He would repeat the phrase "Howdy partner, welcome to Las Vegas" by the time he finished saying that the arm had completed from going up to his head and came back down.

People loved that. Later they changed it to where he quit saying that and the arm just moved. The people who lived there wanted to keep it up. The people who visited there kept complaining since it ran all night and all day. They would be having hangovers from their drinking and couldn't stand hearing that all night or all day. Like I said, I heard all these stories I could give you a tour of each one. I don't think it is something for a little kid should memorize or bother to learn instead of school stuff.

Third Grade

When I started third grade I kept getting picked on at school since I would have seizures in class. Back then I was told I had epilepsy, but I had trouble pronouncing it. Teachers didn't understand it. Back then they didn't classify it as a medical problem like they do now. Some teachers and other adults would keep me from doing things in school and others would care less. They would treat me like an equal even though I had epilepsy. During this year in school I noticed something was different.

The kids who picked on me because I had epilepsy would become even more aggressive at me. They had done this each year in first and second grade. Some of the same kids that would kick me in the leg would be back. Of course, I expected that since they were back again. But this time they would kick me harder.

It was an automatic reaction to chase them. I think I surprised them since I was able to keep up with then and catch them this year they weren't expecting it. Now the group that was doing it grew. Instead of one kid doing it there was a group of four of five of them kicking me in the leg. For some reason they kept aiming the same leg too.

Of course what did I do? Ran after them. I was determined that if I caught one of those this year that I would kick that kid back just like they did me. Maybe if they got kicked like I did then they would know how it felt and they wouldn't do it again. It was only third grade and I was already tired of going through this every year. I had a friend of mine who was a boy and he would help me a lot when this happened. He helped me the last two years. Again this year was different.

Now instead of defending me like he did before, he would be one of the kids who would be kicking me in the leg. I went to the office everyday and tell the lady in the office of what happened. She said "Okay Betty" and told me to leave. I don't know why, but I guess I must have reported stuff to them so much that they acted like I was the kid who cried wolf. So they never did anything and brushed me off. I finally figured I was on my own and took matters into my own hands. So I finally chased them so much that I was determined to get a kid and find out what was going on. I did manage one day to get a hold of a kid and asked him. The one I grabbed was the boy who used to defend me. I got him pinned down to where he was against a tree and couldn't move. I asked him. "Why me?"

"Why are you even doing this to me?" He was tired from running he was trying to catch his breath. I told him. "You used to help me."

"Why are you being a mean person and kicking me now?"

"You used to help me."

"Why are you doing this?" His reply. "Everyone else is doing it." He just wanted to fit into the group. I just couldn't believe what I was hearing. He ran off and I noticed now my leg was hurting more than it ever did. I had trouble walking, like someone with a limp. I put my hand down on it and rubbed it. I finished going to school and went home. Limping all the way home. My leg swelled up so much that the next morning my mom took me to see the doctor. They put some stuff around it to help with the swelling; I was even told not to go to school till the swelling went down and the leg healed. It didn't break, but it was getting to the point where it would have soon from the kicking they were doing.

Normally the school calls to find out why the student wasn't in school that day. Especially if the parent didn't call yet. My mom never did call the school and they never called the house to find out why I wasn't there. After that the office people took it more seriously when I told them there was a problem. Unfortunately it took them four years and several injures later for them to figure that out. To this day, I can feel that my leg has not been the same since the incident. Plus it happened that it was also the same leg I broke when I was four.

Crossing Guard

I would walk home before and after school. I took the same route every time. So I ended getting familiar with the cars that were parked in the driveway or next to the house. I started memorizing the license plates on each vehicle like it was a challenge of some sort. Sure enough I was able to do it.

Now days I've noticed it is easy for me to memorize numbers easier than memorizing someone's name. I can picture someone really easy and know where I've seen them before, but their name is the last thing I remember.

There was a crosswalk guard stationed at certain areas so you can across from the school to the residential area. There must have been six of them. The closest one to my area and the others would be mean to me. Call me names and do other stuff. The nicest one was the last one and farthest away from where I needed to be get home. My mom would complain "Don't take that route."

"There is too much traffic it isn't safe." But I would still take it. Even though it was more dangerous none of the others would be nice or even talk to me. It made a big difference to a little kid. I would rather be hit by a car and had talked to the nice guard than take the safer route and be treated like garbage. (putting it nicely) Believe me a little goes a long way.

Dishes

We would switch off doing chores. Each week one of us would take care of the animals, one would do dishes, etc. When you do the dishes the rules were to wash off the dish before putting them into the dishwasher. One time (when I was seven) I was doing the dishes and Dad put his mixed glass on the counter. He would have cans of beer he drank all day. Then he switches to mixed drinks after the cans were gone. Either he made them with Jim Beam or Jack Daniel's and Ginger Ale.

It was more important that the Ginger Ale was saved for his mixed drinks. If we had an upset stomach we couldn't have it, because he needed it for mixing his drinks. I was having an upset stomach one time and my mom told me I couldn't have the ginger ale. I looked at where the ginger ale was and we had plenty of bottles for him and us. Again it was saved for him and we had to suffer. I quickly learned which one in the house had priority. If he was finished with his drink he would set it down on the counter next to the sink. If he wasn't done, he wouldn't put it there.

One time, when I was doing the dishes, he placed it on the counter. So naturally I washed it and put it into the dishwasher. He came back afterward and wanted it. I told him he put it on the counter.

He yelled at me for washing it. Told me I should have known he wasn't finished, since there was some left in the glass. (It was about one third of a cup of his mixed drink left.) "I wasn't finished with it yet!" He yelled. He then grabbed my shirt. "Didn't you know that?"

"No." I replied in a frightened voice. "You should have!" Then he punched me in the face. "Either leave it there or ask your mom next time!" He shook me, made another drink in another glass. "Now don't wash this!"

"If it is like this next time ask first!" He then left the kitchen in a made rage. I could hear him yelling at my mom in the living room. I began crying and wishing I didn't have to be doing this while he was around. I didn't want to do the dishes anymore and was terrified of it. I was scared whenever he came in and I was doing the dishes, totally terrified from all of this. After that I would ask if he was done. He would reply. "Good."

"Now you remember to ask first."

"Good girl." To this day I hate seeing, Coors Beer, Jack Daniel's or Jim Beam ads. All I think about is how much they affected my dad and how much they ruined my family and my life.

Earthquake

On February 9, 1971 San Fernando, California had an earthquake that measured 6.6 magnitudes on the scale. The earthquake could be felt all the way Las Vegas, Nevada. It caused power outages in Las Vegas, the house swayed and the bed moved several feet by itself. The aftershocks weren't felt that far away, but the quake itself was. People clocks fell off the furniture, beds were moving etc. No was killed from the quake in the Vegas area. People knew about the Nevada test site and thought maybe it had been a bomb they were testing that cause it. The radio stations had to keep reminding the listeners that it was an earthquake and not a bomb that went off at the test site. I don't see how people managed to sleep through it in Vegas.

In California it was different. Forty-nine people were killed. A hospital was one of the places that got a lot of damage from the quake. Because of this quake a law was passed in California raising the building codes to prohibit locating buildings that will be used by humans across the active fault lines. This would prevent more lives being lost. It was passed in 1972.

Since we were living in Vegas at the time, there wasn't much damage to the place. None of us ended up getting hurt from it. Just shaken up and surprised that we felt it. Afterwards we found out that we were on a fault line when we didn't even know it.

Piano

We had a piano in the living room while we were living in Las Vegas. It was a requirement that when we turned eight years old that mom would teach us how to play the piano. She would make sure I was sitting on her left side knowing that I had trouble hearing in my left ear already. "Can you hear me okay?"

"Yes." I nodded. All of my sisters ended up learning how to play the piano without having any problems. Thinking back now with my bad vision I can see how it would be difficult for me. Maybe if the notes were labeled it would have helped.

Back then I was wearing glasses. When it came time for me to learn. My mom made it feel like a chore. She would try to teach me something called middle "C". I couldn't understand what she was talking about. She would point to it on the book where the note was. I just saw a lot of notes. I couldn't tell one from the other. Then she would show me where it was on the piano. I just saw a bunch of white keys. She told me it was on a key. She would play it and I said "okay".

She replied "No, you have to play it." Of course I couldn't even remember where the note was. So I pressed the wrong key and she yelled at me. She would get frustrated at me for it. She kept it up every day for a few days trying to teach me how to play the Christmas song "Joy to the World". (You will see later how this song keeps popping up on me during emotional times.) I got as far as playing the first four notes since you start with the right side and only have to go to the left playing one note right after the other. I was able to handle that. After that I kept getting lost on whatever she was saying or understanding what she was even referring to. It took her a few weeks just to get that far. So she got frustrated at me and yelled at me for it. "You have no music talent whatsoever!" I said "Fine, I didn't want to learn this stuff anyway!" Got up and left the living room. I never wanted to play the piano ever again. I wanted to learn the drums when I got to be twelve, but my mom kept reminding me that I don't have any music talent whatsoever when I mentioned anything about it again. She said "You can't play the piano."

"How are you going to manage playing the drums?"

All of my other sisters ending being in some kind of band. Showing which ones in the family have music talent. Cynthia played the flute and clarinet. Debbie played the clarinet, Liz played the flute. Mary ended up playing the clarinet. Me, I ended up not being in any band when I was in school.

In fact I didn't pick up any type of musical instrument until three years after my mom died. I finally got the courage to try the drums after she died. I ended up playing a trap set every so often at the second church in Maryland. Because of my rotating schedule at the Vet Clinic I couldn't do it every week.

Honor Roll

In high school they would have what schools referred to as honor roll cards. You would get one if your name was on the "A" honor roll or "AB" honor roll. Your name would be in the newspaper. Plus you were allowed to leave to go to lunch ten minutes earlier. You could leave school ten minutes earlier also.

My sister thought that the greatest idea she ever had was to get one of those cards and not do the work. Debbie didn't want to do the hard work that would be required to study for it. So when the time came to take the test, she would fix it so she would answer the questions wrong. Be put into a class of any subject that was classified for people who didn't do well on the test.

Debbie would of course ace the class work and pass the tests without having to think of the answers. End up getting her name in the paper, get a card and get out of school earlier than the others. I remember her being so proud of getting the card that she would show it to me a lot. "You can get these when you are in high school." I would hear. She ended up convincing Liz to do it and wanted rest of us to do the same thing. It ended up affecting her score for college later so before you think of doing the same thing remember this. Some things come back to haunt you later. Just like drinking and driving don't mix. Neither does doing stupid things.

Perry Como

Debbie and Liz, Mom and I (when I was eight) went to see Perry Como and his Orchestra at a Las Vegas Hotel. He was singing "And I Love You So" I wanted to go up stage and get his autograph so I can get back down. One of my sisters wanted the autograph. My mom said if they didn't want it she would take it. Mom told me not to go up there until he was finished with the song. She knew that would be his last song he sang. When he finished singing I went up to get the autograph from him using one of my sister's autograph book. He asked me for the name and I told him one of their names. He gave me the autograph and I started walking off.

He called me by the name I used and I didn't think he was talking to me since that isn't my name. He called me again and I had a surprised look on my face since I'm not used to someone calling me. He looked at me and wanted me to come back to him. I did and was still surprised. He held the microphone to me and asked me what I wanted to be when I grow up. I answered a dancer since I loved to dance. He said where? I didn't think of anything so I said "here".

He laughed and said "You mean this hotel or Las Vegas?" I answered "Las Vegas" He replied "Okay why wait?" I looked around and confused. He gave the orchestra a signal and told me to dance now. I still had a stunned look on my face. "You can dance right?" I answered "Yes"

"Then let's do it." The orchestra started playing for a minute and I started dancing the same thing I do at home. I got into it that he had to stop me when after the orchestra finished. He told the audience. "Let's give her applause." They did and then he mentioned my name again. I was like excited and stunned that someone did that for me. My mom and two sisters were excited for me. I started crying because someone actually took an interest in me. In 1978 He had a Christmas Special on TV entitled "Early American Christmas".

My mom reminded me of him wanting me to dance on the stage and I forgot about it since all I remembered was my dad's abuse. I thought he was some dude with a Christmas special. I'm glad now I remember it. God lets you remember the good times also.


Neighbors


Since we lived in Las Vegas all the neighbors in this area were rich. Keep in mind this is in the 1960's. Back then one million dollars went further. We were the only middle class family living in this neighborhood. Probably because we were the first family to move into the neighborhood. Everyone had at least one pool, two jobs, and slot machines, etc. They mostly worked at the hotels so they made a lot of money. Kids would pick on us since we weren't the rich family like them.

First. There was a married couple who lived in the corner house on my street. I forgot about what happened to him till I was living in Maryland. The elder of the church wanted to help me with a problem I was having so he told me to read Psalm 54. As soon as I got to the third verse I started having flashbacks. Here is what psalm 54 says: 1 God, save me because of who you are. By your strength show that I am innocent. 2 Hear my prayer, God; listen to what I say. 3 Strangers turn against me, and cruel men want to kill me. They do not care about God. 4 See, God will help me; the Lord will support me. 5 Let my enemies be punished with their own evil. Destroy them because you are loyal to me. 6 I will offer a sacrifice as a special gift to you. I will thank you, Lord, because you are good. 7 You have saved me from all my troubles, and I have seen my enemies defeated.

During the part where strangers turn against me, and cruel people want to kill me. I was remembering a night where a helicopter was shinning its lights into our bedroom window during the night.

I asked my mom about it later. She was surprised I remember that considering how young I was. Apparently the wife found out that her husband was cheating on her so she shot him. He ended up getting wounded in the arm and drove himself out of the neighborhood in a hurry to the hospital. The wife was running after him with a gun trying to finish him off. (Almost sounds like a story for a TV show) She ran off and the police were trying to find her and that is why the helicopter was shinning it's lights in our window.

Second. There was a neighbor who lived almost across from us. They ended up having a reputation in the neighborhood from what they would do to everyone on the street. They had some idea that when they bought the house that the sidewalk came with the house.

So if I own the house I own the sidewalk. It is well known that the sidewalk is used for pedestrians to move from one area to another and is available to everyone. Unfortunately for the owner she didn't believe it. She assumed that when she bought the house that the sidewalk came with it. So if I walked on the sidewalk in front of her house she would call the police on me. (This is before the 911 system) They came out to see what was going on. They would inform her that the sidewalk is public property and that anyone can use it. Unfortunately she didn't believe them.

They had to come out about four more times. She still didn't believe them. After the fifth time she called them the police never bothered to come out again. She would be standing in the kitchen doing something. As soon as she saw someone on the sidewalk she would go to her phone and call the police.

Third. The neighbors next door had a maid. She was the only one in the neighborhood who actually talked to me and was nice. Like I mentioned earlier she would listen. I would tell her about what my dad would do. She knew what was going on, but didn't know what to do. Back then you couldn't report it like you can now. So she would take time out of her schedule and actually listen to me. Something I always cherish and never took for granted like a lot of people do now days.

Fourth Grade

I could tell there was something wrong with this teacher I had in the fourth grade. She would send me to the corner a lot of times I felt like Willie on "Little House on the Prairie". I ended up having repressed memory from it that when I was in my twenties I finally remembered what happened. I came out of a complex partial seizure where you just stare. The teacher, I'll call her Miss Smith, had a long pointed she used to point to the chalkboard with that had a rubber point at the end. She would hit me with the middle of the stick on my hand so hard it was an automatic reaction to pull my hand away from her really quick. One day she held my hand down on the desk so I couldn't move it away and slammed my hand over and over again till it was bleeding.

On the day my memory came back. I noticed I came out of the seizure and she asked me to tell her what she just told the class. I didn't know what she said since I just came out of it. "I don't know" I told her. She didn't say anything and took a step back. It was an automatic reaction for me to go to the corner as if I did it a hundred times. The last time we went through this she said "no" I was surprised and she told me to go to the desk. I did it and was wondering why. She had a furious look on her face. "Pull down you pants!" I was confused and the kids laughed at me. "What did I say?" She asked me. I didn't reply and pulled down my pants like she said. Slapping noised I heard behind me and I started crying from the paddling I was getting for having a seizure in class. Now I can see why I had repressed the memory for years. Just when I thought the worse was over. I still had to go into the normal corner and stand there until she decided I had spent enough time there. I was crying for so long that she kept me in there longer than she usually did.

The next day I went to class like I usually did. She must have had a talk with the office about it. She told me when I came up to the door. "You are not allowed to come in." I asked "Why?"

"Follow me." She replied. I didn't think anything about it and followed her. She took me to a different classroom. I would ask her "How come?" She told me "No talking." in an angry voice. I was in shock when I read the door saying "Special Ed." I couldn't believe it when she purposely put me in that room without telling me. The teacher was happy to see me since we were already friends. My fourth grade teacher snickered and then left. My new teacher was introducing me to the class.

I've seen these kids before. I didn't know their names, but their faces were very familiar to me. These were the kids who were bullying me on the playground or had a physical disability. I wanted to leave the room and the teacher stopped me. Like usual it was an automatic reaction for me to leave the room.

Since these kids had disabilities they were given more free periods than the regular kids. They weren't allowed on the playground so they had to play in the classroom or watch TV. Again like someone babysitting us. I couldn't stand it so I ended up helping the special ed teacher with her secretarial type of work. She couldn't understand why I was in there and after the year was up recommended I be put in a regular fifth grade class.

One time I was outside with the kids just walking around helping the special ed teacher do a few things. Like go to the office and mail stuff. I ran into former teacher Miss Smith and said hello. She gave me a look like I had a contagious disease or something else and quickly left me in a hurry. I called her name and she still ignored me while walking away in a hurry. I was upset from it and told my teacher when I got back to the classroom.

My special Ed teacher explained to me that she couldn't understand why she acted like that and told me that there was nothing wrong with me that it was her fault. I shouldn't be upset from her. I noticed afterwards that while I was in the special Ed class that the amount of seizures I was having dropped by at least half than when I was in the Miss Smith's class getting abused by her.

## Pick Pocket

Today when I do something like pass a person and they have a wallet in their pocket all I can think of is they are an easy target. They are going to lose their wallet and their money without them knowing it. But how to go up to someone and explain to them that they are an easy target when they don't know it and you are just trying to help them? They are more likely to call the cops on you when you are just trying to help them.

Back when I was living in Vegas it was like a game to see how many people we could confiscate their wallets without them knowing it. I just enjoyed the part of getting their wallets out without them knowing it. I would hand them off to someone else and they would take it.

I got a certain amount of money for doing it. I couldn't see why God would have me learn such a bad thing considering how it goes against something that is written, but thinking about it now it makes perfect sense.

There was an incident where my mom was driving and having problems. I was able to convince her to drive to the emergency room. I told her if she wanted to leave in five minutes we would to it. She wanted to leave right away after what I said. "I'm ready to go now." So we were supposed to leave. For some reason she couldn't find her keys or wallet.

After she got in they had to give her oxygen and some other things. Again she wanted to leave. She spent more time looking through her purse and trying to find the wallet and keys. I ended up lifting them before she got to the counter to sign in. It took her couple of hours to finally figure out that I took them. I told her she wasn't getting them back till the doctor releases her. She kept telling me to give them back. I told her no and that since she was oxygen she wasn't getting them. Once they released her I gave them back to her.

Just like it says in the bible. You are supposed to rest on the Sabbath, but if you need to do something to help someone it is okay. Here I was learning to steal, but it ended up saving my mom later. So God does take something bad and uses it for good later.

Girl Scouts

Since my mom had five girls we were supposed to join the girl scouts. One person who was a big supporter of the girl scouts was Debbie Reynolds. She would invite the entire local troops to a hotel and we would have a party before going out to sell the cookies. We would be able to go swimming and have snacks and cookies. Everyone got an autographed photo of her every year.

I remember that we had to dress up in the uniforms to enter to the floor of the hotel. We would be paired up. I was paired up with Lori. People would be watching all these girl scouts walking around the area where the slot machines were. (It was the only way to get to the elevators) So people who were plastered and gambling would say the meanest, rudest and profanity stuff to us while were in two rows trying to get to the elevators. Lori didn't understand what they were saying. After living there I understood what they were saying. She would repeat what she heard and asked me what it meant. I made up some excuse. When Lori asked me where I heard it before. I told her I heard the same thing at home.

This was an annual event with the Girl Scouts so you think the hotel staff would have done a better job of trying to keep some of the gamblers away from us or schedule us at a different area. There were ways we could have gone in a back way and avoid all of that.

Then afterwards the Girl Scouts would be in our bathing suits and beach towels having to come downstairs to go through the same route again. Then the profanity stuff would be even worse.

Sometimes the drunks would really try to hit on us or even worse. I still don't remember any of the staff trying to help us. Sometimes I wonder if they told them to look for us. I remember the looks on those people's faces were like they were in shock seeing us. They would point to us and laugh at us like we were freaks. Then later when we came down they were so excited to see us.

I remember Lori getting propositioned by a guy who was so drunk. He even gave her a fifty dollar bill. Lori didn't even know why she was given that I had to tell her to take the money and run out. The guy ran off after the two of us. Since he didn't get what he paid for he wanted his money back. I told her to follow me and run like the building was on fire. She fell tripping on her towel so I had to go back and help her. He was so mad he ran out of the hotel while carrying his booze with him.

The security ended up catching him for stealing the booze and trying to leave without paying for his stuff. Again no one cared what happened to us. They were more concerned with their "guests". Again God gives us "tools" to help someone in time of need. I told her later to put the money in the savings account.

Another incident involving the Girl Scouts had to do with my sisters. I wasn't there, but Mary and her troop were. They were outside of a local store that was near our area. It was like an old day Wal-mart to best describe it with slot machines added. My mom was the troop leader and they had a table set up to sell cookies. This guy went into the store with three body guards following him. My mom recognized him right away. If my Cynthia, Debbie or Liz, were there they would have gotten his autograph before he went into the store.

My mom asked him if he wanted to buy some cookies. He said he would when he came back out. It was in the paper later that there were threats on his life. He was a famous singer and had a concert to do that night at a hotel in Vegas. So he went inside of that store because it was the closest one that he could find that sold guns. He came out later with a brown bag. He pulled the gun out and loaded it right there in front of the kids.

My mom again asked about the cookies. He told one of his bodyguards to buy some boxes. They asked the guard what type of cookies he wanted. He just handed some money and said he didn't care. The Girl Scouts bagged up some boxes for the guard. He took the cookies and thanked the singer for buying the cookies. My mom asked him to autograph a box for her. Sure enough he did and he signed it with his name. Elvis Presley.

Fifth Grade

Next year I was in fifth grade. This time I was in a class with normal kids and not in special ed. Kids didn't treat me as bad as they did in the other years, but I was finally one of the bigger kids and not the younger/smaller ones. They had events during the year for track. I decided to try out for that since I do enough running at home and other places.

Sure enough I was right. I ended up winning second place in a 440 yard dash. First time I won something for running and didn't get yelled at for running. It was an unusual experience for me, when someone else would have enjoyed it.

They called us out through the PA system at school. As soon as my name was called the first thing I was thinking was that I got in trouble again. The only time they call me is when I'm getting yelled at for something. This time I was getting an award. Something I never thought of.

Now that I knew I was good at running I used it to my advantage. I would do stuff like the pick pocketing, hotwiring and be able to outrun the cops when they came up to us. By now I was seizure free so I wanted to be off the meds. I wasn't having Miss Smith that was giving me problems anymore and I couldn't see why I was on the meds. So I was told I can quit taking them.

The cops knew I was a good runner whenever they saw me. I also figured I could be on the track team in school. But this year it was too late to join it. I figured I could do it next year.

Apology

Mary and I were sitting in the kitchen/dining room of the house that was separated by a bar. She was telling jokes and I was laughing.

I already had food at the bar area and was eating something. (When I was ten years old) I was laughing so hard I couldn't eat my food.

Dad came in the house in a very mad mood. He started yelling at me. Mary could tell he was in one of his mad moods, that she quickly got up and left the kitchen area in a hurry. She was worried he would yell at her or worse, getting beaten up so she left. I wanted to get out of there in a hurry. Before I could, dad ordered me to eat my food. I had trouble stopping from laughing, but tried to eat.

Apparently it wasn't fast enough for dad. "Eat it!" He yelled at me. I tried to eat it and it still wasn't fast enough for him. So he got even angrier and started taking the food. With the spoon, he took it, pinched my nose with two of his fingers and spoon-fed me with the food. Like I was baby and didn't know how to eat. He did it really fast and hard so he would be able to get it done in a hurry. Since according to him I was taking too long. I couldn't breathe from all of this.

I tried getting him to stop, but I still couldn't breathe or talk. He kept shoving the food while keeping my nose pinched. I finally used my hand to push him off. I wonder if I didn't if he would have kept it up till I passed out. He always had a bad temper. Combined with the alcohol was never a good combination. He yelled at me again. "Aren't you going to finish that?" I nodded yes.

"What did you say?" yelling at me again. "Yes." I answered while crying. "Quit crying!" He kept an eye on me while I tried to eat as fast as I could to get out the kitchen and go to my room. I was determined to do anything to get away from him. I didn't want to be near him anymore or ever again. When I was finally done, it seem like forever, I left the dishes and ran to my room as fast as I can. I could hear him yelling. "Betty!"

"Come down here and put them in the sink!"

"Damn!"

"She never listens!" He put them in the sink. I heard crashing. "I know you can hear me!' I then closed the door and locked it. I cried and never came out again. My mom came in and tried to check on me.

I told her I wasn't going to go down there, as long as dad was down there. "I know what you mean, but he lives here and he is your father." She replied. I was determined never to leave my room again.

After I calmed down I ended up playing in my room and still never left the upstairs at all. Just left my room to go to the bathroom and quickly went to my room to avoid being seen by my dad. I was getting hungry after not eating for over seven hours. I was too terrified to come down and get yelled at by my dad or even worse. I couldn't even imagine what would be next. My mom came up crying, trying to convince me to come down. I even wondered if she was crying because my dad was yelling at her since I wasn't coming down.

After a few more hours my dad came up to my room. I was horrified to even have him knock at my door. "What was he going to do now?" I kept thinking to myself. "I couldn't have done anything wrong now."

"I've been in my room all day."

"I couldn't even have done anything wrong."

"Now he is probably going to yell at me for something I didn't do again." My mind was going crazy trying to figure out what I did this time to get hit with the belt or get thrown across the room. He finally came into the room. I backed up against the wall as far as I could go.

He kept coming closer and then stopped. I was so terrified of him that I grabbed a toy and started playing with it. If he was going to hit me I didn't even want to see it. He had a hard time trying to talk, like he had to speak in front of a crowd or something.

Very nervous type of talking, he didn't say very much but was something I don't think I was ever going to forget. "I'm sorry." Then he left the room in a hurry and shut the door. My mom told me later. That he never heard those words from his father. I should be very grateful he said that to me.

Afterwards my mom came back up and wanted me to eat dinner. I didn't want to, but I ended up doing it. Dad was already downstairs in the kitchen reading the paper. My mom gave me a plate and handed it to me. Dad quickly left the table. I don't know if he didn't want to talk to me or didn't even want to see me after what he had to go through to get me down there. I think my mom had a lot to do with coming upstairs and apologizing.

## Rape

During this time. My older sisters Debbie and Liz were getting in trouble and my parent's first concern was taking care of them. They did a lot of shoplifting and ended up in jail. My mom had to go to bail them out, go to court and take care of school matters dealing with them.

In one way I can't blame them. They were teenagers. You have to take care of three teenagers and two kids at the same time. What would you do? How would you handle it? The teenagers were keeping them busy. Getting phone calls for being in juvenile detention for shoplifting or something else. My parents had to come down to the station or courthouse and bail them out over and over. So they were already preoccupied.

Personally I don't know what I would have done in their position also. All I know is this is a traumatic part of any girl's life no matter what age she is when this happens to her. Whether they are five or one hundred and five. Every girl/woman doesn't want this to happen to her, but the last I heard it was one in six chance that this will happen to her in her lifetime. One in thirty-three chance for the man in their lifetime. I praise the Lord that it hasn't happened to some of them already and pray it won't happen to anyone ever again.

This occurred shortly after the school year started. Our regular teacher, Mrs. Jones had to leave. No one liked her, but for one reason or another she had to leave. (I don't remember why she left.) So of course we got a substitute teacher. I keep thanking God that I don't remember his name.

He was the kind of guy "everyone liked". He would tell us jokes and we would be laughing. He made it feel so you looked forward to coming to his class. If you didn't like any of the other classes you went to you loved coming to his and seeing him. Like I said everyone liked him. We would even talk about how great he was and that we looked forward to going to his class and couldn't wait.

I had developed early and was already wearing a bra by now. Sometimes I wonder if that is what attracted him to me. All the other girls were still looking like a little kid and didn't look different.

We had recess a few more times, so he dismissed the class. This was within the first month of school. Thinking back now I can see a few "signs" popping up. One is when we were put in a seating arrangement by our last names. In alphabetical order we had to sit in a certain chair. Normally the teachers go by your last name. So I should have been put in the back. After I was in his class I got moved up to one of the chairs in the front row. He never did tell me why, but later I definitely figured it out.

One day he dismissed the class early and told me he needed my help. The kids were so excited they left in a hurry. I was about to get up out of my chair and he told me to stay there. He watched as the kids left and came up to me.

He relaxed me by touching certain areas around my neck. I kept having these weird feelings and didn't know what they were. After knowing what happened I wonder why I never had a seizure. I must have froze up after the hug I got from my dad earlier and was terrified when the teacher touched me.

He then put his hand down my blouse and unbuttoned it. He was doing all of this so fast I didn't know what to do. No one had a talk with me about this stuff so I didn't even know that this kind of stuff was wrong.

After he was finished with playing with me he ended up pulling down my panties since I was wearing a skirt and raping me. I could feel what was going on, but almost like I was watching it and not being able to do anything about it. I'm so good at running, but this was one time I stopped and couldn't move. All I could feel was pain to the point to where I closed my eyes and was crying. Again all I did was become a frozen statue. Like I said it wasn't very long, but it seemed like it lasted forever.

He had to pull himself away from me and wanted me to get on the floor. That is when I ran and left the room with my blouse undone and going into the bathroom. Again God was helping me by having me being a good runner and getting out of there before anything else happened.

I spent a lot of time in the bathroom and cried all day. Not knowing what was going on or what to say to anyone. How do you explain this when you don't even know what is going on yourself? Plus with the stuff I've been doing and running from cops who are going to believe me? I ended up catching the bus and going home.

That night I told my parents what happened. Guess what my dad did? The same thing as usual. Swear every word in the book like he did everyday. Yell at me like it was my fault. He told me they would try to figure out what happened. This meant I was going to get yelled at every night. I wasn't going to go through that, so the next day I went to the principal's office and reported it.

Things are so much different nowadays compared to then. Today they have the police come by and check everything. They take you to the hospital and get you checked out to see if you have STD's and other things. Back then it was like they wanted to sweep everything under the rug and try to keep it quiet as much as possible.

That night all I could think and dream about the whole night was what happened. I kept trying to think of something else, but all I could do was remember every little detail of the whole thing. I couldn't forget anything no matter how hard I tried.

The next day I went to the principal's office and told him what happened. Of course I had a hard time explaining it. Telling him what happened since I didn't know what to say. I was already nervous from the whole thing. An office lady came in and jotted down the notes of what everyone was saying. The only people in the room were the office lady, the principal and me. At first it seemed like the right thing to do. Now after everything is over I don't know if it was the best thing.

They ended drilling me everyday over and over again. We kept rehashing every little detail over and over. My story never changed.

I'm sure the teacher's story never changed either. Even though I never did find out what he was saying.

I would go home and rehash the same thing over and over again with my parents. So it was a constant circle of going through this. Then at night I would relive the whole thing again in my mind when I was supposed to be sleeping. It was a process that lasted twenty-four hours a day seven days a week for nine months. My mom ended up dressing me up in clothes that were harder to undo. Mainly to have the teacher take longer to undress me in case he tried to do it. The guy was still teaching. I can see where her idea came from and it being a safety measure, but considering what I went through, I would be upset a lot and it took forever for me to undo the stuff to even go the bathroom I would either give up or have problems being able to go the bathroom in time. People were making fun at me for it, which made things worse for me.

Everyone at the school was asking me if it really happened. My so called friends, other teachers, etc. They would ask me everyday like they had doubts, I thought once I said "Yes." That would be enough, but I guess not, over and over every day they would ask me the same thing. It was a never ending thing.

The school ended up removing him from the class. Our regular teacher, Mrs. Jones came back. When the students found out that he was gone. Mrs. Jones didn't say why, but looked at me. The students ended up blaming me for the substitute teacher leaving and took it out on me.

Finally I got to the point where I didn't want to go through this anymore. At home or school. I told them the same thing over and over "Why are you doing this?"

"I keep telling you the same thing." It didn't matter with them. They are going to keep this up till one of us breaks.

The day after the rape I started my period. Again I didn't know what was going on. I didn't even know if the rape had something to do with it. Of course that is the first thing I though of. My mom didn't even want to talk to me about it. She just handed me a book and told me to read it. I didn't even want to look at it. Gave it back to her. She asked me if I read it. I told her " yes" so she wouldn't make me look at it anymore. All of this just seemed like one nightmare after another.

It just never seemed to end. I was becoming the talk of school. People were going back to calling me names. My relationship with my family was getting worse each day. Then I was being told that no guy would want to have me later in life since I already had sex before marriage. I still didn't even know what it was, but I knew it wasn't good. I just ended up crying myself to sleep each night. Another thing that became routine with me.

It seem like those nine months of school took forever to go by. Even at church they were treating me different. I couldn't understand what was going on. People were giving me looks and whispering about me. Being called a liar at school, home everywhere I went. When it got closer to the end of the school year the principal had to make a decision. The teacher and I were sticking to our stories. So what did he finally decide to do? Fire the teacher, made me confess that I made up the whole thing. I found out later when I was in seventh grade that he put in my school records that I was mentally ill and recommend that I need to see a shrink from what happened here.

I didn't want to confess to the whole ordeal. I wanted to keep it up, but he wouldn't let me. He was determined to keep me in his office till I finally gave up and confessed.

Once I did then I was allowed to go back to my class. Since I had missed so much school work they ended up putting me in a low score class for several subjects like I was so uneducated that I couldn't even handle a simple math class.

So ended up the way he wanted. No bad teacher, the kid was punished and taken care of and the whole thing went away in his opinion so the mess was all cleaned up. Ready to face a new school year. For the longest time I even believed it. My parents were even more furious with me from that than they were before.

The following year I ended up flirting with guys thinking that was normal and girls should be doing that. If we stayed in Vegas I probably would have gone into the oldest profession there is. Prostitution.

To this day my family believes it happened if they are in a good mood. If they are in a bad mood they don't believe me. Some don't even believe me today. I give up let them believe what they want. A few people know the truth. The teacher, me and God. I figure those are the most important anyway.

I can see where God has had his hand in things through this. I never did remember what the guy's name was. If I did, I doubt if I would want to name any kids with the same name. In my writing I wouldn't want to use the name and other things like it. So I can even see where he is protecting me still from the whole ordeal.

Christmas 1969

My grandmother was dying of colon cancer. This was my dad's mother so we took care of her during her last few years of her life. Christmas is on December twenty- fifth of the current year. She passed away on December twenty-third of 1969 so it was a hard time for us. My dad wanted to get it over with as quickly as possible so we could have a good Christmas without thinking about someone dying.

Since I wasn't told anything about death or dying all I could visualize was myself being put in a coffin and being buried. No one explained to me about the afterlife or heaven. So all I knew was that you die get buried and that is it.

It would have been a good time for my parents to explain about Jesus, death and heaven then. If they felt they couldn't they could have taken me to a minister and have him explain it to me. Instead if I asked about it, my dad would just yell at me again. My mom would have just told me to leave. As far as I knew it was a horrible situation I never wanted to be in. I was going to live for as long as possible. I never wanted to die and go through what my grandmother went through.

Again Christmas had come and gone and no one really said anything. My birthday was after Christmas and I was getting ignored since it was too close to new years even. My dad's birthday was after new years so I just pretty much kept to myself. The only time people wanted me was when it was time for the birthday cake.

I kept dreaming it every night reliving the same thing over and over again. Getting scared of dying and no one to help me. Another perfect opportunity God gave everyone to help this family to get saved and they blew it off as if it was just another day and not do anything. How does that saying go? God opens doors, but if he closes one he opens a window. Believe me you'll see a lot of doors being opened, closed, and windows being opened throughout this book. It is also praise that God doesn't just give us one chance and forget it. He gives us numerous opportunities to learn about him and accept him. I am so fortunate that he never gave up on me.

Sixth Grade

In 1971 a Supreme Court decision from the court case of Swann v. Charlotte- Mecklenburg Board of Education made it official to make sure every school was desegregated. Meaning a school couldn't have all one race of kids at one school and another all another race at another school. In other words all schools should be integrated.

This didn't happen to me until I reached sixth grade. The busses ran us from the school that was closest to us to one that was all the way across town. All this time we went to a school that was close to us and we could walk to school. Not anymore, by the time we got home from school and rode the bus home. It was too dark to go outside and play basketball or do some exercise. I wasn't on the seizure meds so I wasn't hyperactive anymore either. So I ended up putting on weight and begin looking for other activities to keep me busy.

One of the things they had at this school was failing notices. It says on the back of the paper is to have the parents sign it. I was terrified of that. I already get in trouble at home for stuff I don't do. I don't need that now.

I took the paper home and my parents yelled at me again. What's new? Later they signed it and I gave it to the teacher. It turns out I wasn't supposed to let my parents see it. I was supposed to sign the paper, but not my parents. Why? This school district is different. You passed school with a third grade education. It didn't make a difference. You can pass and not learn anything or you can pass and be a genius.

The main thing they were concerned about was that you signed the failing notice. Not anyone else. No one told me that. Of course I got chewed out for having my parents sign it. "Next time don't let that happen!" Mrs. Jones told me. "Yea right." I kept thinking to myself. I was counting down the days till school was over. The sooner the better.

We were given lockers to keep our stuff in. I never saw anything like it at all. This was so new to me. There were metal bars over the windows to keep people out. I would keep my stuff in the lockers. So far nothing happened. Then came the time for Christmas break. We were going to be out of school for two weeks. Some kids kept their stuff in the lockers and others took their things home.

Everyone was back after the holidays to find out our stuff was gone. They broke into our class rooms, lockers and removed anything they wanted. Windows were broken and glass was all over the place. I have never seen anything like it before. I never got my stuff back and now was determined to make sure it didn't happen to me again. Now I was determined to get even. I was already pick pocketing, but now it was different. By the time I finished sixth grade I had perfected this to the point where nobody was going to take my stuff and not being able to figure out who was doing it.

I would distract people while they looked on way and I confiscated what I needed. I couldn't understand why girls had purses. I never did. I knew how easy of a target they were. I could put my hand in and get what I wanted.

If they did figure out it was me I could out run them. This was definitely a year I wanted to get back at people for what happened to me. No matter what the cost was. From the way I was being treated and what happened. I kept it in too long and it finally built up.

Hotwire

As far back as I can remember I always wanted to learn stuff about cars. My dad would fix the cars and change the oil. He would always tell me to get away and that he was too busy. I thought if I was a guy maybe he would be eager to teach me this stuff, but that never happened.

I ended up teaching myself this stuff and just like the pick pocketing or gambling. You had to either teach yourself this stuff or learn it from someone else. Even today when I am with someone and we look at a car dealership I have a hard time looking at cars and trying not to notice how vulnerable the car is. How easy you can break into it or do something else to it. I may not be able to drive it, but I know how to and how the mechanics of it works. It is just harder now because of the computer systems they use since I've done these things.

A few friends of mine and I would ride our bikes around the neighborhood and other places. We would go to parks, apartment complexes etc. Check out the cars that are parked. All we needed back then was a metal hanger. Bend it and use it to unlock someone's car. If one of us couldn't work on getting it started, the other one could. Same with breaking in and starting it. I rather be doing this than staying home and get beaten up. There wasn't anything else for us to do. Since everything is geared for the adults.

Even before we unlocked it, we would look inside and see what was in it. Praise the Lord they have tinted windows now. Those help discourage people like me who were younger and doing that nowadays. I keep thinking if my dad had me help him on the cars maybe I would have been discouraged from doing this. I was becoming a tomboy and was interested in the same stuff he was. I was being neglected more and more by him when I was interested in the same stuff he was. Everyone in my family at one time or another has wondered if he wanted a son and maybe that is why we were treated like that.

If anything good was to come out of this I think I finally found it. If someone was to buy a car I can tell them how easy of a trap or how good it is not to break into it. Plus I used the same technique to break back into my house or someone else's car when I get locked out.

Energy Crisis

During the 1970's the Arabian government decided to attack the United States where it hurt. By not letting us have oil or gas, because we were helping Israel. In 1973 the United States had an energy crisis from the shortage. People were forced to cut back on what we used for normal activities. You have to think about this one for a minute from Vegas' point of view. Las Vegas was a type of city that ran twenty-four hours a day, seven days a week. Everything was open and it was a city that never sleeps.

People were told not to keep the TV on after a certain point. My dad would read his book at night like he always did. As soon as it was time for us to come into the living room and watch TV. He told us we couldn't because of the energy crisis.

I looked out the window or glass doors and see other people using electricity. Their TVs would be on and the whole family would watch on TV. I couldn't believe it. On Saturdays we would sit in the living room. My parents wanted to watch Hee Haw. It was a musical country western show. Some of us wanted to watch it. Others didn't. Since the parents were in charge it was either watch it or nothing. Since I was the youngest all the chairs were taken and I used the floor. To this day people wonder why I sit on the floor. Some habits die hard I guess.

They were building a new hotel called the MGM hotel. Every night the spotlights would be out every night for some event. The same kind that you only see at big events. At Las Vegas they did it every night. Some big singer is at a hotel performing or something else.

I was so used to seeing them, I could sleep at night. Well during this time period the Government told everyone to cut back on usage. This included the hotels. The whole city that would be lit up at night, twenty-four hours a day, was in total darkness.

Something I have never seen before. It was so different. It reminded me of blackouts they would have in a war. The only lights we did get to see were the building of the MGM hotel. They worked on it twenty-four hours a day, everyday. They had portable lights on so they could see during the night and do the construction. It was the first time I can remember what the sky looked like. You actually got to see stars, the moon and everything. All these man made things took over everything that God had made and moved us into another universe of some kind.

Every night we could see how much of the construction that had completed on the hotel. Since they were the only ones who were lit up in the dark, you could tell they had completed a floor every night. It looked so strange. Each floor looked like the roof at night. In the day they looked like they were doing the interior. At night they were doing the walls or shell of the building. It was so awesome and so bizarre to be seeing it. Like I said the rest of the city was in total darkness, but being to see God's creation for the first time is awesome. Everyone shouldn't have to wait till there is an energy crisis to see it.

Pay Toilets

About 1970 they started a new program called paid toilets to help cities get reimbursed for the use of water, paper products and other things used in the public restrooms. It ended up becoming a strange thing in Vegas. Fortunately it didn't last long. If you wanted to use a stall you had to put a dime in the slot, then you could open up the door and use it. Then when you finished the door would close and you had to pay again unless you were able to find someone who would keep the door open for you so you didn't have to pay to use it. Ninety-nine percent of the time no one else was there to let you in so you wouldn't have to pay. I saw them all over the place, hotels, and stores even the airport.

Since I was the youngest, no one wanted to pay a dime to use the toilets so I had to crawl under the door and then open up the door and let my older sisters in. I'm sure anyone reading this could imagine what was on the floor already. One by one I kept doing it until all them got to go in without having to pay to get in. No one would let me use one after they did so I had to either pay a dime or crawl under the door so I could use one.

No one was happier than I was when they finally stopped it since I was the one who had to go on to the floor and get a door opened. It didn't matter how clean or dirty the floors were. No one was going to pay for it except me and I'm not talking about money.

They ended up getting rid of them since Americans didn't want to pay for something that was a necessity. It seemed like it took forever for it to reach Las Vegas. One person told me they weren't making much money out of them. Probably because of people like me who were taking the round about way to avoid the situation of giving them money.

Television

It was like a twenty minute drive to a local TV station. They would record the Merv Griffin talk show at this station. At that time there weren't that many talk shows on TV. Not to mention anyone had heard of cable so the only stations we could get were the local affiliates for each network. Plus an independent station from Henderson.

My mom already knew what time they finished filming the show. Everyday she would call down the station and asked the guy working there who were their guests. They would tell us the name of the people who were scheduled to be on the TV today. Not who was already at the station. She called up so much they recognized her voice and they finally gave her the answer she wanted. They would say stuff like we just finished filming (give the celebrity's name). She would say "Hold on." to the guy on the phone.

Then she would ask us if anyone wanted to see this person. If it was someone we wanted to see she would say we were going to be there in twenty minutes. If there wasn't anyone there we wanted to see, then she would say "Thank you." And then hang up. If it was someone there we wanted to see she made sure we had pen and paper handy to get their autographs. That is one thing I never see anymore, autograph books. They seem like antiques now.

Most of the time they would be people my older sisters wanted to see. Like Wayne Newton, Tom Jones, Engelbert Humperdink and so on. I could never understand why they liked them so much.

Mash

There was a show on television that was just starting out called Mash. There was a character on the called Radar. He was the kind of person who would help all sorts of animals. Pet kinds and wildlife. He would today probably be a PETA member the way he felt about animals. I noticed how much I liked comedies since it made me laugh and took my mind off of my problems.

When I was a kid I watched the show and was able to relate to Radar so much. When I saw him helping a turtle or a rabbit I kept thinking now there is something I would love to do. Take care of animals. He would name even the wildlife. I can see where God was listening to me then too. He did it in a round about way, but I ended up getting a job at a vet clinic. What did I end up doing? Taking care of wildlife and named them just like Radar did. Every time wildlife came in they would call me and say something like "Thumper is here." So I knew that a wild rabbit came in and I had to go take care of it.

News

People already know about the different unions and that some of them go on strike, like the Writer's Guild of America, Screen Actor's Guild, etc. Well when we were living in Vegas the same actors would be working at the hotels. Doing night shows and some other stuff. Sometimes they got paid for it like a stand up comic does. Other times they would be gambling so much that they ended up getting themselves into debt and the only way to repay the hotel was to do stand up acts and some other works to pay it off.

All we had to do is drive by somewhere in Vegas and you would see on the billboard signs that Tom Jones would be at the Landmark hotel (for example) and that they would be posting the dates he would be there. It the actor was there for a long time it usually meant that they had a big bill to pay. If they were there only for a weekend then they were getting paid as a gig like other actors do. My mom was already familiar with which actors had the gambling debt. She would see the person's name on a billboard and say the person's name is here because they have a bill to pay. It took me a while to understand what she was talking about.

One time we saw on the news that the actors and other celebrities were on strike. They were picketing outside on the strip during the day holding up signs and moving in a circle like people do when they are on strike. My mom saw it and told us to load up the car.

We couldn't figure out the commotion was all about. So we loaded up and went down there. After I got down there I could see why. Everyone's favorite singer, actor, etc. Were all there striking. After a while walking in circles they were tired. So if we wanted an autograph they were happy to do it. They wanted a break anyway. So we ended up making a killing on autographs then. I think we ran out of paper and the autograph books got filled really quickly.

Again I can see God was setting me up for the career he wanted me to have, but doing all of this work and practicing it now for needing it in the future. For example being able to communicate with celebrities…

Career

Looking back I can see where God was getting me ready for this career. If you were raised up talking to celebrities like they were "normal" people and didn't even think of those like "higher power" like a lot of people do nowadays. They think they are idols and people who are "higher" than them. I can't get over what people say.

I was raised up to where I went up to them. Especially at an early age. To go up to them and get an autograph for my sisters. So to I saw them as normal people. Not idols. I would always be told to get an autograph for an actor, for example. I was told to get him to sign it with my sister's name. I went up there and they would ask me "Who do I make it out to?"

I would tell them Liz. Or whoever the autograph was for. I would be bored waiting for them to write it. I didn't know who the person was. I was a kid. This would be someone a teenager wanted an autograph for. I was like "trained" to do this. Then the actor would write down something about me. Like: "You have a sweet smile". Then he would sign his name.

So the autography would be in three parts. My sister's name. Something about me and then their signature. One time a celebrity saw me come up and wanted my name. Since he knew I was being forced to do this against my will. He ended up signing it to me. I didn't know who this was since I was a kid. Debbie and Liz were mad at me since it wasn't for them. Took the autograph and tore it up into little pieces. The only time I was wanted was to help someone get an autograph from a celebrity. So now this is how I see them.

They are normal people who have a job just like you and me. The only thing that makes them different than like your next door neighbor is their job. Before you go running off thinking so and so makes x number of dollars per episode and has a huge house than you do there is a difference. A lot of showbiz people have to start at the beginning like you did when you got a job at sixteen for example. Some actors quit because they can't even make a living out of it. They quit and do something else. The ones you are thinking have been in the business forever and have a reputation now or are so well known that they can get paid so much.

I can see now where God was just getting me ready for the job he wanted me to do, but in order to do it I had to get used to being around these people so I can accept them as normal people and talk to them like normal people so I can handle my future employment.

Presidents

While I was living in Las Vegas Nixon was President and the Vice President was Spiro Agnew. It seems strange now remembering that far back. I had to do a report while I was in Mary's room. Agnew was resigning so I had to do a report on it. In my opinion the guy was speaking jibberish. I couldn't understand a word he was saying. I had to ask Mary to explain it to me. So I could write up the report.

It was a short time between Nixon not having a Vice President and until he found another one. He came into Vegas to give a speech. We went to the convention center and he gave a talk. It was also the first time I had someone check my purse and had to go through a metal detector. Otherwise I never saw one.

He gave what seemed to me a boring speech, but since I was a kid, it probably isn't s surprise. The only thing I remember beside the security check was all these secret service people and guards they had. I kept my eye on them the whole time counting how many there were. Police and other security type of people that were there. It was so unusual for me to see so many people like that in one place.

Ford

Shortly afterwards Nixon got a new Vice President named Gerald Ford. It wasn't much longer after that Nixon resigned and then Ford became president. What happened afterwards? Ford came to Las Vegas to give a speech at the convention.

I was starting to wonder what is wrong with this country. We go through Presidents like people do with potato chips? It was unusual. I was trying to figure up how long Ford was going to last as president since the others were leaving right and left.

Labor Day Telethon

In 1973, Jerry Lewis moved the Muscular Dystrophy Association Labor Day Telethon to Las Vegas, Nevada. I remember the Sahara Hotel is where it was filmed at. He would raise money for the charity. It would be filmed in Las Vegas after it was originally started in another state. Every year we would go there to see an hour of it. Every hour they would change audiences so we can only be there for that time period. I remember one year seeing Telly Savalas, from the TV show "Kojak", my mom tried telling me he was sitting in the right side of the room a few rows down from us.

At that time I was familiar with him, but I couldn't hear my mom since she was on my left side so she had to speak up. By this time he heard her and was looking around to see who was yelling. He didn't want anyone to know he was there until he came up to the stage. She quickly put her hand down hoping he didn't see her. I don't think he did since he kept looking around our area trying to find out who was blowing his cover.

Maybe if he had worn a hat it would have helped. My mom loved it when the guest stars would show up. Like Dean Martin, Frank Sinatra, she would try to get their autographs. We would end up going to one audience and come back a few hours later. They never know we came back more than once.

One year Jerry Lewis was complaining that the number board wasn't going as fast as it should have been. So he walked around the audience trying to get people to put their cash in a square plastic box that had sharp edges at the bottom. He was moving so fast that he went past some people who still wanted to donate. He would stop by when a kid wanted to donate a dime and whiz past adults in a rush. One guy yelled out "I've got a hundred!" So he quickly came back to the guy to get his donation. But in the process he took the plastic container and hit my mom on the head.

She was hurting so bad we had to leave in a hurry. Her head was bleeding a bit from the sharp edges from the box. Jerry Lewis never did check on her or anyone associated with the event. The security noticed us leaving in hurry and my mom holding on to the side of her head. No one did or ask us about anything. To this day I still don't watch it because I think about that incident.

Nevada Church

At this church we went to you graduated from Sunday School when you were ten years old. All we did in Sunday School was play with kitchen toys like you see at toy stores. They look like small versions of sinks, stoves, etc. That three year old kids would play with. Never learned bible verses or anything that people would learn in church. Then after you graduated from Sunday School you were expected to go to Church and listen to the preacher.

I got bored with the preacher and fell asleep a lot. The only time during the sermon when I woke up is when the preacher yelled or slams his hand on the pulpit. The choir was sitting in a raised section above the preacher. The men sat in a box on the right. The women would sit in a box across from them. They were facing each other instead of the congregation.

The minister couldn't preach on gambling, prostitution or alcoholism as a sin since the majority of the members of the church worked at hotels (where there was gambling, alcohol, strippers and prostitution, celebrities being idolized going on outside or inside the place) So what were they supposed to preach on? Not much except complain about the other churches in the city and how better they were compared to the others. They didn't even preach on how God made things. When you lived near Lake Mead, which is a man made lake and they never did let you forget that. Mentioning all the time how many men, labor and scientifically how they went about making this lake for your convenience.

In 1971, my mom was elected and became a deacon of the church. My dad did a letter of transfer from the previous church to this one, but never attended. He would spend his Sundays working on the cars and drinking his beer. To him that was his day of rest. No bother with the kids for a short time while we were in Sunday school and everyone was at church.

My mom was re-elected as a deacon for a second term in 1974. According to the church's records she remained as a deacon till 1977. She already left the church and we moved to Texas in 1975. So how could she be a deacon from 1975 to 1977 is something I can't understand. She couldn't attend meetings or do anything from another state.

When she had to go to deacon meetings, my dad was supposed to take care of us, but he would assign the older sister to baby-sit us since he just wanted to drink his beer or mixed drinks and then go to sleep after working all day. The majority of the time it was Debbie and we dreaded it from the way we would be treated. Personally I didn't know which was worse. Dad or Debbie?

My sister, Liz, got saved in 1971. From listening to a rock opera called "Jesus Christ Superstar". The opera debuted on Broadway in 1971. It starts out on Palm Sunday and goes through Easter. A lot of people got saved from seeing it or listening to the music. Liz was so affected from it she was trying to teach me stuff about the bible. he was good about taking this stuff and putting it in simple terms so even I could understand it. Kind of like a bible study. Neither one of us liked how the church was so we would skip church and have that at home on Sunday mornings in the backyard. It was fun.

Sooner or later our parents found out about it. My mom yelled at us telling us that if we wanted to learn that stuff we would have to go to church. I wonder at times if it was my mom's idea or my dad's. Either way we had to quit it and go back to church. I dreaded doing that.

Because of all of this I ended up becoming what some people refer to as a "Submarine Christian." Only showing up at church on Easter and Christmas. I didn't even want to come to church for those events. Why should I? "All they are going to do is telling us the same story every year." I said to my mom. Sure enough I ended up going just so she would quit telling me. We went and guess what? They ended up telling us the same story again. My mom would ask "Didn't you like the service?"

"No." I answered. "They told the same story they did last year." We argued in the car about it. I kept thinking to myself. "I'll never go to church again even if you paid me."

I learned earlier that there is a higher power named God and that he was in charge. From the biofeedback and the trailer, but after all the bad things that were happening I kept blaming him thinking that if he was in charge how could he have let all this happen. He could have prevented the rape. He could have prevented me from all these injuries I got from the abuse. If he was as powerful as everyone said. He would have sent me to another family that would have loved me for one thing.

So even if I didn't attend church I knew there is a God and that he was in charge. Even my sister Debbie would tell me there wasn't a God. She told Mary and me the same thing. (I don't remember what Mary's reply was.) She wouldn't let either one of us out of the room until we said we agreed with her. I didn't want to, but I didn't want to get hurt again – getting hurt by everyone else at school, church, and home was bad enough.

Finally, I made my decision before she could beat me up. I ended up telling her there wasn't a God, and saying it to her face so she could hear me. I felt bad about it, and ran as fast as I could to my room. I shut the door, and locked it to keep her away from me, and then I prayed to God to help me through all of this. And I asked him why I was even alive, why he put here if I had to go through this. Again, I was thinking I would be better off dead than going through it all. I was being spiritually abused at home and persecuted even before I'd accepted Jesus as my savior. I was seven when she did this to me; this was when she was baby-sitting us, and she was in charge.

If you think about it though God gives you challenges and trials he knows you can handle. If you can handle step one, he leads you to step two and so on. In order for me to get to step two I had to pass this step one. Each time you pass a step you grow in spirit and are able to handle another trial or challenge. The only time these challenges stop is when you find yourself home in heaven. Trying to kill yourself doesn't get you there quicker. It sends you down to another path in another direction. The only way to get to heaven is by following God's direction and stay on the path He has set up for you.

At times the minister would refer to God as our Father. Every time I heard that I was scared. He would say things like going to heaven and being treated there the same way as your human father would treat you. All I could do is think about a heavenly father beating me up, drinking and yelling me for stuff because he was drunk. If we did say a prayer at night my mom would suggest one. I was scared to say any of them. I didn't want to spend eternity in a place getting yelled at and beaten up forever. I would rather stay here on earth. At least I knew my dad would die and if worse came to worse I would have to wait till he died to have the beatings stop then. In heaven I wouldn't know when that would happen.

My mom would teach me a prayer to say before I go to sleep. Now I lay be down to sleep... I'm sure everyone has heard that one. What bothered me saying that one was the part where you would say ... if I die before I wake I pray the Lord soul to take. I was already afraid of dying and spending eternity in a place with someone hitting me all my life like my dad did so reciting that prayer didn't last long. I pretty much gave up on that really fast. When she wanted me to say it in front of her I began crying when we got to the part about dying. She finally picked up on and said I didn't have to say it. I ended up not doing prayers before I went to sleep until after I got saved.

I never heard of people singing hymns in a place like this until after I graduated from Sunday School and this didn't happen till I was ten years old. I could never understand what kind of stuff the choir was singing since all of this felt like a foreign language. I didn't know which was more boring, the sermon or the singing, My mom tried to show me in the hymn book and how to follow everyone else. Again it was a lost cause. I gave up and just looked at the stained glass windows. I was so bored.

The one thing I liked was when the handbell choir showed up. They had two of them. One of they were group of girls who were about the age of high school kids. The second group was an adult group. I loved hearing the sound of them so much. I kept thinking to myself "Now there is something I would like to do when I was old enough." Of course we moved to Texas so that never happened. Looking back now I can see where God was listening, because he made that possible. I don't think the handbell choir director could get me to leave that even if he wanted to.

Babysitting

While I was growing up there was a girl who I was friends with. Her name was Robin. She was what they refer to now as a mentally challenged person. Since we were little girls we would play with dolls. My older sisters were told that they would baby-sit this one lady's kid and they got paid for it. Who really did the babysitting? Me. Who got paid? The sister. It would start with Cynthia and worked down to Debbie and Liz. It didn't matter which one. I played with her and they got paid.

I did notice one thing different about this family. The mother knew that I was doing the work. I didn't mind. I enjoyed playing with her daughter. So she ended up "paying" back not by paying me but taking her daughter and me out. I ended up seeing theatre plays in Vegas. They would be dressed up in fancy dresses and wore long white gloves that matched their outfits. Everyone else at the theatre was dressed up as nice and I looked like I was in rags. I didn't have any clothes that would classify to wear to the plays.

The mother paid for our dinners, tickets and refreshments. When I asked Robin if this was something new for her she replied. "We do this all the time." My mom ended up buying me a nice outfit to wear to the plays after that. I asked mom what did dad say about the clothes. She replied. "Don't even worry about it." She was more concerned about me having the outfit. Robin's mother didn't pay my sisters as much and after that we ended up going to more plays. Of course my sisters didn't like that and yelled at me for it. By the time I was twelve I saw a lot of plays. People today can't or won't believe that I have seen so many plays before I turned thirteen. I can see where God was rewarding me for good deeds. I wasn't expecting anything like that.

I went to Robin's house with her mom. I couldn't get over how it looked. They had a spiral staircase that wasn't even attached to the floor. When I was climbing up it. I had to hold on to the railings on both sides. The stairs would move and I would think it was the coolest thing. When I got to the top. Robin told me to come down. She was used to using them she would run up and down the stairs. I was nervous about it and she said we could use the elevator. I was so surprised she had an elevator. After this, Robin's mom would pick me up and I could spend the day at her house and get me away from the house. Of course my sister's didn't like it. Now they didn't get paid.

Eventually Robin's mom quit coming over and picking me up. I asked my mom and she didn't tell me. Robin's mom came over and told me she passed away. I was so surprised. I didn't know anyone could die at such an early age like that. I ended up going to her funeral. Her mom was happy that I came. It did make her feel better. I felt like I had lost a true sister instead of a friend. Especially after thinking a family beats you up and a friend helps you. This was my understanding of the two.

As soon as my sisters were old enough to babysit the rest of us, they took advantage of it. Debbie would pretty much yell at us all the time. If she was doing something in her room and we were watching TV she would have us turn the TV down to where we couldn't hear it.

We had to sit in the back on the living room, whether we could see the TV or not, sits up straight. Almost like we were in the military. Sitting that far back we couldn't hear the TV. So we got yelled at again for turning it up too loud. If I couldn't see it and moved in closer to watch it, I got yelled at for it. It would be amazing if we didn't get yelled at by her. One minute she would be nice, the next minute she would be yelling at us. If it wasn't the slot machines now the TV was our babysitter.

Mom and dad would hear that we liked it when she babysat us. We were told if we said that to them we would get something. Like money or junk food. Guess what? We never did. After that we dreaded having her baby-sit for us. I don't think our parents never knew what was going on.

One time my mom was heading out. Debbie was babysitting again. I wanted to ask mom if someone besides Debbie could baby-sit me. She stopped and wanted to know what I wanted to say. Debbie stopped me before I could say anything. She grabbed my arm and put it behind me in the back area and pushed it up into my back. I was hurting she whispered for me not to say anything and she ended up telling mom. "Oh she just wants you to have a safe trip."

"Oh thank you Betty."

"I'll be back." Mom answered. I didn't get the arm out of my back till after Debbie closed the door.

Again I got yelled at and threatened by Debbie for trying to keep her from doing some what she referred to as babysitting and getting her money. She needed the money for something since she wasn't old enough to get a job yet and needed the money. What for I never did find out. But it was worth it for the babysitting and what she did to us. At times I didn't know who was worse. My dad or Debbie.

Christian Camp

Only one time I remember going to a camp was a Junior High Camp that was through the church. I went one time since it was during the summer and I was just going into junior high. I don't know if my other sisters went or not. Mary was excited that she was going for the second time, but no way wanted me to come along. I know older sisters didn't want their younger sisters tagging along, but considering my physical problems it makes sense to keep an eye on me.

Considering this was a Camp put on by Christians, not even going into what devotion it was, you think there would be people being there to correct problems or kids who wouldn't even behave like the ones in this camp was. Since it was new to me, I was excited and ended up having one of the top bunks. I was never allowed to have a top bunk at home in case I had a grand mal seizure and rolled off the top bunk. There would be a good chance I wouldn't even make it.

The counselors knew about my medical problems, but again no one considered any of these things as a medical problem. I guess it was a sign of the times. During the week, we would be going swimming. On a Monday we had a bible study. They asked us how many of the kids read their bible. Mary and I never raise our hands. The other kids looked at us like we were aliens from another planet. They asked us if we even knew what one looked like.

The counselor looked at us and showed hers to us. I spoke "I've seen one of those before". "Good" she replied "Where have you seen it?"

"It's in the living room." I told her. "Where in the living room?"

"Sitting in the bottom part of the coffee table." I answered. "Don't you use it?" I had a shocked look on my face when I answered.

"Nobody uses it. It just sits there getting dirty." After bible study we had to divide into groups and get a bible verse. By Friday night we had to act out the bible verse like a play. We were in groups of four, the head of the group grabbed a folded up piece of paper and pulled it out. When she got to the group she read it and was excited. "Oh good, it's a short one." She has been to this camp before she knew exactly what to do, this is why she was in charge of the play.

On the paper read Luke 21:1-4. 1 As Jesus looked up, he saw some rich people putting their gifts into the Temple money box. 2 Then he saw a poor widow putting two small copper coins into the box. 3 He said, "I tell you the truth, this poor widow gave more than all those rich people. 4 They gave only what they did not need. This woman is very poor, but she gave all she had to live on." the kids in group was trying to figure out how to do the play. They were bouncing off the ideas like they already knew what it was about and everything. I never heard the story or knew what was going on. I was curious and trying find out where this stuff was at. To me it looked like a foreign language. The kids just told me to move aside and not to get into the way.

"We're busy!"

"We're trying to assign parts!" So I heard them telling which kid what they would do. I asked "What did you want me to do?" They looked at each other. Talked between them. "Don't worry about it. We'll just give you a small part. We need to work on it. Go do something else and we'll call you later." They just told me what to do when my part came up. I never did learn the story from doing that and forgot about the story until way into my adulthood when I was in my thirties. Kids usually know this story by heart since it is a short story and is easy to memorize. Whenever it came for the group to practice the part of the play. I would show up because the counselors were busy cleaning the kitchen. I asked to help, but they said no since I was supposed to be practicing the play. When I got to the area they were practicing they didn't need me.

"Go away."

"We don't need you."

"Come back Friday."

"That is when we'll need you."

"Yea Friday." Someone else shouted. So I went swimming and did other stuff by myself since I wasn't needed. When it became Friday I lost track of the time and I came in late so I got yelled at by the girl in charge. She kept yelling at me and others were telling me what they wanted me to do. I was supposed to be one of rich people who threw a lot of money into the box. To do this we used heavy rocks to represent a lot of money and placed it in a coffee tin. When my part came up I dropped it into the coffee can, but got yelled at it for it since they never told me to do it gently so there wouldn't be any noise. When we got our score later I heard we didn't do as good as another group.

So they yelled at me and told me they lost because my rock was too loud. The girl in charge of the group complained that she was in this camp and every year she does these plays and never wins. She just once wanted to win these plays she does every year and now this was her last year she wasn't going to be able to win. So she figured it was my fault that she lost this year. I was thankful to be out of there and actually wanting to go home. We didn't go the following year since we were moving to Texas. Looking back now I can see where they had a golden opportunity to minister to someone and blew it off like a shepherd who doesn't want his lost lamb anymore.

Jesus never did leave his lamb. In John 10: 3-5 it says: 3 "The one who guards the door opens it for him. And the sheep listen to the voice of the shepherd. He calls his own sheep by name and leads them out. 4 When he brings all his sheep out, he goes ahead of them, and they follow him because they know his voice. 5 But they will never follow a stranger. They will run away from him because they don't know his voice."

Jesus was saying this story to people. If you think about it. The people at the camp were like the sheep. They were not listening to the shepherd's voice. It was all over the place, but they refused to acknowledge it. Having too much pride and not listening to people and their needs. In one way it was like they had been spiritually abused to the point where they didn't even notice it and passed it along to others. The same way a virus gets passed around. Till everyone has it.

Our culture is a lot like that. Christians are not recognizing the symptoms and are passing this virus around. They need to wake up from a deep sleep and spend time with others and begin shepherding lost souls and bring them to the Lord who is the Shepherd of everyone and everything.

Everyone is given a golden opportunity to be a minister to someone. Unfortunately these people were given a chance and blew it. Don't make the same mistake they did. They were consumed with table manners, plays and chores that they didn't see what was most important. Jesus!

Pools

Being in the city of course there was a city pool. It ended up being a small circle, where the life guard was in the middle sitting. One summer there was a lot of glass near the pool. I was only five years old and got glass in my foot. My parents ended suing the city for the exact amount of money for the bill. When they got to the courtroom, people were suing for thousands of dollars. (Keep in mind this was back in the 1960's) They just sued for under $100 which is the exact amount down to the penny for the bill. They lost. The people who sued for thousands won every case. My mom kept thinking if they sued for thousands maybe they would have won. When it got to the point where you couldn't do anything but just stand up, we ended up leaving and going to a bigger pool.

The next pool we went to was the high school pool in the summer. We kept doing that every year. One summer, Cynthia, was having a grand mal seizure at the pool. Cynthia was under water for quite a while before a lifeguard figured out she wasn't coming out of the pool. She was taken to the hospital and we never went back there again.

The following summer we ended up going to the hotel pools. My mom would go and play the slot machines while the kids were outside using the hotel pools. One hotel would have a waterfall at the shallow end of the hotel. Another one had a pool in a shape of a champagne glass.

There was another hotel where the pool had two lower diving boards with steps that led up to the high dive in the middle. The high dive would be used so much we didn't get to use it much.

Some hotel pools picked up on it quick that we weren't guests. They would ask for our hotel key and of course we didn't have one. After a while my mom would just tell us to tell them she is inside with the slot machines. Since we weren't old enough to go in there they couldn't do anything.

All the hotels would have souvenirs to give out to their guests. All we had to do is say we are from some state and wanted to get souvenirs. Every time we would go home after swimming we would stop by the desk and ask for souvenirs.

If they figured out she wasn't staying in a room she told them she had to get the kids and then we had to get out. Every year there was one hotel that would see us swimming every day for the whole summer who never said anything to us and we ended going to their pool every year.

Seventh Grade

One thing I noticed about seventh grade was how much the music on the radio was affecting my seizures. I would be listening to the radio as soon as I got home. We got home at 2:30 in the afternoon. I would turn on the radio and a song would be playing. Mostly *"Seasons in the Sun"* by Terry Jacks would be playing by the time I turned the radio on. You could set your watch by this.

Certain songs that were popular would cause my auras and some didn't. Even with *"Kung Fu Fighting"* by Carl Douglas would be played the intro and the same part repeated in the middle would cause me to have auras and the rest wouldn't, which would explain the atmosphere in the room changing from the vibrations in the room. Explaining how the sound would trigger them rather than lights like a lot of doctors blame it on. What I thought was weird that every one of them that triggered my auras ended up being a number one song on the billboards.

It didn't take long for the bullies to take over. I don't know if this was normal or not since this was my first year at this school. The teacher was so terrified of the kids. I already knew these kids had a reputation for being bullies since we have been going to the same school every year except for last year when desegregation went into effect. This was more of a babysitting room for us rather than a classroom. Looking back at this school year I can now see why it was a memory I ended up repressing.

Again I would use my biofeedback to get rid of them. If I had trouble I turn the radio off and the aura would go away. I kept doing this till the aura would stop and I was able to listen to the whole song without having an aura. To this day I can listen to songs and not have an aura.

People today talk a lot about bullies. Some even go as far to think that they weren't around when I was a kid. Believe me they were around even when I was a kid. Here is another example…

Kids Taking Over

This must have been the weirdest part for me about going to school in Vegas. I could never figure it out. Even years later looking back now. The kids were even in charge.

The ones who would be the bullies would rule the classes. Even the teachers would be scared of them. Apparently this is a class that was designed just for the trouble makers. So they figured I was a trouble maker and put me in with them. I just sat in the back row and they left me alone. I just brought a book to read or watch TV. Either way you passed the class. Like I said here you graduated with a third grade education. Who cares what you did.

I literally gave up. Now the bullies who attacked me were even threatening the teacher. What was I supposed to do? If I did anything I would get beaten up. Same thing at home so what is the difference. One is an adult one is a kid. Now even the school was thinking of me as a suspect instead of the victim. I literally gave up. They were thinking of sending me to reform school if I did anything more. Apparently they told my parents this, but not me. So I just sat in the back and try to avoid everyone. Maybe that would help? Boy was I wrong.

Thinking back now I wished I did something to help, but the way things were I would have either been hurt of accused of causing trouble. That is how bad it was. Kids were already bringing weapons into school there. No metal detectors like they have now. So I would have been wounded for trying to help.

The teacher would have what is known as failing notices. I learned earlier that the parents aren't supposed to know about it so I didn't want to go through that again and I didn't want to listen to a bully so I told her "No!" She yelled at me. "What?"

"You can't say that to me!"

"I already know the parents don't see these so I don't have to listen to you." I replied. "You can't disobey me." She said angrily. So she huffed off to the teacher yelling. "Teacher she won't listen to me!" They were talking. I could see her looking at me and pointing toward me. Since I could lip read I knew the bully was saying that Betty is sitting back there and won't sign the paper. The teacher looked at me and told her to leave me alone then. The bully was acting like she was going to cry or something. "Betty has to sign this."

"I don't have anything to do and I'm getting bored."

"If you don't let me make her sign it I'll bring something to school tomorrow..."

I couldn't make out what she was planning on bringing. Plus I was wondering if the bully could pick up the fact that I could lip read. Sometimes she would act like she could and other times she acted like she couldn't tell.

The teacher looked frightened and told the bully she can do whatever she wanted. The bully came over to me and told me "The teacher wants you to sign it." I told her "Go away and then I'll sign it." She looked over to the teacher and told her "She won't listen to me." The bully's head was away from me. The next thing I noticed was the teacher was getting up. "See."

"The teacher will come over and hit you if you don't sign it." I saw the teacher coming over so I signed it. After that I signed every single one of the failing notices even if I didn't do anything wrong and they all ended up on my school records just because a bully got bored in class. After she got me to sign it because she was bored.

I noticed she was making a contest out of it. She wanted to spend her day trying to see how many of us would sign these failing notices. If someone said no to her she would point to me and said "Betty signed one you have to sign it too." I wasn't near them but I could lip read them. After she got everyone to sign one everyday she would give the pile to the teacher. It wasn't long after that she would do it more than once a day.

I remember signing up to five a day. It just depended on how bored the girl was. When the bully was sick and didn't come in guess what? No failing notices to sign. The teacher would say "Thank you." To the bully like she was happy to get them. I noticed the teacher put them in a drawer where there was a stack of them. I asked her later "Do you send those to the office." Since that is what she is supposed to do. She treated me like a trouble maker. "She is just doing her job and helping me." The teacher was confident when she said that.

Then the bully walked out of the room cheerfully saying to the teacher. "I'll see you tomorrow." The teacher replied. "See you tomorrow." In a cheerful voice, but when the girl left the teacher was so relieved that the girl was gone. I tried talking to her about it and she just yelled at me. I figured I had enough of getting yelled at by my family and here so she was on her own as far as I was concerned.

As far as the teacher was concerned, she figured we were all nothing but a bunch of trouble makers and that she was just babysitting us from eight am to two pm. I honestly think if something happened to all of us she wouldn't mind. She never gave us the idea that she would want to see one of us changes or tries to become a better person. We had a dean at this school, but never a counselor. The dean at this school was someone you went to when you got in trouble, but not some one to talk to if you needed emotional support. I was the victim and no one believed me. Just like in fourth grade. I tried crying wolf again and no one heard me.

I started becoming friends with a girl, Alice, who was in my class. So since this was a class with nothing but the trouble makers in it, I'm sure you can guess that isn't a good sign. Sure enough I got into more trouble. If we weren't doing something we were planning on it.

In one way it helped pass the time away. I felt like my life was nothing but days just passing by. Not doing anything. Just getting in trouble for one thing or another, at least this time if I got in trouble I was actually doing something for getting yelled at.

Suspended

Like they say third time is the charm? Not in this case. If you get caught for doing something wrong three times you got suspended from school. Sure enough that is what happened to me. Now, Alice and I, were suspended for actually doing something wrong. I was so surprised but at the same time all I could think about is what dad was going to do when he found out. My parents were already dealing with two of my sisters getting in jail and bailing them out. My family didn't believe me about the rape. What is going to happen to me now?

You weren't allowed to return to school till your parents signed a paper and came to the school to talk to the dean. My reputation for being a fast runner and someone who can leave the room unnoticed he must have heard. I was told to stay in the room outside of his office and not leave. He kept opening the door almost all the time to see if I had left unrepentantly.

My mom was furious when she came out. She said I can go back to school now. I didn't want to go back to school and deal with this anymore. "You have to." She replied. "What am I supposed to do when dad finds out?" I asked. "I won't tell him." She answered. To this day I don't know if he ever found out. Between what was going on with my older sisters he may not have found out. One of the reasons my mom wanted to get me back into school so fast. So he wouldn't find out.

Alice on the other end, ended up at the time staying out of school for a week. I kept looking for her and she didn't show up till the next Monday. I asked what was going on and what happened to her with her family. She was treating me worse than the other kids. I just couldn't take it anymore.

I found out about the ordeal with the school saying I was going to be in reform school. This was the first time I had heard it. Apparently other people knew, but I was the last one to hear this. Between all of this it was a bubble that was ready to burst. Sure enough it did when…

Suicide Attempt #1

The day that my bubble burst was like something you see in a movie. Everything is going in slow motion. You can see every second of what is going on. You relive it over and over and wish there was some way you can change the channel and you can't.

I ditched school and just ran home. I didn't care now what happened to me. If there was something nearby I think I would have used it as an option. The bully wasn't there that day. I was hoping she was. I would have asked her to bring the weapon to school. Believe me I would have used it. Again the only person who knew that I was thinking of this was God himself. By the time I got to the intersection walking home was just a block from my house.

It was a street that was very busy. At this time there wasn't a traffic signal there, but they did put one out later. I started going out to the road and almost got hit by a car. Sure enough there was my answer I figured. Just jump in front of a car that was going by fast. You can do it. Then who is going to blame you? If I was dead that would be the answer to all my problems. I wouldn't have to deal with this stuff at home. I wouldn't have to deal with stuff at school. At least that is what I was thinking. Right when I planned the whole thing. What happened?

No cars came by. Where were all these cars a minute ago I thought? There was a bunch of them. It's like they just vanished. I even waited for a while. No cars. In the amount of time I was waiting I could have crossed the street safely. This was getting ridiculous. Finally a car came by and I ran as fast as I could in front of a ladies' car and sure enough she missed me. I thought for sure I planned it right. The lady made me tell her where I lived and she talked to my mom about what I did. The lady left and my mom was made at me. Sure enough my dad found out. "What is wrong with her?" He yelled. By now I didn't care what happened to me. I figured I did everything wrong nothing was going to get better.

You can see where God is in control. The bully never showed up that day. There was plenty of time for me to get across the street safely. He is control of every situation. Whether you realize it or not.

The following year I was walking home from school with Mary. One of the bullies came by on his bike. I started to panic thinking he was going to do something to me again. Plus after everything that happened he could beat me up and no one would believe me. He ended up riding his bike slow and talking to Mary. I couldn't believe it he was actually nice to her. They talked a little since they knew each other from band. He didn't know we were sisters.

After he found out that we were sisters he stopped bullying me and was nice to me the rest of time while were still going to school there. Of course Mary could never believe he was a bully to her he was a nice kid and I was the one with a problem. Pretty much what I still hear today from my family. Some things never change.

Roller Skating

Back when I was kid they didn't have roller blades like they do now. They had roller skates. When you went to a skating rink they would have some with four wheels. Two in the front and two in the back. If you had some other ones they would be attached to your sneakers and you adjusted them with a key.

You have probably seen people do tricks on ice skates. When I was a kid we did the same thing on roller skates. Skating backwards, jumps, etc. Pretty much what some people do with roller blades, but we only did ours to music. To this day I can recall the routine when a certain song comes on the radio. I can redo the routine on roller blades and tell you which ones I did routines to.

So even back then I was entertaining people by doing tricks on roller skates. They had more rinks back then compared to what I see nowadays. To this day I own a pair of roller blades, but they are the kind that is camouflage to look like a regular pair of sneakers.

The wheels push out in case you want to get away from someone and you can push them back in if you want to just walk in them. The only people who can tell I am wearing roller blades today are the kids and teenagers. Everyone else thinks I am wearing a pair of sneakers.

I still go out and do some tricks with the roller blades that I have now. Some people think it is strange with my vision.

Test Site

My dad used to work at the Nevada Test Site when we were living there. He would drive about seventy miles to get to work one way. It is located northwest of Las Vegas on a reservation area. While he was working there they would test the bombs under ground. You couldn't see them, but you could see the damages from them. He would let my mom know what time the bomb would go off. She in turn would call us to come into the kitchen. You couldn't hear the bombs going off but you could see the effects of it when the chandelier would be moving side to side from it. Like a pendulum.

You could also see the effects or feel them in the ground. Our house would be on the ground and the rugs would cover it up. There wasn't a flooring put between the two. So when the bombs would go off you could feel "cracks" in the flooring or your floor tile would be coming apart after each blast. We knew what was going on, but a lot of the citizens living there didn't know. So they would find these strange things on the floor or under the rug and not know what was going on.

By the time we left Vegas there were a lot of "cracks" in the flooring under the rugs. When they would show the house to new people they never told them about the test site or the cracks in the cement. People would trip when coming in and the realtor would act like there was something wrong with the customer rather than tell them there were cracks or there was a problem from cemented flooring under the rug was breaking up a lot.

Lake Mead

When they built Hoover Dam it created a new way for the river to run causing the water to go another direction. The dam was built during the depression and named after President Hoover who signed for it. In other words a lake was formed. They named it Lake Mead since it holds a large portion of the water behind the dam. So who took credit for it? Man. So no credit was given to God for this.

I still don't understand how they can take credit for something that God did. When God made the water, materials for us to use and end up making the dam, etc. Some people still don't understand that God made the things at the beginning and then we took them further to make metals and other supplies to make the dam in the first place that ended up creating the dam. This in turn helped the lake to appear.

Las Vegas is in a valley. So there are mountains surrounding the city and the lake is at the bottom of the area. Making the city vulnerable for flooding, when friends of mine move to Vegas the first thing I tell them about is the weather and the flooding.

One thing good about this is that you can go to the mountains and play in the snow in the mornings. Then come down to the lake and go swimming in the afternoons. I don't know of many places where you can do that in the same place.

We would always go swimming at the lake. My dad would spend time by himself going fishing when the rest of us would be swimming. My older sisters would be diving off the rocks like you see in ads. I am surprised they never hurt their heads. From where I was they could have broken their necks or something worse when they did their diving stunts.

I would get those free toys they would put in the cereal boxes. One time it was a wind up boat made to be in the water. The only place I was allowed to take it was in the lake. So I would wind it up and let it run. The fish would follow it and it took them away from my dad. Of course I got in trouble for it. He told me to move away from the boat. But when I did the fish came with me and he yelled at me again. So he told me to wind up the boat and leave it there so he would get the fish. I gave up and did what he said. No one would spend time with me since he was fishing and drinking his beer again. He would do that every time we went to the lake trying to catch fish and never did. personally I think it was because he was busy making sure he had enough to drink instead of watching the fish. Some of us were interesting in learning to fish, but he didn't want to teach us so he could be alone with his beer.

Sometimes he would drive the boat back. If he was too drunk he would fall asleep. Two of my older sisters would help get him out of the seat. I would hold the steering wheel until my mom would get into the seat and drive. That would take place a few times. Each of my older sisters would learn how to drive the boat. I think it was so my dad could sleep from the drinking.

My mom was watching my older sisters and their diving tricks so I just went swimming by myself. That is why I can never understand why they say not to go swimming by yourself. I've been doing that for years.

Leaving Home

Cynthia ended up leaving home first by graduating from high school and going into the Navy. I've noticed how quickly these three people left home as soon as they could. Since they were older they could tell things were getting worse and worse by the minute. Cynthia was one of three of the girls who got the least amount of abuse.

Debbie ended up leaving next. She moved into an apartment in Vegas with some friends. At the time we didn't know she had bipolar, but you can see how she "clashed" with dad on everything and her abuse was a lot worse than mine was.

Liz got married when she was only seventeen years old. My parents had to sign a piece of paper so she could get married as young as she did. They ended up eloping so no one was allowed to go to their "wedding". She was one of three that got the least amount of abuse. You can see how quickly each one left home as if they were in a prison and was finding a way to get out. Each one did it as fast as they could.

At times I envied them. They were finally out of the house. No more abuse. Since Mary and I were still there. I kept thinking we were going to get the worse of it now. Who else was he going to beat up? Before he had six people. Now it was down to three. Who is going to get the brunt of it?

# CALIFORNIA

Every summer my dad would get two weeks off from work and we would take a trip, driving around, and see the same things every year. He would drive the pick up; my mom would be in the front holding his beer for him while they listen to the music. The rest of us kids would be in the back. An intercom system would be hooked up. So if we needed to get a hold of them we could just press a button. Plus if they wanted to check on us they could listen in.

### Santa Monica

Every year we would go to the beaches in California. My dad would put us in the water to teach us how to swim in the water. We would kick and scream because we didn't want to be in the water. When it was time to come out we were kicking and screaming because we wanted to stay in. It was the complete opposite.

I remember two of my older sisters trying to teach me to dive through the waves. You have to watch the waves and then time it right. If you didn't do it right you would end up doing three summersaults from the force of the water. They would do it right and dive right through. Me? I ended up doing summersaults each time. I guess I never got it right.

We didn't really have any problems with sharks back then. We would go out far away since a lot of it was as high as your knees. So we would go out to even when the people on the beach couldn't see you.

You would really get to appreciate the beauty of God's work going to a place like the beach and seeing the wonders of his creation. Some people really take that for granted.

Of course, we would stay at a campground. Especially, when we would come this direction. It was like sleeping in the backyard for us. We would have sleeping bags and be in a tent. My dad would be a heavy sleeper at home. He would have a lot more drinking on these trips than he has at home. For some reason when we did the camping he didn't get much sleep. So he would drink more to make sure he did sleep.

Monterey

Would be the home for the Scottish Games and Celtic Festival every year. We would plan our trips so the games would be at the end of the trip. They would either be scheduled just for August or part of July through August.

Monterey was also near the beach. So we could go there and do some swimming before then. But most of the time we would associate this place with the Scottish games. We would attend the Scottish activities while my dad would have his beer. We never did see the city just the Scottish activities. After he got tired with the camping we end up advancing to a hotel.

Cynthia, Debbie and Liz were in one hotel room. Mary and I were in the same room with mom and dad. Dad would complain about the noise in the room next to us. I always wanted to be in their room. Since they were having fun. Dad was busy sleeping off the beer so we had to be quiet. I would see Cynthia, Debbie and Liz leaving their room and going somewhere to have fun.

To me it was scary staying in the room with dad. You had to make sure you didn't do anything. If the TV was too loud, you got in trouble. If we were having fun and he didn't like it we got in trouble. It was a no win situation. We already knew what the consequences were if we got in trouble.

It was times like this I was praying I was older instead of the youngest. I could leave the house and not be dealing with dad and his booze. I wish I could throw it out, but if I did we were supposed to get more.

If dad was getting low on beer, we could get more stuff to eat. If he was in a good mood. If not it was just for him. A lot of times I would get out of the camper just to go inside and be with mom. My sisters didn't like it because now they had to move. I couldn't stand it since I was the youngest and no room in the back. I learned quickly to take up the least amount of room in small places. Whether it is a room, car or a bed.

## Santa Rosa

We would drive from Las Vegas to Santa Rosa. That would usually be our first stop on the trip. Every year we would go to a neighboring town. Dad would go to the wineries and drink. The rest of us would go and see things. I remember dad taking us to go to a place and try to pan for gold. He would check to see if we got something.

If we think we did get something, he would come by and check our little pie pans they gave us. If it didn't work he would tell one of us to go to another area and check that area out.

Being kids we would look forward to the same California trip every year. One year we didn't go. Dad took the trip by himself for two weeks. His job was to drink, pan for gold and bring back as much money for us as possible. Instead he came home broke, drunk and didn't have any gold. He told mom the reason he didn't get any gold was because of all of these "squatters". They would be people who had claim to the area and he was forced to keep moving and try to find another place to pan for gold. He said next year he was going to do it again and be a squatter like them so he can get all the gold.

By the time he came home he needed and shave and was too smelly for us to handle including her. So she yelled at him and told him next year he wasn't going to do it. He was going to take his whole family out and not go through this again. I could hear them arguing about how much money he lost. By going out on his own, they couldn't afford to do that every year where she was stuck taking care of all us by herself. She had to listen to us complaining about not being able to go to California again. It was a regular thing so we looked forward to it. To make up to her dad took us to Cynthia's wedding.

Disneyland

Of course every year we had to go to Disneyland since there was five kids in the truck. Everyone was happy to go to it. Even the teenagers had a place to do something they wanted to do, so it made perfect sense.

One of the attractions we would see was the haunted house. In it you would be sitting in a chair that moved and turned around. People loved it and you would see ghosts dancing on the floor. They would be dancing to classical or what others call ballroom type of music. I always enjoyed listening to the music and watching the dancing. They were doing old fashioned dances that people don't do anymore like the waltz.

There was a section of the ride where if you look in the mirror it would appear that a ghost was sitting in the same chair you were. They would turn their head and look at you. If you looked at your chair you wouldn't see it. You could only see them in the mirror.

Another part of it is where a ghost would pop out at the side of you and scream. Because of the screaming, people would have problems. For example an elderly person with a heart condition would have a heart attack and stop breathing. Several people were having problems when the ghosts popped out and scream at them. It didn't matter what medical problem they had they would suffer from it.

Because of this they turned off the sound of the ghosts screaming at you. Now you see a ghost popping out at you, but you don't hear the screaming too. That was the best part we thought of the haunted house.

Since I was a kid I looked forward to this the most. Dad would either stay in the vehicle and drink his beer. Either that or he would go to the Oktoberfest part. If he went in there he would be drinking beer there also. We would have sandwiches packed in the back so he can eat them. For some reason we would always park in the Chip and Dale section. Again another sign from God. (You'll notice it later.) Like always God gives you hints, but you don't pick up on them till later.

Driving

Every year we would have a lot of beer in the car on these trips. Some in the front so dad could drink and drive. Plus a reserve in the back. If his beer got low up front they would get a hold of us in the back and see how much beer was left. In case we had to stop somewhere and get more. If we were getting low on what we needed, that wasn't as important. As long as he got his beer that was the most important thing.

If we did get stopped by a cop we already knew what to say to the cops. Each one of us had our lines memorized on what to say so we would back up his story. (Sounds like we could have been actors)

My dad would always drive drunk every year especially when we left California and was heading back to Nevada. Back then they didn't have drinking and driving laws. Plus most of the area you would be driving was just desert so the chances of getting into a car accident was very slim. One time it was dark and I remember dad was driving home. His headlights were on. Everyone was in the back camper while mom and dad were in the front.

Incident One

One of our tires got blown out from a flat. The first thing dad did was hand his beer over to mom. "Hold this!" She took it and held it. Like this was the most important thing in the world. All of us in the back got thrown all over the place. We didn't have anything to hang on to. I ended up falling close to a corner of the camper. This would be toward the right side if you were looking from outside. I was hitting the tailgate with my back. This made the tailgate open up and was flat.

Things in the back were flying out of the truck. I was grabbing onto a side to hang on. Liz was trying to grab a few things and pull them in. This way we wouldn't loose things. Even a mattress went flying past me. The vehicle went into the left lane and then back into the right lane. This was a two lane road at the time.

Everyone was frantic and trying to grab stuff before we lost more things. I ended up with my head being flung back. The road looked very close to me. I was able to touch the road with my left hand. My foot was caught on the right side of the pick up. My foot was so securely stuck in that spot and couldn't fall out. My right hand was still clenched on the inside of the pickup as tight as I could. Only God could have fixed it so my foot was in that position when the tailgate went down. Otherwise I wouldn't be here to write this. I was pulling myself up and grabbing the side of the back with my hand. The pickup was still moving from each lane. Finally Liz noticed me and helped pull me into the pick up.

As soon as I was in. Liz and Mary closed the tailgate. My mom had a frantic look on her face when we were wondering what was going on. She asked if I was in now. Liz told her yes. I was just happy to be in the back now close to the head of the pick up. This was when I was eight years old.

Afterwards we had to go back to get our stuff that blew out of the truck. Other things plus the tire. I was in a hurry to go home. Forget the other things. I was too shaken up. People put too much on possessions rather than family.

Incident Two

Another time, when I was seven years old. Our attention was reverted to the front when dad started swerving the truck. Mom told us to stay down while he was driving. Instead we kept asking "What is wrong?" She just kept repeating the same thing. She tried grabbing the beer from him.

He made sure the beer in the cup stayed with him. I offered to help, but she wanted me to stay in the back. We felt so helpless. The truck was still moving from the left lane against the traffic and back into the right lane of traffic every half mile.

She kept asking him to let her take over so she could drive. He didn't want to. Finally the truck ended up in a ditch on the right side of the road. He ended up passing out. I can see now where again God was watching us. It was a blessing in disguise. My mom ended up getting into the driver's seat. It took all of us to move him into the passenger seat. I never saw him wake up during the rest of the trip. My mom took the cup and threw it out.

When he finally woke up a little all he asked about was where his beer was. Nothing about the truck or anything about us. The following day he was mad about the damage on the truck and was glad he could just fix it. Never enquire about us or anything. My mom was mad at him for a long time afterwards. I was surprised since he could have been abusing her about it. I don't remember him abusing her over it.

Los Angeles

Every year while we were visiting California we would go around Los Angeles. It was like a routine or something; we would always see the same cities every year. I could map out our itinerary for you. Day one we would go to Santa Rosa, etc. Since we did they same pattern every year.

Well one place we always went to of course was Los Angeles. See the Hollywood sign go down the Hollywood Boulevard and see the stars of the Walk of Fame. We would do this the day before going to Disneyland since they were both right next to each other. (City wise.)

Sometimes we would drive down Hollywood Boulevard and other times we would walk it. If we drove down the street we would be in the back of the pick up and dad would be yelling at us. If we walked dad would stay in the pick up and drink which means he would be drinking and staying in the vehicle. This is what he liked better. Being able to drink and not having to mess with us talking every five seconds.

People would always try to sell you info on where celebrities live. These are mostly rip off artists. People just make up the maps and say this actor lives on ... Then they tell you the only way you can find out where this person lives is to buy the map. After living in Vegas and seeing people doing the same thing and knowing they put the wrong info with the wrong person we knew not to buy those.

I've done these trips so much I was able to tell people how to get to places years later. Pretty cool that I remember all this info when I haven't even been there for quite a while.

Séance

One thing that was an annual event with us, was the fact that it was an eight hour drive to go from Vegas to California. So we did stuff to entertain us while we were in the back. One thing we did was hold séances; of course we would have to wait till it got dark to do it. First we would take a vote on who we wanted to get a hold of. Then when we all agreed on who we wanted to get a hold of we would hold hands and one person (usually the oldest) would try and communicate with that person.

While the oldest was doing this the rest of us were supposed to be quiet. My sisters would always tell me it wouldn't work unless all of us were in on it. Sometimes I would do it and other times I wouldn't. They would usually try to get some celebrity who passed away. I never even heard of them so I rather go to sleep. Then if they didn't "hear" anything they would take it out on me since I didn't join in on it.

The first year after my grandmother died we held one in the back of the camper like we always did. This year it was different for some reason. I guess because we were trying to get a hold of someone I actually knew. So I joined in, plus I was wondering what she would say to us. If you remember in the previous chapter she died pretty close to Christmas. So this was the first summer after that plus I would have asked her how it was so I wouldn't be dreaming those nightmares again.

I don't know about the others, but I don't remember them getting anything. My sisters would say "Sorry. They don't want to talk to us." Or "I've got something!"

"They say..." and then tell us what the person said. Knowing what I know now it sounds like a con job. Like psychics today. I can even do that if I wanted to with all the stuff I learned back in Vegas.

For a while when I would have an aura, I thought I was psychic and that my auras were some ways of me being able to foretell the future. It took several years to be convinced that the auras weren't that. It took me even longer to find out what the auras even were.

There was another summer where one of my sisters had an idea of who to try to contact this particular year. Liz suggested we get a hold of Jesus. If I remember right it was the same year "Jesus Christ Superstar" was popular which would be in 1972. This shows how we were uneducated on religion. Since Jesus is alive and you use this method to get a hold of a dead person. Anyone could have used prayer to get a hold of him instead of a séance. Liz did get a reply back. "We need to help each other." Is what she was told. We looked at each other and couldn't figure out.

"What does it mean?" Mary asked. Liz had her eyes closed. After a little bit her eyes opened and told us. "We need to bond and work together." I had a shocked look on my face. Like "Yea."

"Have dad beat me up some more?"

"Forget it." and went to another part of the camper. I can see why God would say that to us, but it never did happen. We were too scared from the abuse.

The following year it was just the two of us in the back going to and from California. I asked Mary if she wanted to do a séance and she said they were stupid so we never did them again.

Scottish

Every year we would attend the Scottish games. We would see the girls competing in the dancing section. Dancing in teams of four around two swords placed on the ground in a plus sign. Men usually were competing in the caber tossing games, while some men would enter the bagpipe competition. Some women would compete in a cooking competition and there would be three bands and three drum majors entertaining.

I would spend a lot of time watching the girls trying out for the dancing. It wouldn't take long for me to practice what they were doing. Just like the lip reading and other stuff that I had to teach myself. I can see where God has given me a good talent to memorize things in a hurry. I've definitely been using that all my life. To this day I can still get up and do the same dances like I never forgot them.

I don't remember seeing my dad around when we would be going to see them. We would see different things except the caber tossing. I guess my mom wasn't interested in that. Plus she had to keep an eye on five girls. My dad was gone till we ended up with him when the finale came and the bands were marching.

Each band wore one color for their band. Each band would also have three to four bagpipers per band. My favorite part was when all three bands got together and performed. Seeing the different colors of each band together and performing was so unusual to me. I would be forced to sit between my parents since I was the youngest. You could smell the breath on my dad was so bad that you didn't have to be a rocket scientist to know he had been drinking too much and shouldn't even be there. Those were one of the few times he would be smiling at me and actually hug me. I wanted to get away from him so much since he was drunk so bad, I felt uncomfortable like when the teacher was flirting with me. This maybe one reason why my family never gave out hugs. I always wish we were more like the family would give out hugs. Now I feel like someone who wants hugs all the time.

When we were in the car he was singing to the tapes in the tape player he put in the pick up. He would even have beer in a plastic cup. He would be so plastered he would spill it on me. While he was singing he handed me his cup and wanted me to drink out of it. I was about to when my mom grabbed it from me and told me not to drink it. My dad didn't get the cup back for quite a while, but I don't think he even noticed it was gone.

Another time, he would hand me the beer and wanted me to drink it. I came close to doing it again. My mom took it and threw the cup with the beer out the window. He was so furious. I don't think I ever seen him that mad before.

He quickly pulled the truck over and we were sliding in the front. I felt like the truck was going to tip over. While it was still moving on the grass he jumped out into the road. Barely missed a couple of cars. Was gone for a little bit and came back. Holding the cup that was now full of grass. He handed it back to my mom and told her to clean it. He was yelling at her for throwing it out the window. Made sure she cleaned it good.

If she didn't clean it good enough he would give it back to her. Make her clean it some more while yelling at her. She would be crying so much. I could see her and he would yell at me. "What are you looking at?" After that all I could do is look straight ahead and hope he wouldn't yell at me. After she cleaned it good enough that he wanted, he threw it out the window. Now he didn't want it. They yelled at each other all the way home. Eight hours. I wanted to be in the back. No way was that going to happen. I think my mom wanted to use me to keep him from yelling.

"I'll yell all I want to!"

"This is a free country!" He would yell. I already learned not to cry when dad was like this. Mom never did learn so she cried and this made him mad.

At that time I was on two different types of anti-seizure meds so it probably was a good thing I didn't drink any of it. Another time you can see where God stepped in and protected me by using my mom to do his work.

Moving

My dad got tired of living in the city. So he wanted to live on a farm again so he could grow crops again like he did when he was a kid. We had a chance to either move to California or Texas.

We drove out to California with my parents, Mary and I. We were driving around to find places we could live at. In California there is a lot of driving going on. Twist and turns, ups and downs. So it is easy for one person to handle and another on to get motion sickness. My mom and Mary were both getting sick from the drives. Dad and I loved it. To me it was like a roller coaster ride.

Because they couldn't handle the driving we ended up deciding to move to Texas. If we ended up moving to California we figured no one would be able to handle the roads.

We ended up moving to Texas during my junior high school year. I felt like Noah's ark. We had two dogs, two birds and two cats with us. My parents, Mary and I and Liz moved to Texas.

# TEXAS

The first thing I noticed about moving here was that Wayne Newton was in Las Vegas and I'm now in Texas. If anything good was to come out of this was the fact that I wouldn't have to hear Wayne Newton anymore since he lives in Vegas and I don't.

Again I was wrong. Within three weeks after we moved to Texas guess who was doing a tour? Yep. Wayne Newton. First stop? The city I just moved to. I know, it's a coincidence, but it felt more like the guy was following me in a silly way.

Eighth Grade

I started eighth grade in Las Vegas. We moved two months before I turned thirteen. Again I was put in a class with a bunch of trouble makers. They had me put in a special math and English class. I told my parents I didn't want to be put in that class again. I told them about how much trouble I had in there the previous year. They said I was going into those classes whether I liked it or not. Looking back I wonder if they were ordered to have me in those classes by the school.

One class I was taking again was the English class. After being in there the previous year we had to listen to a story on cassette tape. We could stop the tape when a certain area came up. I was so familiar with the story I already knew what parts were going to be on the paper so I stopped it and wrote down the answers. I already knew what the answers were. I told everyone else in the group what to write down word for word so they would get it right. There was no way I would get it wrong again.

Sure enough I was wrong. The teacher wrote down an "F" on my paper and everyone else's in the group. I told her I did this last year. Every question I had last year been on this year's paper. There was no way I could get this wrong. Miss Collins said she was told to put down an "F" not because of what the answers were, but because of *who* I was. I couldn't comprehend what she was talking about. Again

I said I had every question right so Miss Collins just dismissed me and didn't even answer my question.

This is why everyone else in the group got the answers wrong. Not because of the answers but because of whom we were. There was no way to get out of it. Again I was signing failing notices every day I was in there. If you have ever heard of someone graduating with a third grade education this is one of the places where they do it at.

It is like a quota they have to fill. Make sure a certain percentage of your students are failing. They would have a stack of them in their desk drawer waiting to be used. Just like a teacher would have a pass to use the bathroom. Waiting for a student to use it. If it was because of me why didn't Mary get failing notices also? It didn't make sense.

By the time we moved to Texas I wasn't even thirteen years old yet, but I was good at gambling, hotwiring cars, pick pocketing and escaping from cops. Something I wouldn't want to put on a resume and sometimes I wonder what in the world God would want me to learn all this stuff. Sure enough we moved. If we did stay there I would have gone into reform school, ended up in jail and certainly wouldn't even be here to write this for you. See how God works again?

When we got to Texas I was in eighth grade. I got put in eighth grade classes this surprised me. I ended up excelling in all the classes and actually came home excited and told my mom what I learned today in school. Something I never did in Nevada. I didn't feel like any of these classes were babysitting rooms anymore. Because of my hearing problems I had to make sure I was sitting in the front row. Unlike Nevada where I could sit in the back and avoid the troublemakers.

I was in a Junior High School while Mary was in a High School. Back in Nevada the ninth graders were still in the Junior High School. So she liked this better, but always wished we stayed in Nevada. She never wanted to go to Texas. I saw it as an opportunity from God to be able to start over. I didn't even mention my epilepsy to the teachers. I didn't like the way they treated me in Vegas for having epilepsy so I wasn't going to go through that again.

I ended up keeping it silent and didn't tell anyone including my friends. When we moved into Texas it was during October so we had an elective to pick. During this time there wasn't too many classes left to pick from so I ended up picking music. (Why I still don't even know. Must be something God was planning for me, because even today I still don't see it.)

It wasn't a class to teach you the basics of music writing or reading musical notes, but more about the history of music itself. Who wrote songs and their life story behind it. I loved when we got to the part on classical music. Bach, Beethoven and Chopin were my favorites.

In physical education they were already playing basketball. I was given the position of guard. Not knowing what they do. In Vegas we just played free throw in the neighborhood, but never played it in school

When I was playing basketball in PE the girls played basketball and I retrieved the ball and made a basket on my first shot. Instead of telling me I did a good job, I got yelled at by the teacher and the kids for giving the other team the points. They still never told me what the difference was and I pretty much stayed out of the way during that game. So the rest of the season they figured I don't know how to play basketball.

In the springtime they had us in track. Usually they would have the girls and boys teams separated. There weren't very many girls who wanted to run with the guys so I was one of the few. Most of the girls ran with themselves.

I don't know if it was from living in Vegas or something else, but I was actually running faster than a lot of the boys. Naturally a guy runs a lot faster than a girl. It just happens. So why was I running and passing all these boys during the track part I never did realize.

Shortly after I moved to this school one of the kids hit me so I ended hitting him back. The guy in charge of the area with the soccer stuff just yelled at me since he never saw me before. Again I was being labeled a trouble maker as soon I moved there. He told me I was supposed to stand in front of the flagpole for the whole hour as punishment. I couldn't see going through that again after already getting in trouble in Vegas for not doing things wrong I wasn't going to go through that again. Nor did I tell my parents about it. The chances of them not believing were really good. I couldn't risk it so I ended up going into the library for lunch.

There were two girls who moved to Texas after me and we became fast friends since we were three who didn't know much about the area and had a lot in common. All they served for lunch was Mexican food. None of us wanted their food at all for everyday so we ended up coming into the library during the lunch hour. The librarian didn't mind it. We got to talk, read and socialize with the librarian. I ended up doing more reading on history than if I wasn't there during the lunch hour. Even the librarian would sign our yearbooks "I enjoyed having 'lunch' with you." I thought that was so nice. No one else would understand the lunch part except for a few of us.

Austin Church

As soon as we moved into Austin Texas my mom wanted us to go to a church. We were renting a house so we weren't planning on spending a lot of time there. We rented it month by month so anytime we could be leaving. Since we were eager to buy some land and move into the country. Mary and I didn't want to go every Sunday. Dad quit going once we moved to Nevada so I never saw him go to church. My mom didn't get what she wanted. She just agreed with us and said. "Okay we don't have to go to church here.

We did go to a church for a few Sundays. Not all in the same month, but in between a span of several weeks. After that we really didn't want to go anymore. We'll just wait till me move in the country and go to church there." Mom said. That was the end of our Texas church experience till we moved another city.

I was beginning to feel like this would be the same type of church we went to in Nevada.

Rented House

When we moved into a city we had to rent a house, before we could move into another one. The house in Las Vegas we were trying to sell and couldn't do anything until we sold it.

My bedroom was near the front. The bed I used was under the window. There was a crack under the window that went diagonally under the window and to my bed. We couldn't change the furniture since this would make my dad mad. I learned that back in Vegas. Once the furniture is moved it is going to stay there. No changes. (Probably explains why some of my sisters like to change their furniture every five minutes. Now they have the freedom to do that when before they didn't) If we needed some furniture moved around for whatever reason it wasn't worth it.

During the night there would be an army of ants that would come through the crack and moved all over my bed. I found out soon enough they were called "fire ants" since they would sting and you felt like you were on fire. There would be scorpions that would come through the cracks also and sting me in the bed. I would literally be jumping out of bed screaming and crying from it. Of course my dad wouldn't like it since I would be screaming and waking him up in the night. I never had seen these before, didn't know what they were and getting stung by them every night.

My mom told me we could just paint over the crack and it would stop it. I asked "How come we didn't do it?" She replied "Your father would just paint over it, but since we are renting it we would have to get permission, fill out paperwork and it wasn't worth it."

"Just live with it."

After going through this, I suggested we use ant spray. My mom would talk to my dad and came back saying we couldn't. We rehashed the same thing every night for a month. Finally my dad came in and used ant spray and sprayed it so hard and all over the place. "Now quit complaining!"

He was so mad I couldn't say anything. The smell in my room was so bad I couldn't even breathe. But I couldn't say anything in fear I would get beaten up again. After that I just got eaten and stung a lot every night. I figure it was better than anything dad would do to me.

It made me a tougher person now than I was before. I can't understand why people are afraid of bugs. No matter how small or big they are. Even mice I can step on. I am kind of num from people who are paranoid. I end up helping people who can't even stand having "pest" or anything else in their rooms. They don't understand how I can get up to a bug, lizard or anything else and even kills it. They just don't understand or can believe anyone has gone through this.

### Living Here

You felt like you time traveled into the past. People had party lines on their phones. In other words seven houses could be using the same "party line" and you couldn't use the phone because house number two was still using it. You didn't get a busy signal like people does nowadays. Instead you had to wait until someone was finished with their conversation before you could use the phone.

The only way out of that was if you wanted to pay a lot more for a private line. Being out in the country it didn't make sense. Our own mailbox was half a mile away from us. Again it didn't make sense moving the mailbox to your house and have the postal carrier drive a mile out of their way just so you don't have to go so far to your mail box.

In Texas they had these things called "Blue Laws" which meant you couldn't buy certain items on Saturday and the other things you had to wait to buy on Sunday. This was originally created by the government of the state to keep people from shopping on Sundays. This way you would attend church instead of going shopping. Like liquor wouldn't be sold on Sunday for example so you would stay home and not work. Rest like it says to in the Bible. Other things you couldn't buy was house ware items like pots, pans, can openers, etc.

Our only source of heat was a "Ben Franklin" stove. Not only did we use that for a heat source, but for cooking. You would put the wood in the main area down below and there were four burners to cook on. If you just wanted it for heat you would put the covers over the burners and it were a fireplace. Unfortunately you couldn't touch it. Otherwise you would get burned yourself. It was named Ben Franklin stove since Ben Franklin from the revolutionary war designed it.

The road we lived off of was just put in ten years before we moved down to Texas so we were really outsiders. It had a number for the road instead of a street name. So you can see now why I felt like I traveled back in time to the nineteenth century.

## Thanksgiving

During 1976, we were living in the ranch house. We didn't have much. Most of the money went to the shell of the house and the property. We had a Ben Franklin stove for heat. Slept in the living room to at night to keep warm and had to close the doors in the bedrooms. So Dad needed his beer and stuff. Mom tried to talk to him about not drinking or cut down se we can have money to buy groceries and get food for our thanksgiving meal. She wanted me to watch while she talked to dad. During this whole conversation he was holding a can of his Coors beer like he would always do.

"We need some money to buy groceries." He didn't answer and kept watching the TV. He never looked at her while she was talking to him and kept watching the TV. "Can you hear me?" She asked. "Yea." He replied while still glued to the TV. "You are going to have to limit your drinking so we can get groceries."

"No I'm not!" He yelled while still not looking at her. "I don't have enough to get milk!" He looks around sees me. "What are you looking at?" I was so used to it I just turned my head. My mom knew I could lip read, but my dad didn't. She would always later ask me about what someone said. My dad never did since he was busy doing something else. "You have enough money!" My dad would yell at her. "No I don't! We need eggs, bread, milk…" while using her hand as named each item. Dad gets up. "No we have enough."

"Go look in the refrigerator if you don't believe me!" Pointing to the kitchen. He ended up sitting back down. They whispered something. Mom came over to me. "Come on we're going shopping." I was surprised that he agreed to not drink at least for a while so we could get groceries.

My mom was so excited she ended up getting a whole shopping cart full of food. I never saw so much in a cart for us since we left Austin. After this incident my Mom would keep like forty dollars out of dad's paycheck each week so we could get what we needed.

Like groceries or something else. She kept it in her dresser drawer in her bedroom. Dad never noticed the money was gone. Since he never kept an eye on his paycheck and just made sure he had enough money for his beer and mixed drinks.

Texas Network Church

We ended up moving into a country setting type of church. It was a small town, but since it was Texas there weren't much of any religious churches to pick from unless you were a Baptist. Then you had a lot to pick from.

My mom told me after we moved to Texas that we would probably have to join a Baptist church. Since there were so many of them around. I didn't mind. But my dad had a different opinion. "There is no way in Hell we're joining a Baptist Church!"

"I never joined one and you never will!" I don't know why my dad had a choice in the matter when he didn't even go to church after being in New York.

My mom again reminded him of the choices we have. She mentioned a couple of churches near us. "I don't care." He told her. "Then we can join a Baptist one?" She asked. "No!"

"Go look up one!" He ordered her. I was watching. She grabbed a phone book and looked up the different churches. Each time she came up to a name he would say he didn't care. Again I don't know why it was his decision. She asked him if he was going to go to church again since he was concerned.

"No!" He yelled. "Why are you asking me?" He got up and grabbed another beer. "I don't want anyone telling me how to drink or not to drink at all."

"I'll do what I want to!"

"I'll keep drinking till I die!" My mom was crying thinking we'll never be able to join a church. Since he was so determined to decide what church we can go to.

Again my mom went over some church names. When she got to one name he said to check out that church. I really didn't feel like we got a choice in the matter. After we spent one Sunday there we came home and mom told him what she thought of it. Sure enough we decided to join this Texas Network Church

When we decided this was the church we wanted to join. They asked if we were already baptized. We all were according to their rules. I was baptized when I was only a few hours old. I wasn't breathing when I was born. The doctor just told my mom that I didn't want to breathe. (Like I was having a temper tantrum at that age.) My parents figured I wouldn't get into heaven unless I was baptized so I got baptized as soon as they were able to find someone who could do it.

The only way they baptized someone was to put water on the baby's forehead in a shape of a cross. That is what they were taught in the churches they went to.

They actually had a Sunday School that people would attend no matter how old they were. I didn't understand that, because I had graduated from Sunday School a few years ago. All I could think was "How many times did this guy flunk Sunday School?"

"I graduated when I was ten." The adult classes would use these books and they would learn the same thing every week. I could tell you what they were learning week by week. Nothing changed. You just learned the same thing over and over.

Again being what people referred to as a "Submarine Christian" and only going to church on Christmas and Easter I wasn't planning on going to church except for those days. I can see where God had other plans for me. There was no way I was going to be allowed to do that routine here now. He gave me another chance by moving to Texas and not ending up in reform school. (This is what would have happened if I stayed in Nevada) So now he wanted me to change spiritually as well.

Choir

I was constantly being told I have no music talent whatsoever by my mom. We went to this one church in Texas. So far no problems. They were looking for a full time pastor so most of the time there was an interim that would show up until a new one came in. My mom, Mary and I would sit in the very back pew so we could leave if we wanted to and no one would find out. The choir box would hold fifteen people at the most. At this time there were twelve people in it. It came time for the congregation to sing a hymn. When we finished a song the lady in the pew ahead of us turned around told me I sang well and that I should be in the choir. I was scared and shook my head "no". The lady and my mom kept talking. I kept saying I didn't want to and reminding my mom you said "I don't have any talent and that I'm no good." My mom smiled and said "I know we will talk about it later." We never did so I guessed that it was the end of the conversation. I was so happy she never brought it up again.

It turns out I was wrong. They must have talked during the week. When Sunday came again. My mom was so excited to go to church. I didn't care. So we went. My mom went ahead of me as we entered. I ended up coming in. Two ladies grabbed me. I yelled for my mom, but she kept going. They took me to the area where the choir was putting on their robes. They put one on me as fast as they could. I was terrified and called for my mom. She ignored me and kept on walking. I didn't know what was going on. They finished putting the robe on me and handed a hymn book. I was in so much shock they practiced their song, I wanted to leave. They kept me from leaving and then when they finished they formed a line and walked off. They made sure I didn't leave the line. We came in the back way and formed in the choir box. I didn't know what to do. I pretty much kept my mouth shut. The next thing I knew it I was forced to be a choir member.

I hated it so much I was mad at my mom, the choir, church and God for doing this to me. I couldn't understand why this was happening to me. I would give anything to be sitting in the same old area of the church I was sitting in before. I didn't know what was going on. I didn't read music or even know what I was doing. You could have told me I sang bass and I would agree with you, since I wasn't familiar with any of this stuff.

Again my mom forced me to go to choir practice. I just went and sat in the box, being so mad at everyone for doing this to me. Never sang or did anything. Some of the choir members tried to get me to sing. I even told them the same thing I was hearing for years. "I have no talent whatsoever."

"Can I go home now?" I didn't like it at all. Being forced to do something without asking and totally convinced I can't do any of this stuff for years it would have to take a lot of work for me to ever change my mind about that.

After I was in the choir, my mom started moving up a certain number of pews so she could see me better and hear me. I would have trouble understanding what the director was saying. I never heard of any of these musical terms before. I kept getting moved to where the sopranos were, to where the altos where and even a few times I was sitting on the same row as the men. I was so confused I even tried singing the same notes they were.

There was a lady who came in to help us when we had to do a special. She sang first soprano. When she sat next to me I tried to see if I could sing anywhere near her. I ended up singing the same notes, but apparently she didn't like it. Instead of asking me about it, she would tell the choir director that someone is singing the same notes. She was supposed to be the only one who assigned to sing those notes. The choir director told all of us not to sing those notes. They were reserved for her.

So I tried to hum it and see if I could hit them. Again I got told off not to hum the notes either. I still couldn't understand why they wanted me in there if all they were going to do is yell at me for trying to help.

Again I wanted out of there ASAP. This was definitely not the place for me. I was getting treated badly for something I didn't want to do and something I am not good at all. The choir director just now proved that to me. I didn't even show up for practice on Wednesday nights anymore. My mom made me come to church on Sundays, but I ended just sitting with her.

My mom was wondering why I wasn't in the choir. I told her they are treating me bad and I didn't want to be in this anyway. "It was your idea, not mine." So I ended up staying out of the choir.

A year later I figured I was okay. Nope. Again the whole process started all over again. A lady would be sitting in front of me and heard me singing. Told me I should be in the choir. I told her they don't want me since they have a girl who can sing better. "Who is it?" She asked. I looked around since I still haven't learned anyone's name yet. "I don't see her." I told the girl. "Then you can sing."

"No." I replied "Since they were being mean to me." She didn't say anything after that so again I figured I was okay.

Nope. This has got to be some sign from God again. "Go back into the choir." I keep thinking he was telling me. We ended up getting a phone call from one of the choir members. Saying how they needed me. I ended up answering the phone. They thought I was my mom. I said "No."

"This is Betty."

"Good." One of them said. I was so surprised. No one wants to talk to me. "We want you to be in the choir." I told them what happened. "She is just helping us out." The lady told me. "You are the one we need." Again I was thinking this lady is crazy or something.

"I can't sing." I told her. "Yes you can." She replied. "Just ask my mom and she'll tell you."

"I don't have any music talent whatsoever." I reminded her. "Your mom is the one who told us you can sing and wants you in here." I almost freaked out. I looked at my mom since she was nearby. You should have seen how quickly she left the room since I couldn't follow her and was stuck on the phone. Again you can see how God uses people to get what he wants done.

The lady on the phone started talking to me again. "We know you can sing." I asked her to repeat it. I thought I was hearing things. "I said you can sing."

"We've heard you sing." I ended up interrupting her. "But my mom…" Before I could say anything. "Don't listen to that."

"You can sing."

"We've heard you." I told them "The last time I was in with the men."

"I have trouble singing those notes."

"You were in the back?" She asked. "Yes." I answered. "You shouldn't be in the back."

"Those are for the bass."

"We'll make sure you are in with the ladies." I was more confused than ever. "Just come for practice and see how it is." I was debating and the next thing I was saying was "Yes." without even knowing it like someone was saying it for me.

Okay I went to practice thinking this wont last long. I was sitting with the altos. Of course not knowing where I was sitting. The choir director was going over what we were supposed to sing Sunday. The girl next to me was showing me in the book which area of notes I should be singing. I still didn't understand what she was talking about. Again this was like a foreign language to me.

The girl next to me was sitting on my right so I could hear her. She was singing and I would try to match it. Sometimes she told me I did it right. After being with the men I would be trying to hit lower than I could. So she had to help me sing higher.

So I was an alto now. Sometimes I would be singing and noticed a girl in front me was singing louder than I was. I didn't know she was projecting her voice. I wasn't sure if I should do that or not. So I would only do that at the end of the song. Being afraid maybe I wasn't supposed to do that or not.

Afterwards the choir director would come back and ask me if I was projecting my voice. I told her "No." since I was afraid I would get in trouble and not even knowing what it was. She would tell me. "It sure sounded like you did." After hearing that I wouldn't even try it again until a special event came up and we would sing some specials.

The choir director would tell us from time to time to project our voice. Everyone else acted like they knew what she was talking about. I just kept quiet since she never asked if anyone didn't know. Plus I didn't need to get yelled at by the choir director again.

We finally did a Christmas Concert and they rearranged us. Now I'm sitting in the front row with the sopranos. I didn't understand why and I never asked the director. She told me I would be in this row from now on. "Which seat did you want me to be in?" I asked. "In the very first seat." This is the closest to the congregation. "That will be you're seat." She said. I didn't realize it, but that was a compliment since she wanted me to be where everyone could hear me.

During practice for the concert I would only project my voice at the end of the song. Again she wanted me to project my voice and I didn't understand what she was even saying. "You know what you did at the end?" She asked. "Yes." I answered. "Do that more often." She told me. I had the weirdest look on my face, but went ahead and did it. She would say good when I did it. Then I knew it was something good.

After that I definitely knew I was supposed to be in the choir. I would do solos and duets at times. Those I enjoyed doing as well. There would even be times where I would be the only soprano there and they would grab me in a hurry, but this time it didn't bother me, because I knew they needed me and God wanted me to do this. I still kept thinking I was an alto though since no one explained it to me, but now I am where God wants me. So I stayed in the choir and didn't leave again.

High School

When we would have football games, Mary would be in Band playing her clarinet. In my junior year I was in Pep Squad where we would stay in the stands and do routines. The cheerleaders would do the same routines on the ground. The band would do the same thing every week in the stands, but we would change ours every week. I would even see the cheerleaders watching us more than doing their routines. They had their routine memorized that they would talk while doing it.

In my senior year I was in the Drill Team. They called them the Highlandettes. Mom was able to convince my Dad to come to a football game so he can see us perform. Even in the bleachers we were doing stuff. All he wanted to do was watch the game. He may not have thought of it or realize it, but it affected me. I'm not sure how or even if it did affect Mary. One good thing about the football games on TV or other places are that he did teach me what was going on. So in that way we did have one thing in common that was good. He could watch every game no matter who was playing. For some reason I had to root for some team. Now I can talk about football just like anyone else.

Physical Education

When I started this high school I spent a lot of time in PE. One of the things we had to do was play dodge ball. We were all up against the wall and someone would throw a ball at you. You are supposed to move away from the ball so you didn't get hit. If you got hit you were taken away from the wall and end up trying to "hit" someone who hasn't been hit yet.

We had a range where if you went past a spot you were already counted as out or got hit. I ended up being the last one left. (Sometimes I think is from all the practice of running away from everyone in Vegas.) So one person got a ball went to my left. Another girl got a ball and went to my right. A third person went to the middle, got a ball and on the count of three they were each to throw a ball at me and I would be "out". I knew no matter where I would go I would end up getting hit. So when they counted three all the balls were coming straight at me. What did I do? The last thing anyone expected.

Instead of going left, right, or staying there I went down. All the balls missed me. So I was still safe according to the game. But instead I got yelled at by the teacher. The next year when we played the game. The teacher kept telling them to make sure I got hit right away. Again getting yelled at for doing something I'm good at. You can see where something I learned that is bad ends up being good for you later. God showing you what you can do and where your strengths are.

After that I stopped going to PE and made sure next year I would be in another activity so I didn't have to go to PE and get yelled at for being good at something. After my freshman year, they started letting us play volleyball in the gym during lunch. This made good sense if you think about it. A lot of us would finish eating early and we could burn off all of that energy by playing instead of fighting. Some of the students would be in band and other activities where they don't have to be in PE and this would give them exercise also.

After we signed up, we would be assigned teams and play against each other like a tournament. This made it even more fun than just playing. I had a lot of practice on this game from playing it in Vegas. Sometimes we would play it in the backyard, but that would only be one against one. Not nine verses nine like they do on teams.

In my sophomore year I went into athletics. I figured if I was going to be doing a lot of running I might as well do it instead of getting yelled at by the PE teacher. So I started out for track. Since this was a small town school the same people who were on the track team was also on the basketball team. After what happened in Austin I didn't want to go through that again. So I just went ahead and said I would stick with track.

The coach couldn't understand, but went ahead and I just did track. I still had to learn everything a basketball team member was supposed to learn, but not play. I agreed and ended up practicing. To this day someone will play basketball with me and assume I was on basketball team at school. I can honestly say "No I wasn't on the team." Because I never was. If they don't know, they think I can't play till they find out.

When they said I would have to travel to the games anyway and my parents didn't like it. I had to drop out. They weren't going to stay up, pick me up at school like they did for Mary. They already had one to do. She only had to do Friday nights. Mine would be a lot more because of basketball. I was going to tell the coach when she said we had to run three miles in three days. I couldn't do that either so I ended up dropping out. Using the three miles excuse and the coach thought I was a wimp.

Foreign Languages

I always wanted to learn German. In Austin we could learn any language we wanted to. Since this was a country school. The only foreign language that was available was Spanish. So I didn't have a choice and ended up learning Spanish.

Here is where God shows you what he knows about you. If you don't know something about your gifts he ends up teaching you. I didn't know I had a gift for speaking another language until I did this class. I was terrible in English, but I did great in Spanish. Sounds weird doesn't it? That is what I kept thinking.

I ended up doing well in this class that I took it for Spanish two the following year. Now I keep thinking I could have done well in German also. Every time something to me seems like a foreign language I end up doing well in it.

UIL Competitions

There is an organization called the University Interscholastic League where you can compete in different subjects. You would compete from different schools to the district competition to the regional, state and finally nationals. It is kind of like what a spelling bee competition is like, but other subjects.

At the school I went to all the students would take a test. The top three students were selected to go to district to represent the school.

My subject was always science. Every year I entered I was to represent my school for the district competition.

One year I got fourth place in district. If someone couldn't make it I would go on to regional. Even though I was an alternate, it made me feel good. When I got to the car afterwards I told my mom how I did she was just as excited as I was. I told my mom I didn't want to tell dad, because I knew how he would react. She told me to tell him that he would feel good about it. I dread it myself.

When we got home, my mom made me tell my dad how I did. Explaining to him that I might end up going to regional if someone else couldn't do it. He was busy reading his newspaper and didn't look like he was listening. I knew this wouldn't be good. Sure enough he didn't say anything so I quickly got out of there before he had a chance to yell at me again. I could hear my mom yelling at him and of course they both ended up yelling at each other for something I did again. It didn't make a difference if it was good or bad.

I ended up just staying in my room again. I figured I had gotten myself in enough trouble. It didn't matter to him as long as he had his beer and drinks. I could have been dead and I bet he wouldn't even notice. You would think he would be happy. Then we would be out of the house like we are on Sundays. That is how he liked it anyway.

Seeing how God knows about all of this before it happens. Again he was preparing me for what was going to happen. I ended up needing science to write scripts for sci-fi shows, medical dramas and other shows that required science.

Career Testing

While in High School we had to take a test to see what kind of jobs we were skilled at, had an interest in and what jobs would be best for us. I scored really well in writing, but had no interest in it since all we did in English classes was do research papers on stuff I wasn't interested in. So to me that was boring.

I scored good on astronomy, probably since I was doing well in UIL competitions, but when I looked it up all I found was most of them end up teaching. I wanted to do the research so I gave up on that. You can see where God has led me to my new career since I ended up working for a lot of science fiction shows.

I scored really well in skills and interests animals since I was planning on being a veterinarian's assistant. At that time the people who assisted the vets were called assistants. Now they are called veterinarian technicians. So when I graduated I was planning on being a veterinarian technician.

Another area I was interested in was writing. I couldn't see that either since I didn't like the stuff we did in our English class. Shakespeare really wasn't what I was interested in. If it was something I liked I could see writing about it. Boring stuff I would never do.

Third on interest was acting. I couldn't see that since you have to be on stage. I would never get up there even if you paid me. If I did something that had to do with entertaining it would be behind the camera. Never in front of it. God wanted something else done apparently. Here is where you can see he gets what he wants again.

Red Cross Volunteer

I started out in the Red Cross when I was in high school. They did a program where the junior ones could work at places like hospital, disasters, etc. My sister Mary wanted to work at the hospital. Me? I wanted to do disaster work. My mom wanted to only make one trip so the two of us ended up working at the hospital. I don't remember what the situation was but we didn't stay in there very long.

Mary ended up doing candy striper work at hospitals. Me I ended up doing disaster work with the red cross after I graduated and everyone pretty much left home. I was able to find rides with others from our area that were going to places like Houston and other places pretty much after a disaster hit like tornadoes, etc.

I started working out in the kitchen. Helping people make food or serving. I loved the way you can change things. While we were cleaning up we would talk to people. A lot of people after a disaster just want someone to listen. Some people don't realize that.

Since this was Texas a lot of people knew Spanish so I wasn't needed for that. I kept moving around while trying to find out what area I was best in. There were people who came in and had hearing problems. I was still a beginner at sign language so sometimes I had to lip read what someone was trying to say. Then I was able to translate for them.

After listening to people and communicate with them they started having me listen on one on one with the victims. They knew I was majoring in psychology so they would have me be like a student and study under them. It didn't take long for them to put me in the area of counseling. Now I was able to put all those psychology classes to use and help people.

Whenever a disaster would strike there were some of us already grouped up. Our hours were flexible and we could get going on a moments notice. Somebody would drive us down to like Houston for example and we would be there after a hurricane hit. The first thing we had to do was give out supplies and help people.

After the initial response was done then we went into our areas we were best in. Now I was in counseling and helping them with the trauma of what they were going through. Again God using you what you are good at, taking a bad thing and doing something good with it.

Since these were with the Red Cross and not a missionary trip, they would have ministers who would come out and help people with spiritual needs. This is one area I never felt comfortable in.

What was I supposed to tell them? How choirs don't like you? How it isn't important to go to church like my family does? I definitely wouldn't be a good subject to talk to someone about that. So I just left it up to the guys in the black collars.

The reason I ended leaving is because there was a disaster we had in Texas. In 1997 there was a bad ice storm. Power lines were being taken down by the ice and there were a lot of power outages going on. I called up the local TV station and talked to the news room. I wasn't able to call in my weather reports since the power was out.

They ended up sending out a news crew to our house and we were the top story when they did 3 news stories that day.

I tried getting a hold of the red cross to see if they could help us. They never did. Our church wouldn't help us even though they had power. I couldn't get over it. No one wanted to help us. Our well was the only way we could get water and you needed electricity. We had two dogs, two birds and nine cats at the time. No heat or anything. My sister Cynthia went into work where they had heat and water.

I couldn't get over how no one was able to help us. We had to wait for the sun to heat up enough to get the ice off of the trees to give us some water to drink. We ended up finding a hotel to get to that had some power. We brought containers home full of water. Cynthia would come home and put the animals in the house so they would be warmer than staying outside. Then mom and I would take care of the animals in the day and take care of her animals and ours. She had a dog and some cats at her house.

It was like that for a week. They started in the small towns getting the power back on the areas that needed to be done first. Since we lived out in the country we didn't get power back on till a week later. Since then I don't work with the red cross anymore. I decided that I need to do volunteer work somewhere else now.

The following year I heard that there was a bad ice storm in the east coast. The first thing I noticed is how fast how the red cross got there, put people up in heated buildings and helped them out. I just couldn't get over that. Does it make a difference on the amount of people gets hurt before they come out and help? Or any group for that matter? It shouldn't, in God's eyes everyone needs help. No matter where you live. In the United States or another country for that matter.

Construction

We had a Jim Walter's home so we had the shell built for us. At first dad was in charge of doing that stuff. When he did the hammering it just gave me a headache so bad that I couldn't even handle it after taking aspirin for it. He made the family pitched in and finished the rest. "If you are going to complain about it, I'll give you something to complain about!" He yelled. So by the time I was sixteen years old I already knew how to spackle, duct taping, wallboard, insulation, etc. Stuff that guys usually know how to do and girls don't. If we messed up a little section he yelled at us, rip up the whole wallboard for example and made us do it again and remind us how expensive it costs so we wouldn't mess up next time.

If we cried about the verbal abuse he would do something to the point where he would give us something to cry about. He would check over it and if we did it right he would say "nice" which means we passed inspection and that was as close to a compliment as we got. I actually smiled since I didn't get compliments that often. I did wiring, but when I messed up I would get shocked good to where it felt like I was having a seizure so I kind of avoid doing stuff like that now.

When I messed up to the point where I would get a shock. He would look at me and tell me "That should be your hint not to do it that way." If I got shocked again. "Quit doing that."

"I have to pay for the electricity." I can still do it right today. Since I got shocked a lot to where I got corrected. At the time, when he was yelling, I felt like God was correcting me for it. I kept wondering why He and my dad were yelling at me. It didn't make sense.

Here is another reason I was probably good at hotwiring cars. There are some similarities to the two. But some differences too. You are working with more wires on the house than on the car. I guess I needed some training before doing the work on the houses.

Christmas Concert

When my mom found out about why I got moved to the first seat in the front row she told my dad to come to the concert. Both of my parents coming to see me and they could see me good, I couldn't believe it.

During the day I would be practicing my singing and trying to project my voice. My dad did his usual drinking as if nothing was strange. He would get dressed up in a nice suit. He only did that when it was a special occasion or for a photo at work. Mom was reminding him for the twentieth time to get dressed for tonight. At the dinner table he finished drinking and stated. "Okay."

"Let's get this over with." I could hear him, but I was too excited to even pay attention about how he was feeling. I guess I should have.

There was a pew in the middle of the sanctuary on the left hand side where the congregation was seated that my family would usually sit. People who never saw my dad before acted like they saw him every week. They wouldn't go up to him, but just hello. He smiled and was polite to them. Didn't say much. Acting like he saw them every week also. The pastor wanted to talk to him. My mom fixed it so he had a letter of transfer done. The minister always acted like he died since he never went to church and never joined the church like people do when they ask at the end of a service. People usually assumed he died since he never showed up anyway. After this concert people really did believe us when we said we have a dad. Until then I don't think people believed us. Assuming we were lying or thinking something else. People from church never did come to our house while he was around.

Dad's Driving

After what happened in Nevada my dad didn't change. He still drank and drive. Even when they finally figured out that people like him were handing their drinks over to a passenger they would do breathalyzer tests on the driver. He consumed so much that he would drink a twelve pack a day and then gets his mixed drinks all night. He would drink sixteen ounces each time he drank. After five times he drank I gave up counting. Either I went to sleep and he was drinking or he passed out before then.

The problem with that is that my dad did so much drinking that his body tolerated all that drinking. So he would never look like a drunk. If you did pull him over and gave him a test to where he was supposed to walk a straight line he would pass it. So none of those things worked with him.

Again as soon as he saw the cop car in the mirror he would hand the beer over to one of us and we were told to hold it or even hide it so the cop wouldn't see it. After drinking for years he would be polite to the cops and did everything they asked. Like hand his driver's license over to them. To me he was like a different person. My mom and I were told to keep our mouths shut when this happened. If the cop wanted the registration. It was my mom's job to hand the card over to him as quick as possible. He wanted the cops to leave quickly. After the cop left it was a different story. If he got a ticket for a light being out for example he would take it, thank the cop and tell him to have a nice day. As soon as the cop left and was in front of us my dad would pull out make sure he was behind the cop.

Then he would demand to have his beer back. We would hear every name in the book that he would call the cop. The cop wasn't doing anything wrong, but it shows how much affect it had on me while I was growing up. Another reason I kept running away from cops like it was automatic reaction from what I was hearing. If my dad threw the beer out of the window he would stop, drive back and make sure we got it. That is how important to him the beer was rather than us.

It was a routine for us. We would have to hold his beer whoever was closest to him. That way he knew where his beer was and it wouldn't take long for him to get his beer back. If I was late on giving his beer back, he would take it from me. Since I was taking too long or wasn't quick enough.

Suicide Attempt #2

I was sixteen years old and couldn't handle it again. I went to see the counselor at the high school and tried to have a talk to him about the rape. Since no one believed me about what happened I thought if maybe I talked to someone and told them the same thing everyone else had told me that I made it all up maybe that would make me feel better. This time I was definitely wrong.

After talking to him he told me how I ruined the guy's career and that my life wasn't worth anything anymore and that nothing would help me. I was a hopeless person and that nothing would save me from all the stuff I caused him and his family. I couldn't take it anymore. More people not believing me and that I have failed at everything. More abuse from my family, school everything. I finally gave up and decided to try something else again.

I knew from earlier that running in front of a car doesn't work. So I tried to think of something else that would work. It would have to be something that is available at home. We had a cutlery set at home. The biggest one in the set was a big carving knife in the block of wood.

That one would work I knew. I even checked it out. Again not telling anyone about it, but just saying it in my mind so no one could hear me on what I was planning. This way I figured no one could stop me. If my family found out I knew my mom would at least want to stop me and that is one thing I didn't want. No one stopping me from trying this like last time. Sure enough someone else had a different plan.

I checked to see if the knife was sharp enough. Yep it was. So then I kept trying to think of where to stab myself. I finally decided to do the abdominal area. I figured it would be painless or I would pass out from it and then no one would find out till it was too late. There was no 911 system yet so it would take them ages to get an ambulance out there since we lived out on a ranch area.

Now I am ready to do this I thought to myself. It was a sure fire plan. I took the knife out of the block of wood, positioned the knife toward me so it would go straight into me and do it fast enough so I would get it over with. While I am aiming for the body something was happening. I couldn't do it. So I closed my eyes thinking maybe I am spending time on looking at it and I could get it over with. What happened? I was like a frozen robot. I couldn't even get it in. I ended up opening up my eyes and trying to do it again. Nope I just froze like that. It wouldn't move and for some reason I couldn't move my arms and hands to even do it. I felt like a failure and dropped the knife on the floor. I ran out of the house again. Thinking I can't do anything right and couldn't understand what was going on. Believe me now I know who was in charge of all of this. Again God was showing me who was in charge and telling me "Nope you can't do this".

Afterwards my parents found the knife on the floor and yelled at me for it. My dad got so mad he ended up punching a big hole in the wall on the right side of hallway. As a constant reminder to me and everyone else of his temper, what happens if you do something wrong and what can happen if you disobey.

I was also wondering what he would have done if I was in the room when he found out. Would he have put the same size hole in my face? Would he have done it to my abdominal area? Kept it up till he got it out of his system? Having me end up in the hospital? Even today I think abut it in the back of my head.

My dad never did bring up the subject again. Yelled at me for it. I never brought up the subject either. So only God knows what happened afterwards.

Going Blind

I could tell something weird was happening to my vision. Keep in mind this was before computers. I was in a class in high school called Typing 2. You were required to type on the manual typewriter doing at least thirty-three words per minute. Since it was continuation of the Typing 1 class. The faster you typed the better of a grade you got. By the time you finished this class you should be able to type seventy-seven words per minute to get an "A". If you did sixty-six words per minute to got a "B" and so on.

We would get a quiz every day as soon as we got in. "Turn to page fifty-one." The teacher would say. Right away we were given a few minutes to type the whole page. We were given a lead way of three mistakes. If you had more than that you got part of your score taken off. I was doing well on this that the most mistakes I would have would be three. I remember doing well on these till I hit fifty-five words per minute. If I typed more than that my vision started doing crazy things. One time I remember the words on the page of the book I was looking at would vanish from the book. I would rub my eyes and then they were back on the page. As soon as I started typing fifty-six words per minute or more the words would vanish from the book again. My teacher would wonder what was going on. She figured I just needed new glasses so my mom took me to an eye doctor.

It turned out that it was worse than I suspected. Just needing glasses wasn't enough. My eye doctor referred to a specialist. Of course a lot of tests were done. In the end neither specialist could figure out what was happening. No decision was made. Should she have new glasses? Get eye drops? Nothing. Just go back to school. So what happened? I couldn't type faster than fifty-five words per minute so what ended up getting an "A" in class when the class started. I ended up getting a "C" in class by the end of the school year. Even though it wasn't my fault I got yelled at. "This is your second year in this." My dad would say to me.

"You picked this class!"

"Don't you know how to type?" As he yelled. "Yes." I replied. "Then prove it!" He got out the typewriter loaded it with paper and began typing on it some. "There it works!"

"Now type something!" I typed whatever he said. Of course being upset it made it harder for me to see, but that didn't phase him. He just kept reading something from a book. Expecting me to type it without making more than three mistakes. Faster than fifty-five words per minute. He would ask my mom if I was typing fifty-five words per minute. She would be checking me with a stop watch. Then she would answer yes or no.

If she said no he would yell at me and tell me to type faster. If I was doing more than fifty-five words per minute then he would check the page. If I had three mistakes or more than he would yell at me again. "God damn it!"

"When are you going to learn how to type?" Then he would have me do it again. I was getting more upset messing up more. My mom and I felt like prisoners that couldn't escape from this place. I wanted to tell him I knew how to type. Even if I did, he would never believe me. From seeing what I just did. It was already hard to explain to him what was happening with my eyes. If I told him the words disappeared from the page he would never believed that even though it was the truth.

When I messed up on it, I was told to go to my room until he could figure out what was wrong with me. Both my mom and my dad were yelling about me in the kitchen. I could hear everything from my bedroom.

The louder he got the more fearful I got about what he would do. Especially if it involved that belt again. I quietly got out of my room and headed down the hallway. My mom saw me. I was signaling to her I wanted to get out of the house. She shook her head "no" tried to get me to back to my room. "What are you doing?" He yelled at my mom. "Nothing." She replied while giving him his full attention. She had been trained that if she didn't give him his full attention she would get hurt in some form. He got mad, left the table and began making one of his mixed drinks. I saw a perfect opportunity to get out of there and ran out of the front door. "God damn!"

"What is going on now?" He yelled. He quickly ran toward the door. "Betty!" My mom yelled. I kept running I didn't want to even look back and see what was happening. I knew he wouldn't be able to keep up with me and eventually would go back into the house. I knew he would take it out on my mom, but at the time all I could think about getting out of there. That was more important to me than anything.

When I finally got back into the house I found out that I was going to pay for it dearly. My mom was already yelled at and beaten up for what happened. Of course it wasn't her fault, but she got it good. Me I not only got beaten up, but thrown against the wall in the hallway where there wasn't much room. My head hit the wall and my back got hurt. I wanted so much to do something back to him, but I knew he was strong than me plus I didn't know how drunk he was. Sometimes when he is drunk he is a lot stronger than people I know. Other times I could beat him up and he wouldn't even know it. This time I definitely could tell he was in a rage where I would lose and he wouldn't break a sweat.

This was one of those times. My mom would yell at him and he would yell back. "Stop it!" She yelled at him. "Why?"

"You want to be next?" He yelled. "No!" She answered. She got out of the area and I didn't see her again until much later. I just closed my eyes and gave up. I got my head pulled and thrashed around. I didn't want to even see what was going on. I cried like usual, but had to stop it in a hurry. I would use my index finger from my right hand to stop the crying as soon as possible. (To this day I still use the same method to stop my crying in a hurry.) I had to take it as a man even though I was a girl. There were no excuses for crying. We learned that back in Vegas.

My face swelled up a lot after that. Sometimes I think back and wonder which one of these times is where I got the damages on my nose from. I think it was from when I did the dishes since it was the earliest I know of and I was still growing.

I must have passed out or went to sleep since I don't remember much after that. I woke up later to see my mom hurt. Of course like usual she wouldn't talk about it. She wanted me to talk about it, but between the two of us not much was said.

I ended up going to the eye doctor later to see what was causing it. Mainly since my work at school was being affected. I went from one eye doctor to another. Having so many tests being done that I can't even remember. Every doctor couldn't understand why my vision was acting like that when I got passed a certain speed on the typewriter. They just told me to slow down and not to go passed fifty-five words per minute. I did that, but then my grades slipped since I couldn't get up to seventy-seven words per minute. Everyone else ended up getting an "A" in the class. Me? I ended up getting a "C" in the class since I couldn't get up to the right speed like everyone was able to. This was like a warning sign from God that I was going blind. But like usual we didn't notice it. We had other things on our minds.

Driver's Ed

I took the written test for driver's ed in school. That was easy. I couldn't take the class when I was fifteen like some people do since it was only offered in the spring so I had to wait till I was sixteen and in my senior year.

I took the driving part after I graduated and the instructor was having trouble with me. He kept an eye on the speedometer. So if I went up to fifty-six miles per hour he would tell me to slow down. If I got down to fifty-four miles per hour he would tell me to speed up. This was before they had cruise control in the cars. The way he kept an eye on every little speed did nothing, but makes me nervous. He kept it up so much and getting angry about it.

I had to keep an eye on the speedometer instead of the road since he kept nagging at me about the speed. So I wasn't able to concentrate on other cars or the road. My mom tried to teach me some more about driving. Just like the piano I didn't have any interest in learning how to drive. So she kept telling me how to drive. We were going toward a small town and she told me to slow down to thirty-five miles per hour since we in the city.

"Slow down." She yelled. "Now what?" I asked. "The speed limit sign said thirty-five miles per hour." She said. "It did?" I asked. "Didn't you see the sign?" She asked. "What sign?" I asked. My mom had me pull over and I did. Then she was asking why I didn't see the sign. I told her I never saw it. Then that is when she figured I had a vision problem.

After we discussed it I prayed to God for an answer. I couldn't understand what was going on. I ended up having a dream about it.

In the dream I was doing something and was slowly watching my vision getting worse. It was like a slow motion film I was watching. I was outside in the yard and doing something. Then the stuff outside was disappearing. I didn't see the grass, the sky and everything. I ended up looking at the sky and even that vanished. I woke up when I couldn't see anything anymore.

I spent the next two weeks crying about it. My mom could tell I was crying and wanted to know what it was about. I just told her "Nothing." And didn't mention anything about the dream. Since I never finished the drivers ed class my parents never did their deposit back. "Well there's fifty dollars we'll never see." My dad told us. Since now he won't get his fifty dollars back because of me. Just like usual it was my fault. That is all I ever learned from this family. Nothing will ever change. Money is more important. Just like his drinks.

Hospital

Since my vision was going I ended up spending two weeks in the hospital. They kept testing my vision and my seizures. Because of my epilepsy I was put on the fourth floor with the neurology patients were. I didn't have a problem with that, but there was one nurse I kept having problems with. After what happened when I was nine no one would believe me anymore so I had to keep quiet.

The nurse was a guy who kept sexually assaulting the female patients. The least he would do is kiss you. The worse I don't think anyone wants to hear. At the time I was only seventeen years old. I don't know if that is what attracted him to me or if it was something else. I was already scared by what was going on with my vision.

Of course he was the kind of person who would listen to you, talk to you and ask you questions. Perfect for his type of job, but when he would take me to get tested he would come and get me take me back to my room. Afterwards he felt compelled to get a kiss from the female patients for taking them back to their bed. Every time he would kiss me I would have flashbacks from what happened and the teacher when I was nine. So that didn't help either. I tried telling Liz about, but because of what happened she didn't want to listen to me or even believe me. "I believed you when you said the other guy raped you."

"I'm not going to make that same mistake again." She got mad and left the room. Never came back to visit me. So now I knew I was on my own with this nurse, no one to believe me even if I told them. This is the first time since I at the hospital that I'm now mentioning it since people stopped believed me about this stuff ages ago with my family.

If another nurse came in they would check my vision. This male nurse came in too, I was at the point where my blood pressure would go up when he came in and went down when he left. I went into this hospital as a person with okay vision and left it as a legally blind person. This was in October so it happened five months after I graduated from high school.

There was no way I could tell my dad about it too. I already had a fear of him and got abused so much from him at home I didn't need anymore from him or anyone in the family for that matter.

There was a girl who was on the same floor that I was on. She had brain surgery so she was mostly confined to her bedroom and couldn't leave. I went ahead and visited her since I could get out. I had to do it without the nurse finding out otherwise I would be required to kiss him (at least) for him taking me in a wheelchair or escorting me.

When I got to her room we were talking and becoming good friends. We ended up discussing about the nurse. Sure enough she was going through the same thing I did with the substitute teacher. She asked me if she should report it. I didn't have any advice to give her since I reported mine and no one believed me. I ended up telling her not to tell anyone. I told her that no one believed me and what he was doing to me and my own family didn't believe me either. Back then they didn't do rape kits and not many police departments believe the victim still. We both felt trapped and embarrassed by the whole thing. I never did visit her again and I never did find out what happened to her.

Once they figured out I lost all that vision the next step was to release me from hospital. They figured they did all they could and the next step was to send me to a rehab center for the blind. My mom came up to me when it was time for me to leave. She ended up asking. "You knew this was going to happen didn't you?" I said "Yes." She was so surprised that I was the only one in the family who wasn't crying about my vision loss when everyone else was. She asked me when I knew and I told her about the dream I had.

Texas Lions Camp

They wanted to send me to a rehab center for the blind, but they couldn't do it till I turned eighteen. I was seventeen so they couldn't do anything. The state commission for the blind said they usually send someone my age to the school for the blind, but since I already graduated they couldn't do that either. So I pretty much sat around the house and didn't do anything. Finally it became the following year so I was able to go.

In January first of the next year I was able to attend a rehab center put on by the Lion's Camp. During the nine months of the year it is set up for the blind adults who need to learn the basics. During the summer it is set up as a camp for kids who have medical needs. My mom said if we were living in Texas when I was a kid I could have gone there because of my epilepsy. I keep wondering what it would have been like to be around other kids with the same problem. No getting picked on, being able to talk about seizures with other kids, etc.

I had to learn the basics that everyone already knows. How to cook, clean house, and do everything as a blind person does. I learned how to read Braille, use a white cane and use a pair of shades to keep as much light out as possible. In other words I ended up looking like the same type of blind person you expect to see on TV or in real life.

In Braille we would use a Perkins Brailler. It is a device that looks like a typewriter. But when we use it instead of seeing letters you would see bumps for the Braille. Six dots that blind people use to read. To me it was like learning another language. I was told to ask my counselor for one. He said he would send me to another rehab center. Until then to just use a slate and stylus. The slate is smaller and takes longer to use. Like using a pen and paper instead of a typewriter to write letters.

Criss Cole Rehab Center

This rehab center was a lot different then the other one. It was geared more for kids who were going to college. So there are more people who are closer to my age than the previous one.

They had a few people at the center who were both deaf and blind. So they were showing us how to communicate with them. I started learning grade one sign language. This is faster and shorter. It consists of doing a sign for a whole word instead of using the letters. To me it is easier to learn since you are substituting one word for another. Just like learning Spanish in school. After the two people left they quit offering it to us. So if I wanted to learn anymore sign language I would have to teach myself.

One thing different about this rehab center is that they make you talk about your vision loss. You can't do anything until you talk to a psychiatrist about loosing your vision. I already knew what they thought about me from the rape. It was put in my records that I am mentally ill and I should see a shrink. So there was no way I was going to tell this guy anything.

I ended up drinking a soda and sitting there for the whole time. (You are scheduled for an hour) He kept trying to get me to talk. None of it worked. I kept checking my watch. Counting down the time till I get out of here.

"It's not going to work." The psychiatrist told me. "What's not going to work?" I asked. "You're staying here till we talk."

"Yea right." I told him. I was getting ready to leave since the hour was up. He quickly got up and shut the door.

"Hey."

"My hour is up." I told him. "It is a requirement that I talk to everyone about their vision loss." He told me. "That's nice."

"You can talk to the next one." I told him. I tried to open the door and he stood in front of it. I walked over to the window. Nope it was too high. "You can't jump out of there." He quickly told me. "I can see that I told him."

"Tried killing yourself before?" He asked me. I just sat down again and didn't say anything. I looked around the room to avoid looking at him. "I've got plenty of time." I hate it when they say that.

"Don't you like psychiatrist?"

"No." I told him. He asked why and I told him. That after what happened no one believes me. He asked me to tell him. I told him after what happened when I was nine; they put in my school records. That I was mentally ill and recommend I see a shrink. He was the first one to reassure me that what happened when I was nine. Wasn't my fault and I am not mentally ill. Never heard that before. Then we preceded to talk about my vision loss.

At this rehab center they would teach us how to use what little vision we have left. So if you can only tell the difference between light and darkness they show you how to manage that and still get around. It was at this center that I learned how to walk around like a sighted person.

They would show me that I didn't need to use a cane. How to hear which way the traffic was moving and watch for the pedestrian walks. Look down the stairs where the steps are divided with the different color strips and other methods. Because of this people don't know I am blind or even forget that I have a vision problem. Doing this also helped me with my self esteem since I wouldn't feel like a helpless person and get around like other people.

## University of Texas

When I started college I wanted to be a counselor. I originally thought about being a counselor for the blind since I have lost so much vision I figured I could help the same type of people. During my schooling I found out that these people's positions were being cut by state budgets. Because they were classified as state employees. So even if I earned my degree the chances of getting a job would be slim. So I figured I should have a minor as a back up and possibly help me get a job.

I already knew my minor was in criminal justice. I could get a job as a juvenile counselor. I already knew what the kids had gone through after all the bad experience I went through in Las Vegas. This would be easy.

I ended up taking classes at this school. I was getting a prescription for an allergy medicine. My doctor told me I had a drug addiction problem. He told me to quit taking the meds and that I needed to get counseling. I did and went to a drug addiction support group.

I went to a few of their meetings. At these places everyone knows you by your first name. For example your name can be John Smith, but you only tell them your first name. I learned very quickly to just mention my first name. Everyone was sitting in a chair that formed a circle.

We would talk about things and one session the counselor wanted me to share my addiction. I told them about how my doctor said I have a drug addiction problem. They wanted to know what the medication was and I told them. Some had a strange look on their face, because they never have heard of someone being addicted to that medication.

After I told them what symptoms I was having. Several of them gave me weird looks. I was confused. "What's wrong now?" I asked them. The group counselor asked me. "Who told you that you are addicted to this?"

"My doctor." I told him. "He's wrong." A girl answered. "What do you mean?" I asked her. "You are not addicted to this med." The group counselor told me. "I'm not?"

"Nope." He answered. "Then what is wrong?" I asked. "You are allergic to it."

I couldn't believe what I have heard. I looked around and everyone else in the group was agreeing with him. "It's true." Some of them said. "You don't need to be here." The counselor told me. I thought I was hearing things. They were explaining to me that the symptoms I was having were from an allergic reaction.

Then they started asking me some questions that a drug addicted person feels. I answered "no" to those. "See?"

"You're not addicted." After what I've been through I didn't know who to believe. I ended up seeing my neurologist. He agreed with them. I'm allergic to the meds. Now I even have it listed on my medical alert bracelet since I'm allergic to an allergy pill that even ER doctors give out right away for an allergic reaction.

Because of this I had to go to another college…

Central Texas College

It was at this college that I was studying to be a counselor. My minor of criminal Justice. I wasn't doing so well in school so people told me I wouldn't do well in college, from teachers to my family.

I ended up staying in a dorm which I loved since it was away from the abuse. I only had to come home on the weekends. Those times I dreaded.

During one semester I was taking a class. I was having an aura. The teacher paid attention and asked me "What was wrong?" I was having trouble talking again from a complex partial seizure so I couldn't talk even if I wanted to. She had one student take me out and watch me. She told the students what to do and how to arrange the desks.

The guy stayed with me until I was better. When I came back to the room the desks were arranged in a circle. The teacher told me to go to the nurse's office. I told her I was fine, but she wouldn't listen to me. I was told to clear out of school and not to come back till my seizures were under control. I've been kicked out of different things all my life. Now I was kicked out of college for a having a seizure. This was before the American's Disability Act was even thought of.

Spiked Soda

It was toward the end of 1984, while I was going to college. My boyfriend and I heard there was a party downstairs in the foyer of the dormitory. He wasn't planning on going, paused and then asked me if I have ever been to one. I replied "No."

"Do you want to go?" He asked. "Sure." I was so surprised anyone had even asked me to a party. Certainly never had that happen before.

We ended up going to the party. He introduced me to some of his friends. The two of us walked over to the table where the refreshments were located. I started heading toward the punch. He stopped me and told me it probably was spiked and not to have any. I believed him and we went over to the sodas.

The sodas were already poured out into plastic glasses for us. He grabbed one glass and I took one. We began drinking and I noticed two guys sitting on a table, pointing toward us and laughing. Ever since that night I kept wondering if they were responsible for what happened.

The two of us got tired of standing around and not caring for the music they were playing. So we left. He knew that I had trouble seeing so he helped me down the stairs. He stopped at a trash can and threw his soda out. "Mine is flat." He stated after throwing his away. "Did you want to get rid of yours?"

"No." I answered. I have had flat sodas before and finished them. So that is exactly what I did.

We ended up going back to his room. His room mate and friend were there. The four of us ended up playing board games while talking. After I finished the drink, things were clear and others were blurry. I remember the four of us playing games. I don't remember how I got back to my room. I woke up in my bed the next morning.

This is before the date rape drug was around. I had college algebra that morning. This meant a pop quiz. I never studied them, but always passed with at least a "B". But today was different. I had a headache like I never had before. It was too weird to even describe. I wore contacts then and I ended up loosing on that morning. Things looked so blurry I would never be able to find the contact even if I tried. So I gave up. Didn't eat breakfast from the way my stomach hurt and just took my meds. This included five different anti-seizure meds at the time. I never forget to take those since I know how important they are.

I took the quiz and not surprisingly flunked it. With the way I was feeling I just wanted to get out of there. I ended up getting to a pay phone and called up my neurologist. The nurse answered and I told her how I was feeling and what happened. She said what I was feeling was a hangover and that someone spiked my soda. Of course no one checked the glass, so the best she could guess was Everclear. That was the most popular one people were using during the time.

The nurse did get concerned about my seizure meds though. "Did you take them?"

"This morning I did." I answered. "Good." Still sounding worried. "What about last night?" I had to stop and think about that one. Things were still blurry. "Lets see."

"I take them at nine o'clock."

"Yes that is what I have here." She stated. "No."

"I wasn't in my room." I heard a sound of relief on the phone. "What's wrong?" I asked. "No."

"It's good."

"It is." I asked. "I never forget them."

"I know." She stated. "That is why I was worried."

"Huh?" I couldn't understand. "I don't know why I forgot to take them."

"It's like clockwork for me." I told her. "Well."

"Someone is watching out for you." She told me.

"What do you mean?" I asked. "You would have been dead if you took them last night." I was like in total shock. "The only reason you are still alive is because you forgot to take them." I still couldn't believe what I was hearing. "I know you."

"You never forget to take your meds."

"You probably are one of the few patients I know who does take their meds."

"In order for you to forget like that is if God knew what was going to happen and kept you from taking them." I was so shocked I couldn't say anything. "Betty?" I just hung up the phone and ran to my room. "Dead?"

"Why am I still here?"

Anyone reading this can think of a hundred things that could have happened to me that night. Again this shows how God knows what is going to happen and protects his children from harm. No matter where they are. I always take my meds. After thinking about the conversation I checked my purse. There was my meds in the pill box I use in my purse. I could have taken them and still drank the soda. But God has other plans.

Weather Reporting

After majoring in science in high school, I was always fascinated by weather. I ended up calling the weather man at a TV station in Texas. It was an ABC affiliated, but since I was in college in another city they didn't use my info too much.

When I was finished with college I tried doing weather observing for another station in Texas. Some stations already had some that covered my area. When Fox ended up getting smaller numbers on the TV, CBS ended up getting the higher number in different cities. So they needed weather observers for Austin and surrounding areas. I ended up becoming the weather observer for my area.

Wilson, the chief meteorologist, gave me so much creditability on my reports. That usually when someone reports a tornado warning for example, there would have to be at least two people. These two people report it in to the police or sheriff's department before it gets listed to the weather office. Wilson said my creditability was so good, that my report counted as if two people reporting in. That is how much they counted on me and my reports.

One day I reported in a temp of twenty-eight degrees. That afternoon we went up to eighty degrees. Wilson kept asking me if those temps were right. I said yes and he said he would get back with me. He never did call me back. The next thing I heard was my mom calling me.

Instead of calling me back he went on TV and explained the variation of the two temps. He must have spent somewhere near ten minutes on the weather segment telling people about it and explaining why we had so much of a variation in the temps for one town in just a short amount of time. I was surprised he would go to such great lengths to explain to everyone my weather report like that.

We became fast friends. Again it was like having another step brother. We would do practical jokes on each other. See each other at stores and he would tease me by asking a weather related question when I call up. He would give out a question during the weather segment on the news. So he would use me as a gunny pig for his question. Just like a brother.

I kept telling him I didn't major in meteorology. He said "Don't worry anyone can answer this." Yea right. It ended up being a question you needed to study for. After that he would quiz me to see if I could answer it. If not he changed the quiz question before he went on TV at ten o'clock.

The news department knew me really well. As soon as I call in, they would recognize my voice. We would talk for a bit before they transfer me to Wilson. Every year they would have a booth at the local mall. To help raise money for a cause. I would go down there to talk to everyone. I didn't say anything, but they would give me an autograph picture. I thought that was sweet.

Wilson? What did he do? He would treat me like a celebrity. I just wanted to socialize. "Oh here is Betty."

"She doesn't live far from you."

"You know Betty don't you?" If they answer no he would ask them "Why not?"

"Everyone else does." Great. More embarrassment.

After it was over my mom asked me how it was. I told her "I was humiliated." She replied. "Good."

"We should do this every year." I think she was planning on making it an annual event or something.

Suicide Potential

Because I tried killing myself in 1975 and tried it again 1979, the next time psychologically and according to police would be when 1983 are. If you think about it, it makes perfect sense. Four years between each one and so I should try it again five years later which would be in 1983.

Even after learning about psychology in college and other classes I knew I was going to be a potential so I wanted to beat it all costs and throw everyone off. I didn't care how or what happened. Just being able to prove these people were wrong would be worth it. I tried running in front of cars and that didn't work. I tried stabbing myself with a knife and that didn't work. I was more convinced than ever to find some method that would work. I was so determined and mad that the other two ideas didn't work. "I've got to find something this time." I kept thinking to myself. "Now what would work?" I was thinking.

So I wanted to do something different this time to make sure it worked. I never told anyone about it till years later. At the time the only one that knew what I was planning besides me was God. Each time it was just the two of us. The only one who could stop me from planning it was him. Even avoiding me from accomplishing what I was thinking was God himself. Again it shows how much he knows about us better than we know ourselves. If anyone was going to stop this idea it would have to be him. I was still trying to figure out how to kill myself. Before I could even get an idea into my head, the next thing that happened was...

Getting Saved

Sure enough God had other plans. I kept trying to figure out what to do. I started planning this in June of 1982. Figuring no one could stop me and this would be the answer to all my current and any other future problems. Nothing else made sense. I was in the church choir for a while so I ended up singing the songs, but they didn't seem different. Like memorizing a song you hear on the radio. You know the words, you sing it and that is it. No meaning or anything different.

You can sing something and your heart is not in it. I can sing to a song and have no expression. Just like studying for a test. You know the answers, pass it and then it is over. You are glad you did a chore and now it is done.

You will get tired from it and it is like cleaning house. You are glad it is done. You did your chores and go lay down. It is just a job you don't like. Work, work, work. Nothing else. You want to even change careers. Nothing makes sense.

Until something finally makes sense. We were singing a song for the invitation or alter call for the whole month. It was titled *He Lives* by Alfred Henry Ackley. I sang that song a hundred times, but this time it felt different. I must have paid really well attention to the words or God was again trying to say something to me that day like "Wake up and pay attention girl."

"I am saying something to you."

To this day when I hear the song, sometimes I cry or can't concentrate on anything else because it has affected me so much now. Here are the words. I serve a risen Saviour, He's in the world today; I know that He is living, Whatever men may say; I see His hand of mercy, I hear His voice of cheer, And just the time I need Him He's always near. Chorus: He lives, He lives, Christ Jesus lives today! He walks with me and He talks with me Along life's narrow way. He lives, He live, salvation to impart! You ask me how I know He lives: He lives within my heart. In all the world around me I see His loving care, And tho my heart grows weary I never will despair; I know that He is leading Thro' all the stormy blast, The day of His appearing Will come at last. Rejoice, rejoice, O Christian, Lift up your voice and sing Eternal hallelujahs To Jesus Christ the King! The hope of all who seek Him, The help of all who find, None other is so loving, So good and kind.

You can see how these words affected me differently that day. As soon as it hit me I couldn't even sing or stop to sing the words. My mind was somewhere else. I was too busy listening to words to notice anything else. The building could be on fire and I wouldn't even notice it since I was so spiritually focused on it. That is how much of an impact it was having on me that day.

Let me try to explain it to you if you haven't gone through it yet. You feel so different. It is like an emotional release. Any problems you have or had are totally useless now. They are not important. What is important is the time you are spending listening to what is going on. Especially at this moment. If you think of something else or try to, you can't. You're mind is at a blank. You are at an emotional high.

Spiritually you are so high that you cannot come down even if you wanted to. Believe me you don't even want to try. Physically you are not in any pain. The holy spirit is taking over your body. You are so fill with joy that it is like the endorphins have taken over the brain. Sorry chemists. It isn't just the brain that is affected. The whole body is now relaxed. Unlike the endorphins that ware off. This continues to stay in effect. Becoming a part of the person. Physically, emotionally and of course spiritually.

Anyone who has already been saved knows what I am talking about. After reading this, if you are not saved, wouldn't it feel good to be like that? It is an awesome experience that everyone would want to feel. I am not saying you feel like you are on cloud nine. *You really are there*. It is a wonderful experience. Just like I want to share the bad times in this book. I also want to share the good ones. This is the best one of all. It is so uplifting and carefree that everyone will want to have it. Plus it won't cost you a penny to have it. Something that everyone should have. I'm even willing to share it with you.

The next week I was planning on going up and did the alter call and got saved when I was nineteen years old. I did it over the phone instead. When I called the minister he said I didn't have to come up to alter since he knew I was a shy and quiet person. The minister knew what my dad was like so he said I could just do it over the phone. I was so happy. Usually they are kids who do this not adults. I would have been embarrassed, gotten ridiculed by my family. Not to mention the stuff they would have said at church.

About me being saved at such an old age compared to them. It made a big difference in my attitude about trying to kill myself also. Any idea or thought about killing myself went out the window. It is so hard to explain it, when someone hasn't been through it being born again. Thinking back I keep wondering how I can even think of trying to kill myself when he has other plans for me.

I never think about it again and use my experience to stop others from trying to kill themselves also. So maybe some good can come out of a bad experience. You don't feel the same way anymore. At first you like an excited kid who just wants to play with a new bike. Some people stray away for a while like they are tired of the new bike. But you have to stick with it or the bike stays in the garage and never gets used again.

Just like if you know how to speak another language you forget it. If you use it a lot then you remember it. I will be the first to admit that I don't know the entire bible. One reason is that it takes me forever to read something because of my bad vision. I can't use that as an excuse when there are versions of the bible on tape, CDs and video. So I can at least use one of these methods to stay with the reading.

People refer to this as your conscious. This isn't true. It is the holy spirit trying to tell you something. If it wasn't how did I know to do biofeedback at four years old? I hadn't been saved before then, but even I could tell there was something different. Once I got saved it was much easier for God to speak to me and I could listen to him more without distractions or other things being in the way.

Because of the abuse it was harder for me to accept the fact that he was a father. But as time progressed and having grown more as a saved Christian. It is a lot easier to communicate with him. I can ask a question and he answers. Whether through the bible, friend, a thought or even the TV. Believe me he knows how.

As you grow more spiritually you want to help. You don't want to stay in this position that you are in now. You want to get involved and do something. Just as someone wants to help out when a disaster strikes they donate money to the cause. The cause here is salvation. Helping is being more involved in His work.

I've seen some people who can't do much, but do pray for others. Some can do more and do as much as possible. Others I know just don't do anything and just show up for church. The more you get involved in church the more you can emotionally and spiritually grow. People who don't do anything aren't growing. God gave you certain gifts to help him in his work. Some of them you can see as talents. Others aren't so noticeable until someone points it out to you. If you are not using them you are not growing spiritually and not helping Him in His work. Both here on earth and His kingdom.

1983

As I mentioned earlier, this year was different for me compared to other people. Even though I got saved and decided not to kill myself. I was still statically labeled a suicide potential for the whole year. Usually people always say this year went by faster than last year. To me this year took forever to go by. I could hardly wait for this year to be over.

I had to keep checking in to see if I was still labeled. Sure enough the police and other people would say "Yes."

"You are still listed." Someone could come by, kill me and make it look like a suicide and sure enough they would believe it. They would never think it was a murder since I was still labeled.

I would keep praying that I wouldn't be labeled anymore. For me this was a challenge or trial itself. I had to overcome this big obstacle to get passed it. It was like blocking my life and I couldn't accomplish anything that He had planned for me till it was gone. It would never be gone till 1984 came by.

I would try to think of something else and it wouldn't work. If I turned on the TV there was something on a show about a person killing themselves or discussing it. I can see where Satan was using this as an attack on me since I just got saved at I was vulnerable at the time. Making me see this over and over throughout the whole year.

Like I said this year didn't go by fast. I didn't even think about my birthday. All I could do was count down the days till it became 1984. People celebrate the new year the same way each year. For me it was the best new year's day ever. It wasn't the same anymore.

I wasn't labeled anymore. My faith grew since I was convinced God was protecting me from all these tests I was having. Now challenges are an excitement for me when others dread it coming. It had a profound affect on me. In more ways than one. Especially spiritually.

God keeps giving you more challenges as you grow. So you need to pass each one to grow. Think of them as a test you had in school.

If you didn't like tests think of them as something you did like. For example a sport. You had to learn to play with a ball before you tried out for a team.

Austin Community College

I ended up going to this school when Central Texas College wouldn't let me back in after I had that seizure. So I ended up going to this college. Because of what happened at CTC I couldn't have my records transferred. If I did ACC wouldn't let me take classes there either. I was majoring in counseling at the time and my minor was criminal justice.

So I had to start out as a freshman at this college when I was already a sophomore. I was taking a psychology class when a TV show called Knight Rider was on. They had an episode that was on I thought was so horrible. I was saying the same thing any fan of a TV show would say. "I can write one better than that." So I tried doing it.

I would always come in early and so I would get started on writing a story for it. I didn't have any plans on writing a script for it. The teacher, Mr. Bracket, would always see me writing something down. He noticed I wasn't talking to anyone and was by myself. Mr. Bracket tried to read it upside down and had trouble with it. He finally gave up and asked me what I was writing.

"Nothing much." I told him. "Just a story about Knight Rider." I replied. "I watch that show." Mr. Bracket said. "Is it any good?" He asked about the story. "I don't think so." We talked about the previous episode that was on the week before class. Neither one of us liked it. "So I thought I could write a better one."

"So that is what I'm doing." I told him.

"Can I read it?" Mr. Bracket asked. I was surprised when he said that. "I don't think anyone would like it."

"I just want to get it out of my system." I told him. "I'll give you ten points to your grade just to let me read it." He told me. Again I was definitely in shock now. Someone wants to read it? I thought to myself. "I'm just writing junk." I kept thinking to myself.

While I was thinking of it, "Do we have a deal?" He asked. I finally said "Yes."

"Good."

"Let me see it when it's done." Mr. Bracket stated. "Sure." I replied. I went back to writing it and sure enough I was finished with it. I gave it to him while everyone was turning in their papers. "Why is this pile so thick?" He was saying to everyone. Mr. Bracket looked through the stack he was holding. "Oh that is right."

"I've got this manuscript." People in the classroom were wondering what was going on.

The next time I saw him was in class and he returned the papers back. I was surprised. I figured he would take a long time to read all of that. He liked reading it so much that he finished reading it in a hurry. Mr. Bracket wrote on it "Here are twenty points toward your grade."

"I thoroughly enjoyed reading it."

"Would love to see it produced." He also wrote "Ten points we agreed on."

"Ten points for enjoying it."

"Equals twenty points." I was in so much shock. Someone actually liked it and wanted to see it produced? Maybe I'm on to something here.

In other words those score tests that I took in high school were right I had interest and skills for writing. Again God tells you something. The question is are you listening to him when he is talking to you or are just watching TV?

Surgery

In 1985, I was having dinner with my family. My mom, dad and Cynthia were there. Everything appeared to be normal. I finished my dinner early since I wasn't feeling too great left the kitchen and went to my room.

A short time later, I was vomiting like crazy. I figured since it happened right afterwards that it was food poisoning of some sort. My mom was concerned that something was wrong. My mom felt my forehead and figured I was warm. We never did take my temperature. She then asked what was wrong so I told her I was thirsty.

Cynthia brought out a glass of water. This was a glass that could hold thirty-two ounces when full. I drank it all. She asked me if I was still thirsty. I nodded yes. Each time I drank a glassful of water she would go back and give me another one. That is how thirsty I was. I went through three of them in five minutes until my mom stopped me.

Cynthia stayed with me while my parents looked up in a medical book to try and find out what was causing my symptoms. I could hear my dad saying appendicitis. I kept telling my sister "I don't have appendicitis."

"It is just bad food I ate."

I got saved in 1982, but I ended straying away for a few years. This is one of those years I had strayed away. I believe God sends us hints that you shouldn't do this. He was definitely giving me a hint here. I just wasn't listening to it at the time.

My parents took me to the hospital. My dad was driving. My mom held me. There was a bucket near me to use until we got to the emergency room, which was a half- hour drive from our house.

Shortly after we got to the ER, I didn't get a chance to say anything. Any questions the doctor asked my parents answered. It was as if I wasn't there. Probably a good thing anyway, I don't think I would have been well enough to answer. The doctor wanted to keep me in the hospital overnight for observation. That is definitely not what I wanted. I never liked hospitals.

They gave me meds for the pain. The next day I wasn't feeling any pain from the meds so I figured everything. Now I was okay and that I could go home. They ran more tests to make sure it weren't anything else. I understand, but I was already dressed and ready to go home. They didn't like that idea. They ended up telling me I can't go home. Of course I wanted to and since I didn't have any pain I wouldn't believe them. They had me lay down, close my eyes and they pressed down on the affected area. I screamed like crazy from the pain.

Now they were proving to me that I can't go home. They scheduled me for surgery and wanted to know who the doctor was that I wanted.

Now I'm in so much pain I didn't even want to answer the question. "I can't believe they did that." Was all I could think about.

During the wait the pain was just getting worse and worse. I asked for some more meds and they gave me some. It was like I wasn't taking anything. After a while I asked for more and they couldn't give me anything more. It might have been a short time before the surgery, but it felt like an eternity.

They scheduled my surgery for one o'clock that afternoon on a Saturday. I could see them wheeling me into the operating room. I was in so much pain that I couldn't stay still. They kept telling me to stay still and it didn't work. When I was in the OR, they kept telling me to count back from one hundred and going out. I have had numerous surgeries since then, but this one was different.

During this surgery, I felt so different. Almost, like I wasn't even here. I could see everything that was going on in the operating room. I was too busy seeing things to even pay attention to something else. I had a hard time comprehending on what else was going on. I saw the two doctors doing the surgery. One nurse was taking a syringe and injecting me with something.

Again it was so clear, which is unusual for me with my bad vision. I wanted to keep watching what was going on. I felt like I was watching a movie except I saw myself on the operating table. I know it is hard to describe, but good vision, no pain, it is like you don't want to leave it. Would you?

The next thing I knew, I was waking up in the recovery room. Both surgeons standing there asking me questions. Like I said, I've had other surgeries and two doctors asking me questions never happened before. The nurse is standing there asking me how I feel. They would ask me how I felt, what happened and other questions. When I asked them what happened, their reply was "Oh it was red and infected, but we got to it before it burst." If that was the case, why are they asking me these questions? They would ask me other questions like "Are you a religious person?" Instead of answering his question I would ask him "Why do you want to know?" After I asked him questions they gave3 up and left.

You would also think that after this I wouldn't stray from God like I did. But this was just one sign he gave me. Believe me there were others. He keeps it up till you come back. He has a purpose for you. You have to find out what it is.

## Writing

Once I realized I could be writing for TV. I bought a book about writing for television. I spent a lot of time watching different TV shows and studying the camera directions. Comparing them to the shows I was watching. Now I'm learning something that is interesting to me and I am good at. Again my family didn't believe me.

I submitted a script and it got returned to me. With a letter stating that I needed to have it sent through an agent. "An agent?" I kept saying to myself. It was a new term for me. I had to keep referring to the book like someone looking up a word in a dictionary. This was like another language to me. Having to try and learn these terms that showbiz people use and other people don't.

Where was my interpreter? I kept asking myself. I had to find an agent. I felt like this was my calling from God. Write things. So I ended up getting an agent and submitted my script. It came back and the company said they already had their scripts for the season. Meaning they already had all the scripts for that season written. "Try again next season." Was written on the letter.

After writing scripts for so long I can see where I messed up a lot. I wouldn't even accept it myself. There are a lot of writers who would tell you're their first one is the worst. It is true. Whatever your job is you get better with each one. Even today when I write one. Each script gets better than the last one I wrote. Since I was a freelancer I could bounce around from one show to another.

The biggest complaint with producers about freelancers is that they do a good job writing the script, but don't watch the show. So their assignment is to go home and watch the show. I couldn't believe it. You get paid to go home and watch TV? I already watch these shows and I could teach someone the characters of the show. So I ended up decided to write for shows that I already watch. Save myself some time. There was no way a producer could complain that I don't know the characters. Or anything about the show for that matter. The producer's job is to buy the script from the writer for the production company.

Again here is something I could do. So I ended up doing scripts for shows I watch already. I would jot down notes for the shows. If I came up with an idea for an episode I would write it down.

When I got to two ideas put together for the same show I wrote a script for that show. I would give it to my agent. He would submit to the company on behalf of me and I would get a copy of the letter.

This is one advantage of being a freelancer. You can pick when show you want to write a script for. One week I could write a comedy script. The next week would write a drama script. One disadvantage is that you don't get paid till you sell the script. So you could write a hundred scripts and never get paid a dime. One thing I found out later is that when the producers find out your specialty is for example comedy. They don't buy a script for drama. Now they know you do comedy. Even though you can do both.

One show I submitted a script for was running their last season. I didn't know that till I received a letter in the mail. They told me to submit the same script for another show. I did that and got a reply back. The executive producer of the show wrote back and asked me to do a pitching session. Here again is God showing you what He wants you to do.

A pitching session is a where you go to the producer of the show. You talk to them about the story idea you have for their show. It is called a pitching session, because you are literally taking your idea and throwing it at the producer. The longer the session the better you are. It also shows you how much they like your idea. They ask more questions the more they like it. It also shows you how much better your chances are of them buying your story.

Since I didn't live near Los Angeles, I was told I could call my pitches in. I would be assigned a producer to talk to. If that person wasn't in another person took the call. When we would be finished the producer would tell me to call up the next day and make an appointment for another pitching session three months later. They liked my ideas, but already had those ideas in their book. So I didn't get paid. I was even told that when I call I should say the producer's name told me to call today. The next thing I knew I had an appointment for three months later.

Normally, your name is put at the bottom the list and you have to work your way back up the chain to get another appointment. For example if there are two hundred names on the list, it would take you years to get an appointment. Which makes sense, but now they liked mine so much that they would let me skip that. So every three months or three times a season I would have a pitching session. This kept up for the whole season of the series.

I ended up becoming friends with some of the people from the show. One even gave me a nickname. So every time I called up for a pitching session he would refer to me with his nickname he called me. Now my name was in the production office and if I called they knew who I was. Even today my name is on file with the company. Again God knows what you need. By giving you friends who are in areas that can help you. Through good times and bad. No matter who they are or what they do. Speaking truthfully about what someone does. Why can't people believe that these people are doing God's work also? Just in a different way.

Dad's Death

My dad was dying of cancer of the esophagus. He had chemo and radiation to battle the cancer. The doctor recommended that he get the chemo done first. Then the radiation. My dad was already in stage three of the cancer. The oncologist figured he would have a year left to live if he didn't do something. Five years if he did do both.

My dad did do both of them, but at the same time. So he would get it over sooner and he figured he would live longer. My mom wanted him around longer. I was so surprised he had cancer. My dad would come home from work. Then say "I want to make out my will." Like he couldn't understand why he was sick. My mom heard it so much that she was sick of it.

My parents grew up not going to the doctor unless you are so sick that you would be on death's door. My mom took him and the doctor was surprised how good he look. Especially when he was in stage three cancer.

He was sixty fifty-nine years old and by the time he was finished with the chemo and radiation he looked like a ninety year old man. I couldn't get over it. He actually went to church a month before he died. People were shocked to see him. Those who have seen him before were surprised at how he look. Those again who thought I didn't have a dad now knew I have one. He couldn't walk and was in a wheelchair. He was the only person who had communion that day.

The day my dad died he was getting worse. He was in the hospital. They were draining the fluid out of his lungs so much. They finally decided to let him go home. We were waiting for the nurse to let him go. As soon as the doctor said he could go home. The first thing out of my dad's mouth was "Can I have my beer again?" The oncologist replied "Sure."

"Whatever you want." That is all my dad cared about.

My mom was already an elder at the church. So she was always told to put a hand on the new person. This was for the person joining the group of elders. This person were being ordained that day. The day of his death he kept saying was "I am going home". It took him a long time to say one sentence. It felt like two years since it took so long. My mom was closest to his bed. Liz, Cynthia, Debbie and I were in the room. But not as close as mom was. We were able to gather around his bed and talk to him. My mom told us to get closer.

His right arm was getting cold. He kept saying to us really slow "I'm going home". We thought he was referring to the ranch house that we were living on. It was like an hour's drive from the hospital. My mom kept reassuring him. "Yes."

"We'll be home in a while." He looked around. I wonder if it was because no one was listening. At the time no one knew he was talking about Heaven. After we had heard that people refer to Heaven as

Home we finally put the pieces together. I can see that God was using him to tell us what was going to happen. Dad was trying his best to tell us and no one picked up on it. I don't know if anyone in the room was spiritually educated enough to pick up on it. Maybe it is another reason he ended up talking to me. Like he was concerned to make sure he ended communicating with someone.

We have never heard of Heaven being called that before. "As soon as the doctor releases you."

"The doctor told us we could get him dressed and take him home." Mom said. The doctor told us he has two weeks left to live so there was nothing else they could do. They were draining fluid from his lungs so much that it finally got to the point it didn't make any difference anymore. So now they said he could do anything he wanted. The cancer won so he could have his beer. As soon as he got home he was going to have some. My mom promised him he could have it. My mom touched him again and noticed he was getting cold in other places. So she sent Liz to get the doctor. As soon as she came back with a nurse, the lady put her stethoscope on him, checked him out and shook her head "no". We figured it meant that the nurse would come back with the doctor.

Mom all of the sudden told us to put a hand on his head like they do in church for the elders. She said later she didn't know why. We later learned that the Holy Spirit was telling her to. Everyone had their hand on his head. There wasn't any room for me so I ended up touching the cold arm.

Since his arm was cold I took my hand off his arm. After a second or two my mom was being urgent. "Betty!"

"Touch his head."

"I can't."

"There isn't room." I told her. "Then touch his arm."

"You can reach that." She stated urgently. "It's cold." I told her. "I know he is getting cold up here."

"Touch him on the arm." She stated in a hurry. I didn't want to touch him since he was getting cold. But reluctantly I did it not liking the coldness of his body.

All of the sudden I could hear my dad talking to me at the same moment when he was dying. "Get your act together and be strong for your mom." He was talking in his normal voice when he couldn't for a long time. Like a soul speaking to another soul. It turned out after he passed away it wasn't the doctor who came in but a minister. The nurse returned with him. It didn't even hit me that he died until I saw the minister. He came in and wanted to talk to us. For some reason he came up to me first. If you think about it, it makes perfect sense considering what had just happened to me for the minister to come to me first. I didn't say much so he went to my mom. If you had seen how he looked, his face was dead; he couldn't have even moved his muscles even if he wanted to. Like people on TV looked when they are dead.

Then I realized my dad had talked to me. I started crying like crazy and ran out of the room as fast as I could. I was in so much shock from it. All my life I can see where God and the Holy Spirit were talking to me. I think finally it sank in when I heard my dad actually says in his own voice. As if he wasn't sick at all. I told my mom what he said and she said "That is definitely what he would have said to you." Since God knew why kind of stuff I was doing my whole life and that I couldn't do that kind of stuff anymore. Plus my mom was going to need my help from now on. Spiritually I was still like a child and couldn't even process that something like that could happen. Peter, my step-brother, told me that maybe in order for dad to be forgiven he was able to talk to me and let me know that I would be needed to be strong and help my mom out later. I can also see that since we didn't pick up on what he was saying. We didn't understand. So now he was using another way to communicate.

I found out later the cancer was caused from all the drinking he was doing. Now he was paying for all of it. He passed away on November 6th, 1990 when he was only sixty years old.

When we had the funeral, my mom wanted some bagpiper music played at the funeral. If you remember earlier, my dad wanted to hear that music all the time. I was the only one who had any bagpiper music on cassette tape. The church didn't have a record player to use there.

On the tape was the song Amazing Grace being played by a solo bagpiper. My mom cried so much when that got played. It was the only thing I felt that I could contribute to the funeral. The minister wanted each of us to say something. My mom talked a bit about her husband. A couple of my sisters went up and said something. My mom kept tapping me wanting me to go up and say something. I had a shocked look on my face and kept shaking my head "no". There was no way I was going up there and say anything.

What was I supposed to say? That this guy kept beating me up. I doubt if they wanted to hear that. Plus a lot of them didn't even know that. Especially since we kept a lot of things about us hidden. We were good at doing that. What they call the don't ask don't tell policy. That would apply to us. Once you did ask we would either deny it or not even mention it. It was like a bad word you didn't use.

My mom was upset later that very few of us wanted to talk about our dad at the funeral. Two of my sisters yelled at me. They felt I should have gone up and said at least one line. I got up and left the room. What did I hear while leaving? "There she goes again." Debbie stated. "Just running away like she always does."

"We went up and said something." Liz mentioned. "She could have done it too."

"Never standing up or helping mom." Debbie mentioned. "Just thinking about herself again." Liz told everyone. I ended up closing the door to my room hoping they would quit."

Again I would think about what my dad said. "Get your act together and be strong for your mom." How was I supposed to do that if I can't even be strong enough to stand up against my sisters? I felt like I was failing everyone. My mom and even God. I just couldn't deal with it.

Shooting

On October 16, 1991, there was a mass murder at a restaurant in Texas. This is now known as the Luby's massacre. It wasn't far from the school where I went to. A man drove his pick up into the place that was a glass wall, and beginning shooting people right and left.

One of the customers pushed a table over and began using it for a barricade. This helped some people to hide from the shooter and not get wounded. Another man threw himself through the glass window/ wall and created an exit for people to get out of. He helped people getting out so they wouldn't get hurt by the broken glass. Twenty-three people died from this. Since then they put up a brick wall half way up so someone can't drive through the wall. Plus a plaque dedicated to those who passed away from the massacre.

Texans, including those who survived the massacre were outraged. They kept repeating. "If only I could have had my gun I could have taken him out."

"If I had a gun this would have been avoided." Plus other ones like that. People back then owned rifles and guns, but were not allowed to carry one in their purse or bring it into a place like the restaurant. So they couldn't defend themselves. The legislators wanted to pass a concealed hand gun law so that if anything like this happens again a citizen would be able to stop the gunman. Which makes sense.

The Governor at that time, Ann Richards, didn't want to, so it got vetoed. The legislative passed it several times and it still didn't get passed. So as soon as the re- election came up she was voted out. In fact this was the first time in ages that a person elected governor didn't win the re-election. She only served one term.

As soon as the election came up, the man running even posted it on the ads, that if he was elected he would sign the bill into law. The legislature passed the bill. George W. Bush signed it and it became law. The people were told to get training before using the weapons. The problem was people were taking the matters into extremes.

Besides using it for matters like the restaurant one. They would get mad at a driver for what is known now as road rage. When a driver cuts them off for example they would pull out their concealed hand gun and shoot at the driver. The majority of the time they were accurate at their firing from the classes they took.

Chip Baby

munchkin

Ivan Smugface

I was so happy to leave that state. You could do something like pass the guy for a legitimate reason. This would make him angry at you. After you in the lane you need. He would pull up to you. Shoot you as he is across from you. The next you know, you are now injured and on the way to the hospital for gun shot wounds. When all you were doing was obeying the traffic laws. It wasn't just the traffic, but other places as well that were getting to be too dangerous for people.

Going Deaf

All through my life they would check my hearing in school. They knew I had a hearing problem and was trying to find out how bad it was. Every year I had to get my hearing tested. I hated doing that. Every year the same thing. When would it end? When we left Vegas I was happy. We never had my hearing checked again. I remember the guy telling my mom. "Make sure she gets her hearing checked every year." My mom agreed and never did.

I forgot about it myself. Till one day, when all of the hearing in my left ear went. Ever since I became blind I was using a hearing aid in my left ear. I was told I would eventually need one for my right ear. When the hearing went out of my left ear, I figured my right ear was next.

They tested my left ear. Sure enough all the hearing in my left ear was gone. I could feel vibrations. According the audiologist. I never did hear anything out of that ear again. They tested my right ear. The hearing in there is normal. I was always told that if the hearing went out my left ear that the right one would be next.

Nope. That never happened. So now I always make sure I have my right ear toward people so I can hear them. If you are at a table with me. You would notice I am moving my head around to hear people at the table talking. Otherwise people don't notice. Half the time I don't think people even notice I am doing sign language.

I don't need to put the phone toward my left ear since I can't hear out of it. I begin teaching myself more and more of the sign language. The audiologist told me I didn't need the hearing aid anymore. One thing I was glad about. When I sleep I just do it on my right ear and I can sleep with no problem on how loud everything is. So in one it is a blessing from God.

### Mom's Cancer

A year after my dad died, my mom got breast cancer. The first thing she thought of was that she was going to die. Mainly because she was without her spouse so that meant she was to go to heaven now and be with him. She really believed this after the surgery. She passed out for a bit after the surgery. I asked her if anything happened. She didn't remember anything and the nurse said she just passed out.

Since now she was on Tricare after my dad died. She would go to the Fort Hood Army base, see the military doctors, and get taken care there. The oncologist that took care of her was a Colonel. Mostly they take of military personnel. So when my mom went to see him, he would treat her like a soldier.

"Patterson!" He would yell and then leave the room. She jumped up in a hurry like a drill sergeant had called her. She didn't know what to do. I just died laughing. She still didn't know what to do. I told her to leave. She didn't see him. "Patterson!" He yelled again and louder. "What do I do?" She asked me. "Just follow him." I told her while trying not to laugh. "Yes Sir." Mom would answer him. She didn't know if she had gotten drafted. "Coming Sir." Again I was just died laughing. I was watching her move from one end of the hallway to the other trying to find his office. "What took you so long?" I could him asking her.

When she had her chemo, mom would have it done at a civilian's office. I would stay in the waiting room while my mom got checked out. One day the oncologist came over to the waiting room to ask me how my mom was doing.

I was asking him "Why didn't you ask her?" He would tell me that she just sits there and doesn't say anything. I went into his office and watched her. Apparently she grew up with a family that wouldn't see doctors. So she ended up not trusting doctors. Would stay there until they didn't leave.

I had to convince her to answer his questions. I told her the sooner she answers those sooner she could leave. If she didn't answer I did. That of course made her mad. Reminds me of when I was at the rehab center. After that I had to go into the doctor's office with her otherwise the doctor wouldn't get any answers.

Neighbors

We had different neighbors living in Texas. It seemed strange the ones we would end up with just like in Vegas. Here is one example.

One lived not far from us. I felt close to this one like she was a step mother. What happened? At first nothing bad happened. Paula would take me to places and drive me around knowing I couldn't get around. She didn't live far so Paula felt like she would come and help me out. Paula even told me she thought of me as another daughter.

It was the first time I heard anyone say that about me. Usually no one says anything nice about me. I thought for sure I was hearing things. We developed a nice friendship. Then it was time for my mom and me to rent my house out to a new couple/people. The last renters left so we put an ad in the paper. Paula wanted it for her kids. Her married couple, relative and/or in-laws. I wasn't sure if I should do that. How many times do you hear don't sell something to your friends, because they won't be your friend anymore?

They were right. I was getting yelled at all the time. Either I was interrupting her family, pestering the kids, etc. If I called them up about something, I sure enough got a phone call later from Paula. I felt like she was the one I had rented the house to. Not her kids.

Shortly after they rented the place my friendship with Paula slowly died down. I didn't even feel like I had a choice in the matter of who to rent it out. I agreed to let them look at it and see if they like it. Me, being the landlord, it was my decision. My mom could even tell Paula was forcing it on us. Paula conned me to let them have it. After the kids left, the kids not only damaged the house. They removed the outlet covers and anything else they wanted. I have never seen that before. I wonder if it was Paula's idea. I lost not only renters, but a good friend as well in the process.

I kept getting the same thing from people. I'll help you out, and then when you need the help they leave you stranded or ignore you. Here is another example...

Sunday Christian

After the surgery, she ended up finding out she had to have chemo for six months. Since I was in the church choir we both figured it would be better if I got a ride with someone for six months and she could stay home by herself for a couple of hours while I went to church.

I had a couple in a small town who agreed to take me to church on Sundays and then I could get to church and they would take me home. It turned out later that I found out they are what people refer to as "Sunday Christians." In other words they act like Christians on Sundays. The rest of the week they act like their normal selves.

For six months nobody came by to see if I needed a ride. No one came by to bring food. Didn't call, mail cards, or anything. If she had died I don't think anyone would have noticed. Since I don't drive I didn't get to go anywhere either. So the two of us were pretty much together. We didn't mind, but I think people need help from the outside world. You don't need to be on another planet to feel the same isolation like we did.

Once she did feel well again we went to church again and we showed up. People at the church treated us the same way as if we weren't gone and had just went to church last Sunday. I had a hard time getting over that. No one asked how she was doing.

Acting like she never had cancer. She even later asked me. "How come they never asked?" I ended up telling her. "Maybe they didn't want to hurt your feelings." She accepted it. I don't know why I said that when I knew the real reason was because they were just being selfish and didn't want to change their routine. After that incident I wanted to bail out of there, but I felt compelled to stay because of my mom.

## Texas Pop Store

At this job they weren't sure if I would be a good employee. I was only having a job for a month since I would only be hired a temporary. So they were taking a gamble by hiring me. After a month they knew I was going to stay, so they hired me as a cashier.

They would sell balloons for the Children's Miracle Network. Each store would keep tract of how many they were selling. When the store I was at would be second place regional wise. They began posting it in the break room.

People liked being in my line since it was longer and moved faster. I would spend a minute or so telling them about the balloons. After a while they figured it was faster to spend a dollar and buy a balloon than hear me give a talk. So I ended up selling a lot of balloons. When the telethon came on the company would present a check to the network. So I got to go on TV and present the check in honor of the store. I was so surprised I wasn't expecting it. People from the local stores were actually yelling "Betty!" I was so surprised.

I had to train the new people to use the register. There was one guy who I had to train. He was a Mexican-American and would stand next to my left ear. I had problems hearing in that ear. I asked him what his name was. He repeated it several times and I couldn't hear him. If I could hear him I would have know what it was. Since I spoke Spanish. During the whole time he was saying "HEH-soos". I pretended I heard him and ended up looking at his badge. I saw the name "Jesus".

You should have seen the look on my face. All these one liners for a comedy show came into my head. I had a hard time keeping from saying them. Another hard time keeping from laughing. Jesus had a hard time wondering what was going on. I had to hold my right hand over my mouth so he couldn't see it. To this day my friends keep teasing me that I had to teach Jesus how to use the register.

This definitely was some of gift from God and proof he has a sense of humor. If nothing else. Probably a test to see if I could keep from laughing.

Their company's rule was that you were a cashier one day and the rest of the week you were a back up and did stocking. I had no problem with that, but they didn't even follow company rules. So I was head cashier for over two years.

This created problems. One of them was I ended up having carpel tunnel syndrome from it. Working eight or more hours a day doing the registers, five days a week for every month for over two years you can see where anyone would end up with that.

The reason they did this, was because I would work so fast at the register. Probably from having two years of typing in school helped. The register line would move very quickly for the customers that they would be in my lane.

I noticed my line would be the longest, but customers would be in this lane with a lot of items and they still moved faster. The managers would put whoever they wanted for that day to be head cashier and who was back up, this one girl, Brenda, who was hired the same day as I was never had to cashier. Brenda was doing nothing but stocking, again not even following the stores policy.

It got really bad near Christmas. With all the sales and shopping. Again my line would be the longest. Another policy they had was that if you work a certain number of hours, you should have a break. If you work a certain number of hours you would have a lunch. Then before you leave for the day, you have to restock a cartload of merchandise.

It never happened. I worked from eight o'clock am to six o'clock pm. No breaks, no lunches, no nothing. Not even a bathroom break. I kept working and my line kept moving. At least they didn't deduct me for a lunch break. When I finally was able to leave a girl stopped me. "You are supposed to restock." Complaining that I didn't restock a cartful of store items. I told her, "give me my lunch and breaks back and I'll restock." She had such a shocked look on her face. "You didn't get a lunch?" I just walked out since I was so tired. I ended up going to sleep in the car till I got home.

This went on for days. Days became weeks. I finally went the doctor. I was diagnosed with partial PTSD. Post Traumatic Stress Disorder. Half of the questions I answered yes to were from work. This could have been solved if they just gave me my breaks and lunches. The doctor gave me a note for work. My boss didn't like it. Since I was keeping the registers going. I left before Christmas and didn't come back till sometime after new year's day. The one time they needed me. They were busy with last minute sales and after Christmas returns.

The store director wanted to know why I was gone. I told him. This wouldn't have happened if you followed your own rules and gave me what was rightfully mine. I gave them a brochure of PTSD and the rules of breaks of lunches. They never said a word afterwards. I lost so much weight from those two months.

I went back to the doctor. He figured my symptoms would go away when I got my breaks and lunches. He never heard of a company doing that before. I reported the store to the next level up. They didn't care. I figured it is just this store. Maybe another location store would be better.

River Boat Cruise

After my dad died. It was pretty much my mom and I in the house. My sister Cynthia lived in the house next door. Since I couldn't drive Cynthia would take me to some places and my mom would take me to usual places like work, store and other places. One day I just happened to get into my room. I turned on the radio and heard them announcing that the eighth caller would get the tickets. I didn't hear what it was for, but I thought I would try it.

I had the number memorized so I dialed it. Sure enough I won it. "You're caller number eight."

"Who is this?" I heard on the phone. Sure enough I was on the radio too. I was in so much shock. I never win these things. (Thinking back later I can see where God was planning this too.) I gave them my name and they told me I won two tickets to the river boat cruise.

They named the group we were going to have dinner with and meet the band.

They were doing the river boat cruise the night before their concert that was schedule for the following night. Kind of like a promotional deal so you would want to go to their concert the following night. Sure enough I would have loved to be on the river boat cruise. I have heard of the group but wasn't really too crazy about the type of music they played. Just winning the tickets were enough for me. When we got on the river boat for the cruise, my sister Cynthia and I were just sitting in an area of the boat and were relaxing after dinner. Watching the sunset on the river.

A guy asked me if I was one of the winners. I said yes and gave him my name. He gave me a copy of the CD of the group. "I won this too?" I asked. "Sure enough."

"Don't you remember the DJ telling you?"

"No." I answered. I guess I was so busy jotting down the information about where to go to and pick up the tickets that I didn't remember what I won. He told me everyone who won was going around and asking for the members of the band to sign their cds. I grabbed the cd and ran off. Sure enough I got everyone to sign the CD.

One guy asked me if I wanted him to sign it. I said sure. He then said. "No one wants me to sign theirs since I'm just the manager and not one of the singers."

"Are you sure?" I said "Yea."

"I'll take it." He then signed it Ice-T. I had a shocked look on my face.

"What's wrong?" he asked. "Ice-T?"

"What kind of a name is that?" I asked him with a shocked look on my face. "It's a name." he answered. "No it's not." I replied. "Yes it is."

"No it's not." I said. We must have done that for 5 minutes.

"Jane Smith is a name."

"Not Ice-T." I told him. "My name is Ice-T. " "Just like your name is Jane." I said "No it's not." He was surprised. "I've been using that as a pen name." Then I told him my real name is Betty Patterson.

Again he was surprised. He told me his real name. We shook hands. "Why are you using a different name?" He asked me.

"I've been using that because I was raped when I was nine."

"I don't want the guy to find me." He was in shock and said. "I'm sorry."

"Now change it to your real name." I asked. "It will be worth more with I-Tea on it."

"Yea right." I thought. Sure enough later on he was right. Then he looked away. I ran into some of the other band members on the boat, but he never came back. I thought he was avoiding me or something. I never heard or saw him again.

Because of what happened to me I always watch Law and Order Special Victims Unit and other type of shows on TV. They help me when I try to get over what happen. Like therapy or something. Anyway, I see this guy show up on the SVU show playing a new detective. I was thinking to myself "That guy looks familiar."

"Where have I seen him before?" Sure enough I finally remembered. "That's him!" I yelled while pointing to the TV. It's got to be God's work that after all of that he is working on that show. Coincidence? You tell me.

STD

One time I was having severe abdominal pain. The doctor's couldn't find out what was wrong. So they sent me to a specialist. Of course he wanted to do tests. He told me he had some theories as to why I was having the pain and other symptoms. But in order to have these problems I would have had to have sex. Since I never mentioned anything about the rape or put it down he assumed I never had it.

After being accused about lying about the rape, I was afraid to tell him. So I didn't know what to do. Should I tell him or not? What if he is right? What could I have? If he is wrong I could have these tests and wasting time and be afraid of lying again. I couldn't have that. My own family still doesn't believe me.

I was afraid and very quiet. "What could it be?" I asked him. He wouldn't tell me. "It doesn't matter you're a virgin." The doctor answered. I cleared my throat. "No I'm not." I answered nervously. He had a shocked look on his face. "You told me you didn't have sex in the last ten years." He reminded me. "I know, but this was earlier." I told him. "What happened?" The doctor asked. "I was raped." I frighteningly replied. "When?"

"I was nine." I told him. "Alight I'll schedule some tests." He quickly got up and left the room. I was still scared thinking he would yell at me too.

This is actually the first time since my rape that someone actually tested me for anything like a sexually transmitted disease. I could have been having it all this time and not even know it. I had to finally go back out to the waiting room where my mom was.

"What did he say?" I had a hard time replying to this question. "He wants to do some tests."

"What are you worried about?" She asked me not knowing what is going on. "I had to tell him." I started crying. "What are you talking about?" She didn't pick up on it. "He thinks I have some disease from the rape." I told her quietly. Then she finally realized that it really did happen. After all these years of not believing me, just like the rest of the family. Again God is giving me a chance to break it to my mom that yes it did happen and maybe I have to pay for it now. My mom was so quiet for a long time. I don't know if it was finally acknowledging the fact that it did happen after thinking it didn't. Or if it was now worried that she and dad had yelled at me for something I didn't do again. Or now worried that I can die depending on what it was I have.

Praise the Lord that didn't happen. The good Lord kept that from happening. The doctor even came out saying that since it has been this long from the rape that I don't have any of the STDs like people talk about. He did ask why I didn't get tested. I told him no one even considered it, and I was never told. "Well I tested you for every single one possible. So now you don't have to worry about anything." I was so happy to hear that I cried this time from being happy. I usually cry from everything, but being happy.

## Children

People keep telling me that at my age, I should have been married by now and having kids. Living here in Texas it was not unusual to have kids out of wedlock. By the time I was in my senior there was only one girl that I knew of that was already pregnant before graduating. Of course she ended up dropping out of school before she graduated and never married the guy. Nowadays that isn't uncommon. Shows the way of the times I guess.

The reason I never had any children is because doctors in Texas told me I never could. I was told that if I had a grand mal seizure at the same time I had a contraction, that I would be dead. Most likely from the lack of oxygen I would be getting to the brain. If I did make it the baby would be dead. From the wrong way I would be delivering the baby while I was having the seizure. Plus if I got pregnant while being on a seizure medication that the baby wouldn't make it either.

Either way it was a lose/lose situation and I was told not to get pregnant. After I moved to Maryland I was asked if I wanted to have kids by my family doctor Bark. I told him what the Texas doctor said about my seizure meds and me being pregnant. He replied "We have new medications you can take while pregnant that won't harm the baby." I was surprised to hear it. It was also surprised that he would be encouraging someone to have a child out of wedlock.

Then I brought up what they said about the seizures and the labor. Dr. Bark seemed surprised and answered "Maybe you better not in case that does happen while you are in labor." Neither one of these doctors ever mention a c-section that would solve that problem and said I could still have a kid. Being doctors I thought they would know that one.

They also seem to be encouraging their patients to have children at an early age. Either that or tying to act like at my age I should have had several kids. Like there is something wrong with this picture.

Apparently God has other plans. I was always concerned that I would abuse a kid. Just like my dad did with me if I ever had one.

### Girl Scouts

My niece, Tammy, was in the girl scouts. So I wanted to get involved in helping. I tried being a troop leader, but the parents didn't like it. Since I am disabled. I kept feeling like it was prejudice and discriminated. When I reminded the parents there was a meeting. The parents gave an excuse why their daughter couldn't come.

So I got involved in another way. Doing public relations for the whole county. This way I could be disabled and no one would care. It was better for me I think. I can see God using me more this way. I would be brave enough to talk on the radio. Handle interviews for talk shows. Be in front of the camera for shows and other events. When a lots of people are scared to talk on radio or TV.

I guess it comes from living in Vegas and being around celebrities. I enjoy it and get a rush and excitement from it. Since my vision is bad I don't even see the camera so I definitely am not seeing it. At first I look around to find it, but once I see where it is, that doesn't bother me.

I ended up doing it for seven years. The radio stations and TV would end up calling me and I would hear my voice on the news for events like even just selling the cookies. I can even see where this would help me for singing in worship teams in church later.

### Foreign Exchange Students

At one time my sister wanted to do a program with a foreign exchange student. My mom and I wanted to do one too. So we applied to a program and began looking. If they accepted us we would be called the host family. After they checked us out we were cleared. We wanted to have a kid who we could share our home and provide a place for a year to help the kid feel secure. Something I never had.

First Year

The first year we started this we got a kid from Denmark, named Michael. Both of us enjoyed the time we had with him. We got to meet his father and bonded really well. I felt like Michael was a son of mine. The girl that my sister had I feel like was my own niece.

I enjoyed the year with those two. We would do practical jokes on each other, but also were able to handle family situations. It was the first time I had even heard of having a family meeting. Where the kid could talk to the parents and not worry about getting yelled at for speaking his mind. Michael was used to it. I didn't even know if it was just a European thing or not. Man I wish we did that when I was younger. Feeling so secure that you can communicate without any problems. There are a lot of people and families that do that already. They just don't know how fortunate they really are.

The day Michael left the U.S. to go home. He bought an airline ticket to go from Texas to New York City. From there Michael was to go home back to Denmark. On July 17, 1996 we didn't think anything would be wrong. He called us on a phone they have on the plane. Michael was curious as to whether the connection would be good. He didn't stay on the phone long.

It was a TWA plane he was on. Leaving New York City around eight o'clock pm. We didn't think anything of it. My mom and I were watching TV when there was a news story that came on about a TWA plane that went down. The first thing we thought of was that it was Michael's plane.

TWA plane flight number 800 exploded and crashed in the Atlantic Ocean. It was first suspected that terrorist attacked the plane. We were in fear. I was calling TWA and the airport every twenty to thirty minutes. I would have called sooner, but it was hard to get through. My mom and I were also thinking that the reason he stopped the phone conversation was because the plane exploded.

According to Michael he was on another flight and saw the plane exploding and going into the ocean. He wasn't far from it when it happened. My mom and I were trying to get a hold of Trans World

Airlines to see if it was Michael's plane that went down. We were never given the flight number or anything. So we didn't know if it was his plane or not.

When he got home to Denmark, Michael did call us back and let us know he was safe. Until then he wasn't able to get a hold of us. I keep thanking God that Michael wasn't on that plane. Years later they did conclude that it was a wiring problem on the plane that crashed, but they never concluded that.

God has really blessed us with these two. We still keep in touch and still feel like family. Even long distances still don't keep us apart. We liked doing it so much we wanted to do it again the following year. This way our family can grow even more...

Second Year

This time it was different. Cynthia wanted to get a girl again and so did we. We ended up getting a girl from a different county. On the information sheet they fill out to the host family, you have to put down information on you. Almost like what people put on a dating site now.

You put down your religion for example. How often you go. What sports you like to do. What activities are you involved in and so on. This girl, Linda, filled out information and stated that she goes to church. Sings in the choir. Is a religious person and others. We thought we found the perfect person for us just from what she filled out. Linda was excited to come over and we became friends.

Apparently, Linda had other things in mind. First of all she lied on the form. Linda told us on the paper she was a Christian. We found out the hard way she was an atheist. Linda decided to drink alcohol when we told her we don't even drink that. Linda called me up one time to tell me she wasn't going to be at dinner. When she called it was ninety minutes passed that. Linda was laughing at the phone and wouldn't even tell me where she was. I yelled at her like a parent would have and told her to get home.

She hung up on me and called two hours later wanting me to apologize for yelling at her. Linda still wouldn't tell me where she was or anything. I told her if she didn't come home that the people in the house would be responsible for criminal charges. (I guess this is where my criminal justice classes came in handy.)

The next thing I knew she came home, but was mad at us. A lady at the church we went to wanted to take the two girls out for lunch after church. She promised to bring them home and she did.

A week later the people from the program came by and told us that Linda was going to a new host family. Apparently she complained that she didn't like being yelled at for something she can do at home. According to the rules you can leave and go to a new host family. I don't know what she told them, but the next thing I knew. Linda was leaving. After that if you want to leave again you are deported. My mom got so depressed from it. I had to help her get over it. Again being strong for my mom.

The girl that my sister had also got taken away. This also ruined our friendship with the church. The church member who took them out to lunch ended up getting the girl from my Cynthia's home. While the church member had the girl she went to a different church. If we asked the members of the church about the girls. They wouldn't talk to us.

Linda ended up going to a different family. We found out later Linda wished she had stayed with us, because it was worse for her. Now she couldn't do anything. If she complained again Linda would be sent back. So now she was stuck with them for the rest of the year.

It just ripped us up so much. We found out also that Linda had lied about everything she told us. Both on the application and other things. The only thing I think she did tell us truthfully about was her name.

If Linda had stayed with us, we could have helped her. So why God let her leave I still don't know. It could have been he was trying to protect us from what else she could have done to us. Only God knows that one.

Network Church Afterwards

As I mentioned earlier. The church was treating us different also through this. The church member who took Linda didn't show up at church anymore. People who were supposed to be our spiritual family was treating us different now.

One guy who was our elder at the time would only talk to us if he had to. This really made it hard on us. There was no minister at the time to help delegate or even help us. So the people were really running the church. It was a rule that if one spouse was on the session the other one couldn't. This makes sense, but again who listens to rules? All of them were doing what they wanted. It didn't matter anymore. Nobody was shepherding this field and the animals were going off in all sorts of directions. No unity among Christians and a spiritual family who was really getting divided. I have never seen anything like it.

If I wasn't spiritually abused already, this would have started it. I don't know if my mom was spiritually abused already or not. If not this was the first time. All I know is that this added to it and made me feel less like a spiritual family and just proved that no one is in charge when someone besides God is in charge. They were not listening to him and just doing what they wanted.

In Mathew 12:25 it states: "Jesus knew what the Pharisees were thinking so he said to them, 'Every kingdom that is divided against itself will be destroyed. And any city or family that is divided against itself will not stand.' " This definitely applied to them. I saw people being nice to each other, talking, etc. They didn't see us coming. We could hear them laughing, etc. As soon as we entered it changed.

People stopped talking, laughing. No one said a word. We didn't get a mad look from them. But no one said anything. They either moved away from us. Walked off without saying anything. If you don't think this is abuse that is your opinion. To me this was abuse from one family you should be able to count on. It definitely changed. Why I don't know.

After the school year was over, the girl went home. The church member who took Cynthia's student came back to church. She came up to us and wanted the name of the program where we got the student from. So she could be a host family for the following year. We couldn't believe it. We mentioned it to the session. They just ignored us. We were being treated like we were suspects in a crime.

I stayed in choir, but didn't show up as much. I don't think anyone noticed. We slowly faded away. Again no one called or checked up on us.

Personally I felt like an outcast at my own church. A place of refuge, that isn't what I would call this place. A jail? You are getting warmer. A place behind bars and no where to go. What were we going to do?

Chip Baby

We came back from a trip and I had lost my one cat. So I ended seeing an ad in the paper for free kittens. I picked one out that was a boy kitten. I fell attached to this one so fast. We came back from a trip to Disneyworld.

The place we stayed at was an area with the chipmunks chip and dale. In the area you ride the bus. One is chip and the other is dale. Ninety-nine percent of the time we would be on the chip bus. I was stuck with that name on the whole trip.

So when I got the kitten what did I name him? Chip of course. I always give the pets a middle name based on the personality. That thing was acting like a baby and wanted to be held like one. So his name now was chip baby.

I trained him to wake me up in the mornings by smacking me in the face. He got a treat for it if I got out of bed. He was raised up with two birds so he had to take the cover off of the bird cage. This way he was waking them up also. He did a good job that he would wake me up at three o'clock am, shows me what he did and wanted his treats. He couldn't understand why he didn't get a treat for waking up the birds.

So he proceeded to wake me up again. He didn't get his treat and wanted it. I learned the hard way I should have declawed him first.

Especially when waking me up. His sharp claws would hit my face and I would jump right out of bed on the first try. He was good at doing chores. I guess I trained him too well.

After a while he learned to wake the birds up after he woke me up first. That way went a lot better. He was too good at noticing what time it was to wake me up. If I didn't get up when the alarm did. He got me up. I think he is more reliable than alarm clock. Believe me you can train a cat to do several things including chores. If I'm feeding him, he's doing chores.

## Dad's Religion

My mom and I would watch a game show called Jeopardy. Just like anyone else. There were categories that my mom would be good on and some I would be good on. When they had a category on presidents I would be good on that. My mom was good on religion and bible.

There was one question they had on books that I answered correctly and she was surprised I got it right. It was about a book that is in every house that is never used. I answered the bible and she was so shocked that I said that. When they announced the same answer I did. She was so surprised that I was right. My mom thought it could never be that answer. I remember from living in Vegas and seeing it collecting dust at home. Plus at the camp that I ended up going to we mentioned it also.

I asked her one time why dad didn't go to church. She told me "He used to be active in church back in New York."

"He was an elder, would usher and help out so much." (I checked the records in New York. He was never an elder.) "Once we moved to Vegas it was different." I know a lot of people would have quiet time by reading their bibles. Dad would always have a quiet time by himself when we lived in different states. He would spend an hour of his quiet time after dinner and just read.

I wonder later if that used to be his quiet time reading the bible. We were always told "not to disturb him while he is reading." After being hit, you don't go into the living room and bother him while he is reading. He never read the bible, but would be reading a war book or a history book. The living room was so big, that we could hold a meeting in there, but again it was reserved for his quiet time. Once he left the living room then we was "allowed" to go in and watch TV or do something.

If a minister from our church came over for a visit, he wouldn't talk to us much, but made sure he got to see my dad. My dad always told us to pretend he wasn't there. During the time of the conversation he was in the garage hiding. He was told a minister wanted to come over like ten o'clock for example. He would say, "I'm not talking to him" . It was scheduled by the minister so he couldn't get out of it. Then he made other arrangements. As soon as my mom told him it was the minister at the house. He would get mad and shut the door yelling. "Get him out of here and don't come back here until it is safe!"

"I don't need his crap right now!" We had like an unwritten script of what to say and how to answer any question that came up. Minister: "Where is your dad Betty?" Betty: "He is in the garage." Minister: "I'll go see him." Mom: (interrupting) "Um... she meant that he was in the garage and left a few minutes ago to get something for the car." Minister: "When will he be back?" Betty: "We don't know. Sometimes he is gone for two minutes or two hours."

If he checked his watch it meant that he had an appointment to get to and couldn't stay longer so we could breathe since he would be gone. Neither of us liked lying to a minister, but what were our options? Hitting or lying? After the minister left mom would go back to the garage and tell him it was safe to come out. Sometimes she would be in there for five minutes or half hour. I could always tell when they finished yelling because she came into the house and grab a beer to take back to the garage. It was like an apology for what happened. Like it was her fault. When it wasn't. I finally picked up on it early in life to already have a can of beer ready for mom to take back to him. She would thank me and go back to the garage. One time I had it out so early that it was warm by the time she got it that I was told to put it back. I asked about it and my mom replied "I did that once (meaning she brought a warm beer out to him) and he hurt me so

I don't do again." In other words she learned her lesson. Or he trained her good. Depends on how you see it. "Put the beer back." She told me. So I did.

It was like once he moved to Las Vegas he quit going to church, spend Sundays drinking, fixing cars, etc. I was like in shock hearing how different of a person he was in New York. He never went back to that person he was before moving there. The only time I remember him going to a church at all after moving was to see me sing in the church choir in Texas. The minister tried grabbing him after the service just to have a talk with him and he didn't like it and vowed never to step into a church again. We had a memorial service so he never did even when he died. Unless you include the ashes.

Sometimes people can't even figure out why I lived the way I did. They think you could have done something. You could have called for help. Think of it this way. The year on the pages. Things were different back then. Items that is available now weren't back then. It seemed like it took forever for us to get a private line. Get a mailbox moved to in front of our yard. Things today that people still take for granted. Sometimes it is like you need to look outside your window and step outside. See things from someone else's perspective.

Again, sometimes it is things like this that show you which are more important. Is it more important that you have to go back to a certain path of life to get a can of beer. Keep moving forward and forget about your past and troubles. Or just press on and stumble over things like a drunk trying to figure out where you are or even who you are for that matter. No matter what type of circumstances you are facing or trying to overcome. God is with you, parking the car, trying to help you up or just give you a hug when you need it. Don't turn your back on him when he is here and waiting for you to put your arms to him and saying "I'm here."

# MARYLAND

Here we go again. I had left Texas and I didn't have to hear the name George W. Bush anymore. He was Governor of Texas and I am here in Maryland. The chances of someone following me like Wayne Newton did in Texas has to be slim.

Nope. It wasn't going to be that way. He was running for office of President of the United States. What happened? He won. So where does he go to? Washington D.C. Not too far from where I am living. This is getting to creepy now. First Wayne Newton and now George W. Bush. Who's next?

If there is any consolation for this was the fact that I was doing weather reporting for Texas and with my luck he probably was watching the same TV station I was reporting on. Guess what? Now I'm a weather reporter for a channel in Washington D.C. With my luck he probably would be watching that one too.

Weather Reporting

Since I did the weather reporting for the TV station in Texas I wanted to do the same thing in Maryland. I called around the TV stations in Washington D.C. Sure enough there was a TV station in Washington D.C. that needed a weather observer from the same city in Maryland. This way I was able to do volunteer work as weather observer from my city. I enjoyed that.

I was told to call in at a certain time of the day and report the high and lows for the day. In the morning I would call in before I went to work. Just like the Texas one I became friends with the weathermen and the news crew over here. I had to learn how to measure the snow here, since we didn't get much of it back in Texas. This was all new to me, but I loved the snow. I can see why God has four seasons. It really makes a difference. In Texas we felt like it was just hot and hotter.

We would always have at least six inches. I used a ruler, measure three different areas and took the average. This way it was more accurate. Just like the weatherman would teach me.

Chip would sink in the snow. A lighter cat could walk across the snow with no problem. Chip would be too heavy so he sank. I had to shovel snow. Another thing that was different here.

On President's Day of 2003. There was an unusual storm that came by. It lasted from February fourteen to the nineteenth of 2003. It covered cities from Washington D.C to Boston Massachusetts. Some places had at least fifteen inches. Some had up to thirty-six inches. I ended up measuring thirty-one inches at my place.

Usually this place is used to snow. They have plows that come by all the time. It is so normal. If it was Texas it would be understandable. This weekend was different. Schools were closed. Everything was at a standstill. No one was moving. People here are fined if you don't remove the snow from your sidewalk within twelve hours after the snow stopped. This weekend no one was getting fined.

The weather man was having problems with the weather observers. After the snow accumulated and packed in. The weather wasn't accurate anymore. If some of it fell off more piled on so they were reporting the same amount. He was encouraging us not to call in unless you had a full proof system. I found one.

I had a rain gauge that I was using for measuring snow. As soon as I could I emptied it. So new snow would fall in. So I kept track of it. Besides the weather service and the studio. I was the only observer who was able to keep accurate count. I didn't think so, but he kept telling me. So the three of us were getting updates on the snow totals. Now they have these systems on computers at the schools so weather observers like me aren't needed anymore.

Maryland Pop Store

I transferred from the Texas store to the Maryland one. Hoping this one would be better. It started out that way. When I moved over here, I was already treated differently. Retailers tell you, you are now part of our family. I felt more of a part of a family with the retail store in Texas than I did here.

I was put up as a cashier since I was doing that in Texas. It didn't take them long to make me head cashier when they found out my line was moving at a faster pace than the others.

Again, according to store policy you should be on the register all day for one day and back up the rest of the week. What did I do? Cashiering all day, everyday, all week, for the whole year, just like the Texas store.

I told them I couldn't do the registers everyday, because of my raynauds. Raynauds is a circulation problem. Your circulation gets cut off when it gets cold or doing the same thing over and over like typing for example. But they did it anyway because I was good at my job. Who cares if my circulation is getting cut off while working? Apparently the managers don't.

I bought a pair of sneakers that were also rollerblades. They pop out and pushed back in when you need to. I would be able to do demos for the customers. Rollerblading in the store and showing them how they work. Yes, they knew that I have a vision problem, but they didn't mind and I didn't have any accidents.

The same thing happened again. You work from one shift to another with no breaks and no lunches. The difference is that they dock you for your lunch. So not only was I working and physically suffering for it. I was loosing pay too. They did this branch different.

In a store as big as it was. They only had three people working. One employee in the customer area, one at the checkout, and one in the electronics. So people who needed help weren't getting it. We weren't allowed to leave our areas if you needed something off the shelves. Nobody was to help you if you had merchandise to pick up. Then they wonder why that location wasn't getting much business. At this location I had to stay and count the tills. Every single one of them. So we couldn't get out till they were done. If we were scheduled to get out at eight for example. We didn't get out till closer to ten pm. Other workers were taking it out on me since it took me longer to do it. Mainly because of my vision. That didn't matter to them. No one offered to help. They wanted to get home. What was that about us being like family?

Finally I couldn't take it anymore. I can handle work, but not without breaks, lunches and now less money. It was a lose/lose situation again. I quit and then reported them to the higher up. Someone investigated it.

I went to a friend of mine who was still working there. "Are things better since I left?" I asked. He replied. "They now pay us if we don't get a lunch."

"But you do get a lunch, right?" I asked. "No. I don't think we ever will." He replied. "But at least now we get paid." This place will never change. So I tried getting a more normal type of job somewhere. Where ever that was.

Maryland Test Church

In the beginning of going to this church my mom and I would be "looking around" for a church to go to. We both felt like this is the one for us. At the time no one could see anything wrong with it. Mom and I had our letters transferred from the Texas church to this one. Cynthia still didn't feel compelled to be a member of this church and wanted to look around. Looking back now I wish we did the same. Since my mom, Cynthia and I were living in the house no man was "head" of the house. The only reason we got the house was because I was the only one with a job. Otherwise we didn't qualify for the house. If that is how you determine who head of the house is than I should have gotten the title.

If you go by the oldest my mom would get the title. Apparently they went by age, but never told us. They would first go by who the man was in the house. If we had a teenage boy in the house they would have called him, head of the house. But since it was just the three girls my mom was classified as the "head" of the household as they put it.

I ended up finding out the hard way. I don't know if any of them figured it out later. At the beginning I picked up certain "hints", but by the time I noticed them it was too late. Even my step-brother Peter didn't pick up on them and he lived next door to me for quite a while.

Getting back to the story, one time I needed to see the minister for something that was just for me. He never answered my calls, returned or anything. So my mom and I happened to stop by the church office. They weren't located near the same place where we had worship. I went in and talked to the secretary asking if the Pastor Sean was in. "No, he's not in his office."

"Can I help you?" she replied. "No I need to talk to Pastor Sean about a personal matter. When will he be in?" I asked. "Two o'clock." The secretary replied.

"Did you want to leave a message with Pastor Sean?"

"So he can call you back?" I wasn't sure since he didn't return any of my other calls. "I guess so." So I gave her my phone number. By now my mom came in and asked "What is taking so long?" Just then Pastor Sean came out of his office. "Did you need something?" He asked. I had a shocked look on my face.

"I was told you weren't in your office."

"Who told you that?" He asked. "Your secretary said that just a few minutes ago." I answered. "My secretary doesn't lie."

"You must have heard her wrong". I didn't think of it then, because I do have a hearing problem so maybe I did hear her wrong. But he didn't let us into his office until my mom showed up. If Pastor Sean didn't want a girl in his office he could have came out of his office and we could have talked. It's not like it was so personal that I didn't mind it.

He never checked to see what it was about. That was my first hint that something was wrong. No one says anything to you unless the head of the household is there. Believe me more hints were popping up right and left that I never picked up till it was too late. Between all these abuses I got from my family and this church I was literally changing. To acquiesce to what they figured is how I should act. Even my family today doesn't like it when my true personality comes out for even when I write my nickname on letters on stuff. They figure I'm being weird or something worse when I laugh and actually have fun, which is what the "G" in Betty G. Patterson stands for.

Home Schooling

People in this church were big on home schooling. I can understand one or two kids being home schooled, but this church really pushed it. I remember one year every kid who graduated was a home schooled. You should have seen how excited Pastor Sean was. This way they can pass their "cult" beliefs on to the next generation. They would speak against public schools. Because if the kids talked about their church, people would let them know what they thought about it. Those they were going to a "cult" type of church. They would never admit and wouldn't let you say that.

If only one kid got home schooled out of a group, Pastor Sean was disappointed. As if it was his job or fault. The church felt they didn't have enough "influence" on the family or on you. They prey on your weakness. So someone who was/is abused this made them an easy prey or someone to target. Whether the abuse was physical or something else. They would try to find out from questioning you what kind of abuse you had. They also try to do it without you knowing you were being questioned.

If a kid came home from a public school and mentioned that a kid at a public school was told the truth about this church; it was the family's responsibility to remind the kid that all the other kids at school were wrong. Again the head of the household was to take care of it. If it was a family it was the father's job. If it got out of hand the church's rep would take care of the father and up the line it went. From the deacon, then the elder, to the associate pastor and then to Pastor Sean. Believe me it was bad enough without Pastor Sean not getting involved.

They would also tell you what movies not to watch. Tell you to protest a movie when a staff member never saw it themselves. Tell you to avoid buying a book when no one has ever read it. Near election day, they would pass out a piece of paper with a list of people who to vote for. You didn't get a choice of whether you wanted the paper or not. Of course they would preach who to vote for and get the paper. They would try to find out whom you voted for. By phone calls or some other method. Don't let you decide for yourself, because it was their job to decide for you.

Again the head of the house had a lot of responsibilities to deal with just for being a member of the church. Not just being head of the family. This would cause a lot more stress on the head of the household. To where it would make someone an easy target for them to control psychologically also. You didn't want a deacon or elder calling you up for a correction and then having a minister calling you up for a correction later.

### Living Here

After living in Texas where things were cheaper we found out that isn't the case here. Prices were higher. We could afford two houses back in Texas. In Maryland we had to combine our incomes to get a townhouse. Big difference if you ask me. The closer you lived to Washington D.C. The more expensive your property was. Plus everything else for that matter. A lot of people had jobs in Washington D.C. and lived somewhere else because it was cheaper.

It took all three of our incomes to get the townhouse. The only reason we got the place was because I had a job. Otherwise we wouldn't have been able to get it. I can see God working on this. If we didn't get the townhouse, the three of us wouldn't have found our step family. Plus we needed to band together to help each other with what would happen later. Physically, emotionally and spiritually.

### Hotel

After I worked at the pop store I ended up getting a job at a hotel. Things here are different. I ended up getting a job in the housekeeping department. There was about eight of us working in the department, plus two maintaince men.

At first it seemed like a great idea. We were told to have certain items on our carts. I always made sure mine was supplied with everything. If you didn't have enough while you were on a floor, you had to go back to the main floor and get more.

People were always grabbing things off my cart. My mom told me that it is good to have to replace a bible in the room. This indicated that someone didn't have a bible and took it home. This is good if someone needed one or didn't even have one. God's word is being taken to a place that is needed or getting used now.

During the whole time I was there I only had to replace one bible. My supervisor, Patty, was wondering why I was down there. "What do you need replacing?" Meaning something got stolen. "I need to replace a bible." I told her. "Oh." She said in a heartless way.

I was excited about it. Now someone had a bible.

Patty has an employee who was bilingual. She could speak Spanish and English. So Patty would train the girls who just got hired, but didn't speak English. Patty didn't like it and wanted them to learn English in a hurry. So Patty sent papers to them in English with the numbers written down one through twenty. Next to the numbers were the words written in English. A maintaince trainee, Juan, knew I could speak English and Spanish. So he came up to me and asked me in Spanish what was on the paper.

I had to tell him in Spanish what it was. Then tell him again in English what it was. Patty assumed that if you write something down in English everyone can read it. "They know English."

"They are just pretending not to." Only a few people there knew I could speak both languages. After getting yelled at so much for things I didn't do. I didn't let others know about it.

The employee who was bilingual was supposed to get extra pay for her work. That never happened. Another reason I never told anyone. Do more work and never get paid for it. Sounds like other places I've worked at. Almost seems like everyone follows this policy. I enjoyed helping people when they needed it. I've heard from a person that is God's talent being used at work. Never heard of it like that before. I like it though.

While I was cleaning one room, there were a lot of things stuck on an outlet. I went ahead and used a wet rag to clean it. I ended up getting shocked from the wet rag mixing with the outlet. The outlet would have electricity moving through it. My right arm would get the shock and blow up. The arm swelled up from the reaction of the electricity moving through my nerves. After that I try to avoid electricity repairs. Especially with my history of seizures.

### Sexual Abuse

I started working a hotel in what is called the housekeeping department. My family didn't like it too well. They wouldn't tell people that their relative is a maid. So they wouldn't call me that much. Of course they call much in the first place. So I guess there wasn't a difference.

There was a man in the maintaince department, by the name of Steve. He was really friendly and wanted to help the new girls in the housekeeping department. Apparently everyone already knew this. I didn't and no one told me either. Including my boss Patty.

He was a nice guy. Offered to help me with heavy things like lifting things, flipping mattresses, etc. When it wasn't even part of his job. He would ask to go out to eat with me and I replied nicely no.

Steve still offered to help me and I told him I could do it, but he kept asking over and over so I accepted it. Finally he was yelling at me. I couldn't understand why. I wasn't doing anything to him. My dad had already died so he wasn't yelling at me. Steve couldn't understand why I let him help me and wouldn't give anything back.

His understanding was, I help you, and you pay me back. Since I was a girl, I was supposed to pay him back by having what he wanted. Sex. After what happened to me I wasn't going to do that. So I went to the Assistant Manager, Keith. I explained to him what was going on. Before I could finish what I was saying he answered Steve.

I had a shocked look on my face. "How did you know who it was?" I asked him. "He has a reputation for doing that." Keith told me. "And you don't do anything about it?" I confronted him. Keith began telling me that women have told him about it, but no one does anything.

I couldn't understand why. I was having all sorts of problems when I was growing up. Nobody did anything, but at least I reported it. Steve heard about it, apologized to me and I forgave him. I guessed he learned his lesson and wouldn't do it again...

September 11, 2001

Another day that will live in infinity some people refer it to. On September 11th of 2001, a group of people known as Al Qaeda took control of some airliners and began their plans of attack on the United States. The first one at 8:46 am crashed into one of the World Trade Center's Tower in New York City.

I was on a floor using the cart and trying to clean rooms. A guy came up to me telling me that a plane had crashed into a tall building. I was having a look on my face like yea right. People staying at hotels have are known to be sleeping it off the next morning from all the partying the do the night before. This one wasn't any different. I told him "When I left the house to come to work that didn't happen."

"If it did it would have been on the news."

"Believe me I would remember that." This also shows how early we come to work and have to be ready for people checking out. At 9:03 am the second plane went into the second World Trade Center Tower in New York City.

He proceeded to tell me his mom called and she hung up. He wanted more information and needed to tell me more. The phone in his room rang and he went to get it. He told me to stay there. Again I was thinking this guy needs to sleep it off and went to my next room.

I was in a room cleaning up that someone was staying in for another night. Patty came in and wanted to check on the rooms that were on my list. I looked over and saw she didn't do anything. "Your rooms aren't on the list." She told me. "What is wrong?" I asked her. "We have thirty rooms that just became vacant in three minutes." Patty sated urgently. I thought I was hearing things.

There is no way people would check out of that many rooms in a short time. It is impossible. I followed her into the hallway and asked her to explain to me what was going on. "I have to check the other girls."

"I'll explain it to you later." Patty left in a hurry. Then the guy who stopped me ran into me saw my cart and came up to talk to me. I was thinking to myself. "Now what?"

He was in a hurry. "My mom just called again." Before I could say anything he was talking in a hurry. "She said another plane just hit the twin towers." I was even more confused than ever. "Are you sure it didn't happen?" I asked him. He told me what happened in New York. Again I told him I haven't heard anything. "What should I do?" He asked in a hurry. I told him that "My supervisor just came in and said thirty rooms became vacant in three minutes."

"I haven't heard anything myself." He started panicking. "Oh my God."

"What should I do?"

"It's up to you." I told him. "I don't know what to do." Panicking again. "I don't know what to do." He was so frightened.

"But my mom wants me to leave."

"Oh my gosh I don't know what to do." He began to move in circles not knowing what to do. I didn't know what to do or say to him. But God finds a way. The next thing I knew God told me what to say to him. "I don't know what you should do."

"If it was up to me I would leave." He finally decided that is what he should do. Then he ran back to his room and began packing.

While I was finishing up he came pass me. "Thanks." He told me while he was leaving. "My mom was hoping I would leave." I felt like I did a good job and was relaxed about it. Like a person does when they do a good job. But then all good things come to an end I guess.

Ten minutes later Patty came back and told me that I had to redo that room since it was vacant now. "What's wrong?" I asked her. "That customer was going to stay."

"He heard you said to leave and he did."

"Now you have to redo the room."

"From now on don't tell anyone anything." Again getting in trouble.

"How many rooms are becoming vacant?" I asked. "I don't know."
"Two girls are having to redo all their rooms since now they are
empty." Patty was hurriedly talking. "They were almost finished too."
Okay. Something is definitely wrong here. "What are you doing?"
I asked "The hotel people are busy checking everyone out." She
answered. "Don't you have a plan?" I asked. "No." She answered.
"I'm busy trying to get these orders done. "I'll be down in a minute."
"We need a plan." I told her. "Okay I'll meet you when you are
done." Patty then left.

So I tried to finished up my rooms. When I was done. Patty and I
got together. "What do you have planned?" I asked. "Nothing."
"I've never seen anything like it."
"It reminds me of disasters." I told her. "What are you talking
about?"
"We need a plan and get organized."
"What are the front people doing?"
"Checking everyone out." She told me. "What do you want to do?"
I asked.
"I don't have a plan."
"What do you suggest?"
"Everyone here wants to leave." Again God is putting words in
my mouth. "I can help the others with their rooms so they can leave."
"That is a good idea." Patty mentioned. "I have been hearing all
sorts of stories and don't know what is going on."
"As soon as a room becomes vacant, I'll come get you."
"That way we can see it on TV and find out what the hell is going
on."
"Okay." I told her and begin finding the other workers.
I went ahead and helped all the girls who were behind on their
rooms. Patty began trying to help in the office area. As soon as one
girl and I got done with a room. I told her to take her cart down and
check out. "When you are clocked out go home!"
"Yes I will."
"And thank you." She would smile. "Run!" I ordered her. She left
in a hurry. I went on to the next girl and helped her.

What normally would have been a few hours for me to do take eight hours to do. Every time I saw Patty she was watching the TV or updating me on what was happening. At 9:37 am another plane hit the Pentagon in Washington D.C. Sometime later Patty came over to me. "Come on!" I was helping a girl with her room. I told her to keep cleaning and I would be back. She was getting worried. "I'll be back." I promised her.

Patty and I went into a vacant room and watched the TV for a bit. "What's wrong? I asked her. "I don't know."

"I need to check this out for myself." She was getting more and angrier by now. She was having trouble finding a local station. "What happened?"

"They said the Pentagon got hit."

"Where is the stupid fucking channel!" She yelled. I was in shock, but then gave her a number to go to. There it was on the TV screen. One of the World Trade Center Towers on fire. I couldn't believe what I was seeing.

Shortly after we saw what was on the TV they mentioned one place that was going to be targeted was Camp David. We started panicking since that isn't far from us. "Okay now this getting closer and closer by the minute." I thought to myself." She turned off the TV. "Okay we are going to have to work faster." She told me. "I'll help they move faster." I told her. "Okay."

"It's like chaos up front." So she went to the front.

I got back to the room. The girl was panicking still. "What happened?" She asked. "The pentagon got hit so we are going to work even faster." I told her. She had a hard time working. Patty began helping some of the girls too. Again as soon as one got done. They were told to go home. Patty and I divided up the work until I saw her with one of the girls.

Patty was getting frustrated when one of the girls she was helping didn't know English. "Why do you come here if you don't speak the language?" She yelled at them. There were two of them working together. Patty left in an angry mood. The two of them started crying. The employee who was bilingual wasn't there.

I spoke to them in Spanish after Patty left. Helped them and they left. One of the guest asked me about the plane that went down in Pennsylvania. "I told them I haven't heard anything yet." By the time I got down there they were going over the list for tomorrow. Keith was already down there. I told her they probably would be empty. She told me they were booked up. Because of the emergency landing the president ordered. Keith was asking me quietly if the girls who didn't speak English were able to leave. I told him yes. He was wondering how I told them. I had to finally tell him I spoke Spanish. He didn't know yet, but kept it quiet from Patty. So she never did find out.

The President ordered all planes to land to the nearest airport and that only military aircraft were to be in the air. So people were trying to find rooms at the nearest hotels. People were ordered to leave their bags on the planes incase they had bombs on them or something else.

The hotel was booked up in three hours. I have never seen anything like it. On the way out of the hotel I saw a taxi coming in from Philadelphia. There was a couple coming to the hotel with no luggage. I went up to them and ask them if they were in Pennsylvania when the plane went down. They said they were from Idaho and had to go to the nearest airport which was in Philadelphia.

My mom picked me up telling me they were trying to get a hold of me and I wouldn't answer the phone. I told her I was needed there. She thought it was more important for me to be home. Cynthia yelled at me too. I shouldn't have been at work when they wanted all of us home and watch the TV. I never did understand that one. I was definitely where God wanted me and used me. I already knew that. They just couldn't see it.

The following day, Patty had all of us meet at the flag pole around noon to have a prayer and form a circle holding hands. That is the first time I saw anyone do that at work. Unfortunately it is the only time since then too. My boss was the one who gave a prayer. People were watching us from the balcony of the hotel.

On May first of 2011, the Navy Seals went into Pakistani and killed Osama Bin Laden. He was the person responsible for the September eleventh attacks. At first when I heard the news, it came through on the prayer list we have at church. I thought it was something with a virus attached to it.

Then I was getting text messages saying that he was confirmed dead. I was crying so much, because I've been waiting to hear this news. I know it's not Christian like to think that. I turned on the TV and kept watching it. I was on cloud nine most of the day. Watching the nine eleven events on TV made me cry again, but seeing him dead made me feel better. It was so traumatic for me and the people who lived in Maryland at the time.

It is like reliving nine eleven all over again when you heard this news. Plus it gave me closure knowing that he was dead. Like when you get when you lose a love one. I didn't loose a love one on nine eleven, but I was working non stop like someone who does disaster work, which you keep it in until something someone says or an event happens and you finally get to release it. I keep wondering if this is what people were going through after hearing Hitler was dead. The following day I was still on an emotional roller coaster from all of this. Being on cloud nine one minute and crying the next.

Secret Service

When I was working at the hotel, we would get all sorts of "guests" staying the place. One group from time to time was the Secret Service. If they are trying to blend in with the crowd or be inconspicuous believe me they need more practice.

They wear a suit, tie and dark glasses. Reminds me of a movie. It is too obvious that they work for someone important. I said "Hello" to all of them or "Good Morning". They had grumpy looks on their faces. One of them actually said "Hello" back. I wonder if he got into trouble later for it.

Later on when they came back, they needed extra towels in their room. I was assigned that room so of course I had to bring their towels up to their room. They just had the door opened a little for them to grab the towels. I could see every type of weapon they used all over the bed.

I looked at them and then to try and cover it up I asked them if they needed anything else. One of them who was putting his gun together told me they just needed the towels and thanked me. So I ended up leaving. While I was walking down the hallway I was counting how many pocket knives, six inch knives, thirty-eights and other weapons I saw on the two twin beds. Believe me there wasn't any room for them on those things.

## Supervisor Threatening

There was a girl who worked in my department and was sixteen years old. She just started working so it was understandable that she would mess up. One of the rules in working at the hotel was not to leave your worksheet at the customer's room. Guess what she did?

Yep left it at the room. Somehow Patty found out and yelled at her. This was her first job so she didn't know how to handle it. Being a teenager she yelled at Patty and called her a name. Patty got mad at her and wanted her to repeat it. Sure enough she did.

Patty was in her early fifties so it would make sense that she would be mature enough and experienced to be able to handle it. Not her. Patty ended up chasing the girl down the hallway threatening her. The girl was scared and ran off. Patty was even bragging the next day about how the girl was so immature at her running skills and that Patty could outrun her with no problem. I couldn't even believe what I was hearing.

The next thing I heard out of Patty's mouth was this: "If I catch any of you doing the same thing I'll come running after you too." I knew now this was the last straw. She wasn't threatening me like the girl, but I couldn't wait to mess up and have her doing the same thing. After doing one room, I went up to the registration desk, gave them the keys to room and told them "I quit." I ran across the street and asked my mom to come pick me up. I couldn't do it at the hotel, because I was concerned that Patty would come after me, yell at me and do something else if she found me.

My mom did pick me up and asked me what happened. I told her and she agreed I did the right thing. I could see Patty looking around for me. Across from where I made the phone call. She found out in a hurry I left and was looking for me.

I took the hotel to the unemployment office and they had a "mini-trial, but them called it a hearing, with Keith, a court reporter, the judge and me. Patty and my mom had to wait outside. It was being audio taped for records. Keith agreed that Steve already has a history of sexually harassing the housekeeping employees. The judge asked him why he is still working there and why nothing has been done about it.

Keith said he would take care of it as soon as he leaves this meeting. The judge asked me if my supervisor threatened me. I told him what she said so he said it was directed at the girl and not me.

So nothing could be done. Keith wanted to shake my hands and wanted to stay on good terms with me. I shook hand and agreed. Even when I got the job at the vet clinic they gave me a glowing recommendation.

I could see Patty asking him what happened. He didn't answer and she was getting furious. Since I could lip read I could see him telling her she would be getting in trouble and Steve was going to be fired. She couldn't understand why and was asking him about it. Then they drove off.

I found out later Steve got a job at the same hotel, but at a different location still pulling the same stunts there that he was at the hotel I was at.

Vet Clinic

A month after I quit my job at the hotel, I ended up getting a job at the vet clinic. Now here is where God rewarded me and shows me he listens. I mentioned when I was a kid I wanted to work with animals and wildlife. Yep that is exactly what I was doing here.

When I was working with the wildlife they would put me in charge of taking care of baby squirrels. Since I had a knack with them, Chip and Ivan enjoyed it. They would look at the squirrel like it was a friend. Can we play with them mommy? Was the kind of look they had on their faces.

I enjoyed this job so much. God knows where your skills are and where you can help others. Because I would talk to the cats at home I would do the same here. When I got a call to take a dog to the back, I would talk to the animal. I would ask him "Do you want to go back with Aunt Betty?" The dog would look at the owner. The owner would say, "She's not talking to me." The dog looked back at me with a look like "I guess so." And then I would take the dog back.

Now, whenever I come and get a pet, they tell the pet "Here is Aunt Betty to come and get you." I would always name the wildlife by groups. Rabbits were called Thumper, squirrels called Dale, deer were called Bambi and so on. One day an employee was teasing me about it. "You can't call the squirrel dale unless you have a chip."

"They go together." My supervisor interrupted her. "She does." Referring to my cat. Then it dawned on her. She was convinced these people at the work place were crazy.

Cynthia's Death

I was working at the vet clinic when the day my sister died. Earlier that morning my mom got a phone call from Cynthia saying she needed a ride home. She drove herself to the ER. They gave her some meds so she couldn't drive home. My mom got the phone call, got dressed and brought her home. Cynthia was in a good mood.

We joked about whose turn it was to go to the ER next time. Cynthia thought for sure it was my turn next time. Lately my mom and she had been going a lot. So I was overdue. I told her she probably was right and went back to sleep since I had to get up that morning to go to work.

When it was time for me to get up and get ready for work I heard her snoring, this is something I don't hear too often. I was happy to hear that. So I went to work and didn't think anything about it.

202  Christine G. Roberts

Once a month we have a staff/lunch meeting at the vet clinic where I work though a lunch time and go over things that need to be discussed. For some reason I felt compelled to bring up about Cynthia being in the hospital. Just like when my dad died. Getting prompted by the Holy Spirit again. Every veterinarian was asking me questions about her symptoms and what tests they did on her. Plus the results of the tests. I gave them some of the answers since Cynthia told me the answers before I went to sleep.

Some I didn't get. After I got home from work my mom was worried about how she was doing. She checked on her and then got worried. Mom ended up calling Cynthia's doctor.

The doctor recommended calling 911. She was too upset to do it so I used the cordless phone and went up to Cynthia's room and made the call. The people on the phone would tell me what to do. One thing they told me to do was to remove the pillows from under her.

I did that, but I could tell she was dead. I had only been working at the vet clinic for a month. I've seen dead animals so much I could see a dead body real easily. Cynthia was lying on the bed with her hands up above her head like a person surrendering.

Again I was doing what my dad told me. "Get your act together and be strong for your mom" I could tell my mom was too upset so she couldn't talk to the 911 operator. I knew Cynthia was already dead. Since rigormortis had already set in. (It usually takes a few hours) I was trying to talk loud enough for the 911 operator to hear me, but quiet enough not to upset my mom. Every so often I heard my mom yelling in an upset voice "What is going on! " "She has to be alright."

"Cynthia!"

"Why aren't you saying anything?"

"Cynthia wake up!" I could hear her and not the 911 operator. I asked the 911 operator to repeat what he said.

"Can you put her hands down?" He asked. "No."

"She is already dead." I replied while crying. "Can you feel a pulse?" I checked her neck and didn't feel one. "What did you find?" He asked. "There isn't one." I told him. "Are you sure?" I already knew from my volunteer work to check the ankles for a pulse.

"Check..." Before he could say anything, I answered. "There isn't one on her ankles too."

"I already checked." From my criminal justice classes I already knew the different codes. The highest priority is code three. Using both the sirens and lights. "You need to up the code." I told the 911 operator.

"I'm doing it." He replied. I could her him saying to ambulance driver. "Code three." Then he told me "Stay there."

"They will be there in a few minutes." Sure enough as soon as he said that I could hear them pulling into the parking spot of the house. I could hear the 911 operator on the phone still talking to me. "They should be there now." While I was rushing down the stairs as fast I could to get to the door. I opened up the door. "Yep."

"They are here." I told him. "I'll let you go." He told me and then hung up. I had to show the paramedics where the room was.

They saw Cynthia on the bed. One of the paramedics had a shocked look on his face. Then they kicked mom and me out of the room. Mom was constantly yelling at Cynthia to wake up. I took mom downstairs and gave her a soda to try and calm her down. She wouldn't drink it or calm down. I felt like a failure and didn't do what my dad told me to do. In less than two minutes they were downstairs and telling us that she is already dead. "If it makes you feel better she went quickly." One of them told us.

My mom ended up having hard time dealing with it. I ended up not having a choice. They offered to call someone for us. Suggested the minister. My mom wouldn't let him do it for us. Since she was mad at him for telling us the bad news. I had to take over and call the pastor's wife and telling her what happened. She called the pastor and our elder to come over and help us.

My mom was asking what had happened. The paramedic answered her "We really can't say anything until the autopsy is done." As soon as he said that. My mom freaked out even more. "An autopsy?" She was having a hard time dealing with it. I had an even harder time trying to help her and not panic myself. Nobody could tell us this was going to happen. Mom got up away from the table and tried to go back up the stairs. He had to stop her.

"Yes Ma'am." He answered. "None of you were here when it happened."

"We're you?" He looked at me. "I was at work." I told him. "What about you Ma'am?" Talking to my mom. "I was home...she was home." My mom answered but very weak and hard to think of anything. "Cynthia!" She yelled to the stairs. The paramedic had to help her to the table. "Why did you do this Cynthia?" She was still yelling. I didn't know what to do with her. Or even what to say either.

"Was she on medication?" One of them asked me. I guess he figured I was the strong one. I was busy trying to help my mom so I heard him, but didn't answer. He repeated it again. "I have to help my mom." I told him. "My friend will help your mom." He told me. "I need to see her meds." He reminded me.

I ended up showing the ambulance people where Cynthia's meds were when the minister came over to help my mom. Again more hints. When Cynthia died Pastor Sean came over to the house which is expected. Again I'm not head of the household so he and my elder, Tom, came into the house and helped her. Me? I was on my own again. I was in shock from my sister passing away unexpected like that. But one thing I thought was that one of them (Either the Pastor or Elder) could be helping one of us since we were both having emotional and spiritual problems from it. Instead they were both comforting her.

The police showed up. The ambulance guys where explaining to the police what happened. I saw them helping the police upstairs. After the four of them went upstairs. I watched Pastor Sean and Elder Tom help mom. Talking to her. Asking if they can help her, etc. Totally ignoring me. As if I wasn't even in the room. I felt the same way when my dad was around. The only difference was I wasn't getting hit this time. Maybe I am being selfish, but I feel like two of them being there, one of them could help each of us. Two people for two people. Makes sense for me.

Finally the mortician office showed up. Since Pastor Sean and Elder Tom were helping me. I went back to doing what my dad told me. "Be strong and help your mom." Don't pay attention to what you need. Help someone else in other words. So I did. I helped the police and mortician's office. Answer questions and watch what they did with my sister.

Since she was having her arms up like she was surrendering. She wouldn't fit in the body bag. So they had to literally, "cut her arms off." They did. Bring her arms down. She finally fit. One of the police officers caught me watching and yelled at me. Told me I wasn't supposed to be there. I told them "I was there to help." Before I could finish I was being pushed out the way. Again getting yelled at for helping. I guess me should have been used to it by now.

I ended up going downstairs since I was getting told not to be there. I came downstairs. Saw Pastor Sean looking at me. Once he saw it was me, he just went back to my mom. No asking if I needed help or anything. By now I was pissed off at him. I guess the anger stage kicked it. I just went outside and walked around in the dark.

No one was going to help me or checked to see if I needed anything. All I did was look at the mortician's car. I couldn't believe there were here to get my sister. It didn't feel right for some reason. Just like not grieving for what has happened isn't normal either.

I could hear people coming down the stairs. The police were helping with the gurney coming down the stairs. The body bag was on the gurney and strapped down. Nothing sticking out or above the head. The mortician was in front of the gurney.

I was supposed to help the morgue people with opening the door and seeing my sister's body being taking out to the coroner's car. The mortician saw me and smiled. "Thank you." For helping him. I guessed he thought I was a nice neighbor just helping him out. I didn't really say anything. I watched the gurney take my sister out to hearse. Cynthia died on December 14th, 2001. Where were they? Both Pastor Sean and Elder Tom was each surrounding her. Blocking my mom's view and helping her.. Why? Again she was head of the household. Today I still get flashbacks when I relive the whole event and begin crying.

In other words Posttraumatic Stress Disorder from Spiritual abuse and emotional abuse. That following Sunday there was no way I was going to go to church. My sister Liz took me. Everyone else wanted to stay home and help mom.

She didn't have to go to church if she didn't want to. Again it was what she wanted. I didn't have a choice. Pastor Sean mentioned about a baby that was born that week. I got upset again thinking a life for a life. Then he mentioned Cynthia dying again that didn't help me. What song did they sing right after that? The same Christmas song I couldn't play on the piano. "Joy to the World" I felt like I was being punished. Between all of this I kept crying and couldn't even sing.

People were looking at me like I shouldn't have come there if I was going to be like that. Liz kept apologizing for me or reassuring people at the church. That I would stop it to them. To me. "You are going to have to quit doing that."

"You are drawing attention to yourself." I gave up and left the room in a hurry. I ended up trying to calm down and told her I wanted to go home.

Finally she gave in and took me home. Elder Tom told her to take me home if I was going be like that. Again apologizing to Elder Tom for me. That I didn't mean to do that. Maybe if I was head of the household I would have been treated different?

Funeral

We had the funeral as soon as we could. Since Cynthia died when no one was in the room or not in a hospital an autopsy was done. Whether we liked it or not. A week later I received a copy of the autopsy report since I paid to get one. When I got it in the mail, I feel like I was reliving the whole day over again. Reliving the 911 call, watching the gurney taking my sister down the stairs, everything. My mom wanted me to read it to her and explain it to her.

That night I couldn't sleep too well while crying. The next day I went to work. I had the hardest time handling work. I called up the church asking for help. They pretty much brushed me off again. I told them "If you aren't going to help me then go check on my mom."

"If she is going through the same thing I am going through she'll need help."

Sure enough Pastor Sean showed up at the house talking to her. She was busy cleaning trying to take her mind off everything. He couldn't understand why I asked him to check on her when she was fine. I never did handle the day at work, kept crying and didn't do a good job. I was in a hurry to get out of there and get home ASAP. Again I'm not head of the household. Needed help and never got it. I still have PTSD thinking about it. Again I think it made my relationship with the church worse. Not that I needed help. But when they got to my house, my mom didn't need it. Like I said, I'm not head of the household. Who cares what I need?

Cynthia's daughter showed up for the funeral. I was in so much stress from what happened and not getting any support. The only way I could compensate for it was by telling jokes. In one way God was protecting me and it helped Cynthia's daughter. She was so much in shock from what happened just like some of us. I think it hurt her more since it was her mom.

Again the church didn't help her. They were busy helping my mom. They supported her, both physically, and emotionally. The rest of us, forget it. All of my sisters showed up to support mom which was good. I think the church should have helped out more. If there is someone you should be able to count on in time of need it should be your spiritual family.

At the funeral people would go up to the body and give their respects. After all I saw with my sister I didn't want to. My mom kept telling me to. Of course she got the support from the Elder and Pastor.

Cynthia's daughter wanted to so mom made me go help her. She didn't want to look at her mom by herself. I went over and saw how Cynthia looked in the casket. Both of her arms were down. They put weights on the arms. Tore the clothes to cover up the weights. So it now looked like she has big arms. When really she didn't. I knew why, but didn't tell anyone. Cynthia's daughter was getting upset. So I told her quietly some jokes. She laughed and that made her feel better. I'm glad I did that. I get nauseated when I remember how she looked in the casket.

Pastor Sean was glad I helped Cynthia's daughter liked that. I just gave him an angry look after all the trash they put me through. Then making me see Cynthia liked that. I wished I didn't have to do that. Be strong for your mom is all I could think of.

As I mentioned earlier we really didn't get along well. Probably from the abuse, or our personalities. You can pretty much guess whatever you want. Ask twenty people and you will get twenty answers is what I always say. With us that is pretty much what you get. If someone is married their spouse supports them. People like me that don't have one doesn't get that either in this family. They pretty much brush me off.

Before and after the funeral we had drivers taking us to and from the place. Some of my sisters were complaining about the drivers they had. So I switched cars with them. I got in the second car this time. We were discussing about Cynthia and the funeral. Now we were leaving the funeral and heading home.

None of us were talking about men. In fact the discussion about men never came up. What got our attention and what we remember since then. Was the talk that the driver told us as we were heading home. All he did was telling us the story about his prostrate problems. Plus how the doctor was helping him. The ones sitting in the back, we all looked at each other. We had looks on our faces like "Is he really telling this to us?" This is the first time I heard a stranger tell me about this stuff. That is the same thing we were all discussing afterwards. Especially after a funeral.

Christmas

This Christmas was different for me compared to others. It was the first one I had after my sister died. I was already having problems with church and the funeral afterwards.

I was feeling like I was being treated different still. My mom the church would have bent over backwards to help. Me? It was like forget it. My mom and I were by ourselves. She was constantly reminding me that it was her that should have died. Not Cynthia. I didn't know what to say to her. I kept hugging her and trying not to cry. I knew that would make it worse for both us. Like dad said. "Be strong for your mom." So I always did that.

My mom didn't really feel like cooking. I didn't even feel like eating. She would tell me to eat to keep my strength up. Especially since I had to work. I told her I wouldn't do that unless she ate. So we were helping each other through that.

Peter and his mom Karen, were living next door. They kept coming over to check up on us. Karen felt like she had just lost a niece. This is when I realized they were more like a family rather than just neighbors. Karen wrote a nice poem about losing Cynthia. I don't know what even happened to it. I wish I had it framed. It touched me so much. Mom yelled at Karen saying "You aren't related to her!" "You didn't just lose a daughter!"

I tried to tell mom that Karen was hurting just as much as we were. Mom was too upset about losing a daughter that she couldn't see it. Karen understood about it and I explained it to her. It is too devastating to a parent to lose a kid before you. No matter how old the kid is. It just doesn't seem right or normal. My mom never did get over it.

Cynthia had bought the presents she was going to give us before Christmas. My mom just handed them to us. This way it didn't hurt as much. Or at least to me, because they weren't wrapped. It still seemed weird getting a present from someone you just lost. My mom enjoyed it. To me it didn't seem right. Like I wanted to give my present back. Or like I wished I never got one. I still have the cat statues in my house. I look at them everyday and feel like they are looking at me. I don't think I'll ever get rid of them.

Birthday

Since it was my first birthday after my sister died. I figured there was going to be some problems when you loose a love one. I wasn't ready for this. The present was wrapped up and there was a tag with my name on it. I saw on the gift tag that it was from Cynthia. As soon as I saw that I started crying. I begged my mom not to have me open up the present. I had already gone through so much with losing her, the 911 call, having the church being so mean; I just wanted to forget about it.

My mom wanted me to open it up. I think it made her feel better by wrapping it. Plus it would help her getting over it if I opened it. She still didn't know about the abuse from the church. Especially, since they were helping her. My mom was crying herself and told me "You'll like it." I finally gave in and took forever to open it.

Cynthia and my mom paid for me to go on a trip. Because I was doing all the work while they were ill in July. A bus trip to New York, dinner, shows everything. I loved it. It was a combination of a Christmas and Birthday present. They bought the tickets in August of 2001. I went on the trip to New York December 4th through the 6th. After September 11th things were still on fire. The fire department was still working. Streets were still blocked off. You could see memorials and dust from everything.

Cynthia told me she would make me some pillow covers for king size pillows. I picked out the material. She never went with me to buy the pillows so I figured that was out. After she died I got her pillows. I didn't want them after what happened to her, but I got them. What did I get for my birthday?

It was the king size pillow cases my sister was making for me. They were made with the material that I picked out earlier. Before I went on my trip. Brown with different cats on it. All I did was cry more thinking about Cynthia dying. It made my mom happy, but made me worse. If I knew she was going to die that month I would have never gone on that trip and spent the time with Cynthia.

My mom could see that I was upset, but felt better that I noticed it was the material that I picked out. She asked me. "Do you like the material?" I replied "Yes." In a hurry since I knew I did. So that made her feel better. She figured I was crying from getting something I wanted, but that wasn't it. Getting a present from your dead sister that she made before she died. I didn't even want to touch it. Don't get me wrong. I loved it and enjoyed it, but the timing was so strange. It freaked me out so much from it. If I knew she was going to die it would have been different. Being so young and unexpected made it seems so unbelievable.

## Chip & Ivan

You know how God rewards you for something you did. Of course you don't know it at the time, but you certainly do realize it later. To this day when I think about these things I still die laughing.

Well one of those times was when I was living in Maryland. I trained Chip to wake me up in mornings. But he got tired of doing all the work and wanted to get the reward. He figured Ivan was getting the treats for not doing any work. Sounds like typical kids fighting to me.

Finally, Chip decided to do something about that. I felt someone smacking me on the face. Usually that is Chip's way of waking me up, but it was different this time. I opened up my eyes and saw Ivan doing it. No wonder it felt different. Ivan was doing it lighter since was new to it. Chip was more aggressive and harder. I guess I trained Chip too well.

Since Ivan wasn't doing a good enough job Chip had to correct him. He would smack Ivan in the face like he was saying "You are doing it wrong." Then smack Ivan in the face again. "Pay attention!" Then Chip would smack me on the left side of my face. "This is how you do it!" He would look at Ivan. Ivan would try to copy Chip and do it again on the right side of my face.

While the two of them were smacking me on each side of my face, I wouldn't be saying anything and watch them. Finally after getting abused by both cats on my face, I would say to them, "What are you guys doing?"

Chip would have a shocked look on his face as if he was saying: "Oh no."

"We've been caught." Chip would look like he was going to get caught. "Run!" Was the next look he had on his face. Then the two cats would see that I was awake. Chip gave a gesture to Ivan. "Run!" Chip then ran. Ivan then ran off following Chip. The two of them ran off in a split second out of the bedroom and into the living room. I died laughing so hard I couldn't even get out of bed.

After that incident. Ivan's new job was to wake me up in the mornings. Chip's job would be to just wait till I woke up. Chip got his treats for not doing anything. The only time Chip would wake me up is if Ivan couldn't do it. Like if he forgot or if there was something wrong. I guess the way Ivan was doing it maybe he had to correct him again.

Worship Team

Since I was used to being in the choir in Texas, I wanted to be on the worship team at the Frederick Test Church. In order to be on it you had to try out. I didn't have a problem with it. According to their rules, if you were a girl you had to sing alto. If you were a guy you had to sing tenor. Anything else you couldn't even try out for the worship team. I didn't know that till too late.

They asked me if I sang alto. If you recall earlier I didn't know the difference so I said "Yes." I tried out a couple of times and then I was accepted and on the team. We had practice on Friday nights before the Sunday service. This was the first time I had to use microphones. Each person had one on the stand, attached to a cord, but weren't allowed to move them. We stood a certain amount of space between the microphone and the stand. There were four of us facing the musicians doing the vocals. There were four musicians facing the vocals. The vocals were to the left of the congregation and the musicians were on the right side. So in all there was eight of us on the worship team. I enjoyed doing that.

Then on one Friday during practice, we were singing a new song for me. I guess they were familiar with it. The worship team leader, David, asked us to project our voices. Because of this song, he figured no one would hear us. With the microphones and that we were singing alto the church wouldn't hear us. I did it like he said. When I did I end up hitting the higher notes without realizing it. I haven't project my voice in this church since I left the Texas one.

Since no one explain to me or even taught me what it was. I was still confused on what projecting was until he explained it to us. Finally it dawned on me what the Texas choir director was telling me. So I projected my voice like he wanted me to do and ended up hitting the notes of a soprano.

I didn't know I was hitting the soprano notes. I was just singing like I did in the Texas church. I thought I was still singing alto. He thought he was hearing things and had me do it again. I ended doing the same thing again. I didn't pick up on the hint that I wasn't singing alto since I wasn't ever told what part I sang. I ended up singing that Sunday.

When it came time for practice on Friday, David came by to pick me up and take me over. In the car he had this conversation with me. I was told to never be on the worship team anymore. Their rules were you had to sing alto. Those are the only ones who can sing. I told him I sang alto, he yelled at me calling me a liar and told me I sing soprano.

Before I could explain anything I was off the worship team and told never to come to practice anymore. I was also ordered not to mention it to anyone about this conversation. I had a shocked look on my face and he said "You're home now." Sure enough he just drove around the neighborhood. Just long enough to have this conversation and I was back at my house again.

"You can get out now." David told me. I got out and was surprised that I got dumped by my own church for not singing alto. To this day when I mention this all I can think of is that I don't think alto. Who cares if I can sing? All I know is that I don't sing alto.

According to first Corinthians 12:25-26 it say: 25 "so our body would not be divided. God wanted the different parts to care the same for each other. 26 If one part of the body suffers, all the other parts suffer with it. Or if one part of our body is honored, all the other parts share its honor."

If you go by this. Than one part of the body is more important than the other. Like the alto and tenors are more important. So the feet and hands of the body of Christ is more important than the body itself? No part of the body is more important than the other. You can't divide the church and live. Just like you can't divide a person's body and live also. If this wasn't true why all of us aren't Pastors then? Or why would we need a choir?

Elders

Everyone at this church has an assigned Elder and Deacon. Some churches have one or the other. At first it might seem good that this church had both. For me it wasn't. Of course there were several people assigned to one deacon and several people assigned to one elder.

Every Sunday there would be two people near the exit so if you wanted to join, have a prayer need, etc. you can go up to them. At this time, my sister passed away, my mom was dead so I was finally head of the house hold like they had for their classification since I was living by myself. Nope that didn't make a difference with them. It didn't matter either way when I finally found out.

One day I went up to the two and told them I needed a prayer. They asked what the prayer was for. I told them I was having problems at work. These two people were saying mean things to me because of my religion. I was being persecuted for my religious beliefs and didn't even know it. They said they would pray for me on the condition that next time I wouldn't ask for a prayer request for something so minor. That they were there for people who had real concerns. I didn't know the difference so I promised them. In the end they prayed for me, but

I never did that again. Since now I didn't know what classification my prayer request would be for. Was it important enough to even get a prayer for? Do they have time to even want to help me? How important does it have to be before they would even want to do a prayer for you? I finally gave up on that too and never asked for prayers again.

When I think back it was more like a policing position they were doing. Whatever you did or said to them went straight to Pastor Sean. It wasn't like they keep things confidential. Ask you if it is okay to mention it someone. See if you would like someone to help you. No it goes to the people higher up and they decide if you need punishment or not. I was literally scared if Pastor Sean called. Normally people are happy to talk to their ministers. Not me. Especially at this church. I would be terrified to answer the phone if they ever called me.

When my mom called I gave the phone to her and they were polite to her. I knew if they called they would never want to talk to me or my sister. One time they did call when the only person at the house was Cynthia. When she answered the only thing they talked to her about was trying to get her to join the church. They kept telling her she "had" to join since her other family members were already members. She ended up hanging up on them.

Sure enough they yelled at me about it like it was my fault she did that. I was ordered to get her to join. Again they wouldn't bother my mom about it since she was "head of the household". I kept trying to get her to join and couldn't. I still got yelled at like I wasn't doing my best and never will. If I didn't get her in the church I was a complete failure for not just the church but for everything.

Presidents

Okay, this time I had President Clinton and George W. Bush to contend with while living here. Yes, this is the same George W. Bush who was Governor of Texas while I was living there. Coincidence? You tell me.

Whenever a president stays at Camp David, it makes the newspapers. If the first lady is shopping, it is on the news. The radio station will report that the first lady was last seen and name the store. What does everyone do? Quickly head over to the store and look for her.

One time there was a lady sitting at the coffee shop. I couldn't believe it. These secret service guys follow the first lady into the shop. While the first lady was getting her order, this one secret service agent starts looking into the customer's purse. Her purse was hanging over the chair the customer was sitting on. She didn't even know the guy was an agent. Even I can spot them in a crowd. It was too funny.

How these people living here never know who the secret service guys are? How do they never recognize them? I'll never understand. They stand out in the crowd so bad. I also don't know how they didn't notice the first lady either. She is seen on TV so much. It's not like they see her in the coffee shop every day. It ended up getting into the newspaper.

## Traffic

There was one time, while I was living in Maryland that a bad traffic accident happened. This one should go into the history books if I had my way. It was a foggy day in Maryland. The President was leaving the White House to go to Camp David. Nothing unusual right? Wrong.

There is a road that takes you from the airport to Camp David. Everyone who lives here know about it. Anyway. I was home listening to the radio. Doing some writing of course. I heard there was accident on the radio. They named the streets. I still didn't think anything of it.

Then they announced that there was a five car accident on this road. I was thinking to myself, "You've got to be kidding." The next thing I heard was a police escort was driving way past the speed limit. It still didn't make sense. The car that was described was an old car that isn't even used anymore. I felt like I was in a twilight zone episode.

They were getting calls right and left on the radio. People were using their cell phones and calling into the station. Describing the crazy drivers of these vehicles and everything else. I was expecting someone to get beeped any minute. That is how bad they were describing everything. Using foul language on whoever was responsible for the accidents. They were getting mad and wanted to know who was responsible as soon as possible. Besides getting off their chest about it. They were hoping other callers had the information and the DJs could tell them.

Finally a D.J. came on and reported the situation. What happened was the marine one helicopter was planning on going to Camp David. It had to stop at the airport, because of the fog. They didn't have any back up vehicles and used the ones from the airport. A vehicle that isn't used anymore and that was collecting dust. All of them got checked out for the weekend. So now if you needed a loaner for the weekend you were out of luck. The President has it.

The radio people were laughing their heads off stating the President of the United States was driving too fast. That all of these old cars were being used by him and his staff. It was short drive, but I guess it was an emergency to cause several accidents. Who is going to believe that? I doubt if the insurance company would. How would you even explain it? I don't know if I would, if I was the insurance company.

Marine One

Whenever the President left Camp David to go back to the White House, his helicopter would always fly over my apartment complex. It wouldn't do that when the helicopter was heading to Camp David. Just on the way back. Just as if it took a different route home. It would make a different sound when flying over that wasn't the same as a regular helicopter. So I could tell the difference even with my eyes closed.

The TV reporters covering a story from Camp David said "The President would be leaving Camp David Monday." But I could tell you he left at 3:00 pm, for example, by hearing Marine One flying over.

Sometimes I could see the other two helicopters when Marine One was going by, but not Marine One. It would be the only one I hear, but not see. Since it would be flying higher than the other two. They would always fly together. Keep moving their positions when together. So if you are in the air you cannot tell which helicopter is the Marine One.

If there were foreign dignitaries at the White House who were supposed to be at Camp David. The helicopters would take several trips. Depending on knowing how many were coming. On the way back I would hear the helicopter go by a few times in the same day. Heading back to the White House to pick up some more people.

Frederick Airport

As you know by now. Marine One can land here if they need to. I've only known of a few times. Usually they land at Camp David. People are used to seeing and hearing those machines fly by that they don't think of it.

There was one incident where one of the three helicopters had to land at the airport. It wasn't the one with the President on it, but people automatically assumed it. They were gathering at the airport waiting for someone to come out of helicopter. The same thing happened again.

The D.J. had to go on the radio and announce that it wasn't the President and that the government was asking people to stay away from the airport. Apparently there was something wrong with one of them. So they announced that the President was safe and sound at Camp David. So they didn't want everyone hanging around the airport and asked them to leave.

Some people just wouldn't listen. They stayed at the airport and waited with their cameras, cell phones, etc. They were disappointed when they found out it was a helicopter pilot exiting the vehicle. If they had only listened to the D.J. and the government. I guess that will never happen.

Women

The women at this church would have bible studies. Since I couldn't drive they would meet at my house. I thought this was great. How nice of these people to help me like this. We would have a bible study and then have refreshments afterwards.

Afterwards I found out why they were being so helpful. They would have it at my place for their own reasons. They didn't know what I was doing at my own place so they had to find out for themselves. They came to my place and would check out the apartment. Look in my medicine cabinet and report back to the elders and other people. If I was on birth control pills for example they would report back that I was taking them.

Instead of thinking I needed them for a medical reason they would automatically assumed that I was sleeping with someone. Automatically accusing me of something instead of checking the facts. As if it is permissible to be looking inside of someone's medicine cabinet is okay in the first place without them knowing it.

Another time, I was scheduled to have an appointment with a glaucoma doctor. I already had a ride scheduled to take me to and from the eye doctor. Tom's wife was a retired nurse so she automatically didn't believe that I have normal pressure glaucoma. Plus she never heard of anyone's vision fluctuating.

I was ordered by Tom and Pastor Sean to have her take me to the doctor. I had to cancel my ride that I scheduled way in advance. Have her drive me to and from the place. I was also told to have her sit with me in the examination room. During and after she asked the doctor questions. She didn't believe me till she heard it from the doctor. He ended up telling her the same things I told her. She asked about the vision fluctuation and he said it fluctuates like other things in your body.

He gave a few examples and I mentioned weight. Then she finally figured it out. She took me home and reported to the Pastor Sean and Tom that I was telling the truth. Why would someone go to great lengths not believing someone is beyond me.

I felt like they were spies for their husbands. They were ordered to check on me for their husbands. Double check with a third person if I suspected they were doing something. Getting another girl to do the dirty work for them and report to Tom's wife so she can put it up the line to get back to Pastor Sean.

Counseling for Rape

I ended up getting counseling for rape thirty years later. I ended up getting it done at a secured location. My mom would drive me to the place and pick me up afterwards. When my mom's cancer got worse Liz came up to help move mom. I asked Liz to drive me to my counseling sessions. That of course was out of the question.

Since she is a recovering alcoholic, Liz needs to go to AA meetings. Alcoholic Anonymous has meetings in different places during the week. I don't have a problem with her going to meetings. I was just asking for one or two rides. Nope. Out of the question. It was more important for her to go to her meetings. So I checked it out and told her when the meetings were. There was one even in the hospital while our mom was there. She thanked me for letting her know and she went to her meeting. Me? I never went back to counseling until weeks later. When I was able to find a ride somehow.

When I saw the counselor she said not many rape victims are coming forward for help. Like me they were told they made up the stories and people back then did whatever they could to cover it up.

She wished there was like a campaign ad to encourage rape victims to come forward for those were raped back in the 1970's and even earlier. People can't become a survivor until they get counseling and forgive the person. Not many rape victims know they can get help whether it happened yesterday or sixty years ago. Here is another difference of thinking of man compared to God. In man's eyes you are no longer a virgin. In God's eyes you still are. Another sign that man should be thinking the same way God does.

One thing we were going over about mine was or is called dissociation. She said the trauma of what I went through was too much for me to handle at the time it happened. So I felt like I wasn't there and this explains why I was a frozen statue and couldn't move. Apparently a lot of rape victims go through this because physically they can't handle it. I can picture God being there to protect us and this is how he does it. Meaning God is saying I'm here and I'm taking care of you girl. You are safe.

Then when you are well enough to handle it, he releases it over to you and you remember it. Maybe in pieces at a time or the whole thing. I've noticed while doing this book that more and more of my memory has been coming back on all of these abuses. I always thank God for helping me write this book. I know he is using me to get it out and use it to help someone. I am certainly not writing these words, but he is to give comfort to everyone who reads it. I can certainly see this as the faster I write these words the more he is in control of the computer and my hands doing the typing.

Some people will never believe this happened to you. The best thing to do is to just forgive them. If you can pray for them. I even pray for the guy who did rape me. I know it is hard or even strange to comprehend at first, but it really makes you feel better, both emotionally and spiritually. You feel like the stress is leaving your body. It will take a while, maybe days or years, but once you do you will feel good. Just give yourself time.

Back then they didn't do rape kits. If they did that would have helped. A lot of people who are accused end up getting released later by the kits proving they didn't do it. Why more people don't use it is beyond me.

Some insurance companies won't even pay for counseling for a rape thinking the victim brought it on like a date rape. Others won't pay for the victim if she/he was raped before and now a second time. Thinking it is a pre-existing condition so the victim is now responsible for the medical bills along with the trauma of what they went through. There is more that needs to be done for them and it is like not much is being done.

Like the old saying goes "The sooner the better." This applies to a lot of things including rape. The longer you wait to report it, get tested, and get counseling. The longer you lose evidence against the person, less likely they will be arrested; you won't get counseling and be relieved of the situation. Even if the case gets thrown out at least you tried. In mine the guy wasn't arrested, my school record was ruined and I didn't get any help till thirty years later, but I feel better that at least I tried to do something. You also won't be a survivor till you accept that it happened and you forgive the person who did it. It is part of the latter of surviving that you have to take to overcome the situation.

Voting

Here is one place where they have control over you. If you didn't feel or see it you should by now. Even telling you who to vote for. One of the things a church as to agree with to get a tax-exempt status is not to tell you who to vote for. If they don't follow these rules they lose that status. Unfortunately I didn't pick up on it till I did this book.

I can see a Pastor suggesting who they think would be good for this country. This church went to the extreme. They would have people standing at every exit. Holding a five by seven piece of paper. It would be white with black letters on it. On the paper would be a list of who you should vote for. Starting with President of United States. Then going all the way down to who you should vote for on the school board.

If you are a visitor and didn't want a piece of paper they didn't pressure you to take one. Me? I was a member and had to take one. One year I didn't one, so they came after me and made sure I had one. If you check the trash cans at the voting place you will see those sheets in there.

The people who would be handing out the papers would be important people at the church. Pastor Sean would give a sermon on who should be voted on the President and Vice President. People passing out sheets would be Elders, Deacons, and even David, my former worship team leader.

Elder Tom was handing out a sheet to one person. The guy stated he was just a visitor. "Oh you are just a visitor?" Tom asked him. "Yes." The guy replied. "You don't need one." Tom told him. "This is just for our members." Tom stated. The guy smiled and left. David wanted me to take one. After he got rid of me on his team. I didn't want anything from him. So I told him "no."

"You have to take one." David told me. "He didn't have to take one."

"So I'm not." David looked at Tom. Tom nodded at Tom. I ran off. David ran after me.

David came after me. I ran out of the building. People saw us. Those who were members just ignored us. Others who were watching looked at us strangely. David made sure I took a sheet. "She forgot something." He told people who weren't members. I took it since I was supposed to. After that I made sure I got one so they wouldn't do that again.

Jefferson wrote, "I contemplate with sovereign reverence that act of the whole American people which declared that their legislature should 'make no law respecting an establishment of religion, or prohibiting the free exercise thereof,' thus building a wall of separation between Church & State". People on both sides have been debating about this for years. When the forefathers started this country. They didn't want a country telling people to have a country run religion like England was having. Which is why it was put in the constitution so quickly. No Government run religion whatsoever.

What happened with me was different. A religion telling me who or what to do. With this church it was more of a "mind control". People still don't understand that a place can call themselves a "church" and use some form of abuse to control you. I'm not saying they are "brainwashing" their members. But getting to the point to where you so used to the abuse that if you get to a place where you are treated nicely. You think it is bizzare.

With the voting. Something didn't seem right. When I didn't want the paper they litterally came after me making me take the paper. According to law they should have been reported and loose their tax exempt status. To them that probably wouldn't make any difference. They would have just kept on going. Remember they didn't do any of this stuff any of the other times of the year. Like putting out pamplets on a table they would do. So you can go over and look at it if you want. They didn't run after you with it. But a voting paper they did.

Transportation

Since I worked on Sundays with the Vet clinic, I told them I wouldn't be able to go to church there anymore and would have to go to a new one. As soon as they heard that they went and gathered up a few families and got them to rotate on a schedule to bring me to church from work or at my apartment depending on my schedule. Again it seemed great.

But later I learned they were doing it to keep me from leaving. No way did they want me telling anyone about this place. They were determined to make sure I stayed in their group.

One of the families that signed up to pick me up on a Sunday was Pastor Sean and his family. He would always ask me questions pertaining to what was going on with my life. This one girl who was my helper, Stacy, ended up getting me out of the church. She used to go to this test church. So Pastor Sean was familiar with her. He would ask me if I had seen Stacy lately. What we talked about and so on. He was really paying attention to what the two of us talked about. If I haven't heard from Stacy or seen her then someone else in the car talked to me about something else.

When I accidentally told Stacy about what kind of questions Pastor Sean was talking about the first thing that was out of her mouth was "You didn't tell him anything did you?" I replied with whatever I said. I was quickly ordered to keep my mouth shut when talking to Pastor Sean about her. She told me he was trying to get information out of me about her. Such as: How they can find her? What information they have on her? Plus if she has been helping anyone else leave the church.

The following year they were able to find more families to help and each family didn't have to pick me up as much. Of course now, Pastor Sean's family still did it. Plus the associate pastor's family, Clark, was driving me too. Both families digging for information out of me. Not to mention, Tom and David. So now I had for people digging for information. While the rest of the families just wanted to have a casual conversation with me.

One Sunday Tom's wife came by my work place to pick me up. I told her I was tired from work and couldn't come. I had been at work since 3:30 am, tired, sweating and wanted to go home. She came and got me and forcible took me to church.

I told her I couldn't go. So what did she do? Took me and made me sit next to her like I was a three year old. She gave me mean looks when I tried to get up and leave. Grab my arm and told me harshly while whispering. "You are not going anywhere!" In a mean harsh voice. I had a shocked look on my face. "What did I do wrong?" She just gave me a mean stern look and grabbed my arm. Then she yanked me. I said "Ow!"

Again she is hurting me in church and thought it was okay. I felt like I was being held against my will. She ended up accusing me for lying to her when I didn't do anything. I ended having to stay at church against my will, started crying and got hit when I did. I kept trying to be quiet about it and I noticed no one was looking at what she was doing. As if it was okay to them. I got lectured for what I supposedly did wrong. Was forced to promise not to do it again. No apology from them for what they did and was told not to tell anyone about what happened. The elders, pastors and my deacon all yelled at me for it and I was taken home and dumped there with no explanations for what was going on. Thinking that everything, anything that happened was my fault and not theirs. Again showing me who is in charge and what happens when you disobey.

Persecuted for Religious Beliefs

Even today I still have some people telling me "You are too religious."

"I don't want to talk to you."

"All you are going to do is tell me I'm doing something wrong, because the bible says not to do it." All I'm doing is speaking the truth. I'm not a judge or jury so why are they are taking it out on me I don't have any idea.

While I was at the vet clinic all I did was wear t-shirts that would have logos on them. Instead of having a credit card logo on it the words on the shirt would read "Jesus he is everywhere you want him to be." So I'm not saying anything. Not bringing a bible to work. Not trying to preach to them like people on TV do. All I did was wear a t-shirt. Others would wear t-shirts that have logos of rock stars or something else and they didn't get yelled at.

One co-worker said "You are too religious." I asked him why he said that. "Look at your shirt." He replied. I looked at it and couldn't figure out what was wrong. "Don't you see it?" He asked. "No." I replied. "Don't you get it?" I was confused. "Look at yours." I told him. He was wearing a t-shirt with a rock star on it. "Yes, but mine is okay. " He told me. "Yours is advertising." I told him. "So is yours." He pointed at the shirt. I then told him "No."

"Mine isn't advertising, it's stating a fact." Then he had a strange look on his face and every time I saw him he would just say to me "Too religious." Even if we just passed each other in the hallway that is all I heard. "Too religious."

Another co-worker didn't like my shirts either. He would see me and do the same thing. Except this person would call me a "Christ Freak." I had such a confused look on my face since I have never heard anyone calling me these names before. Plus no one ever told me this can happen to you.

Everyday it was the same thing. Going into work till I left work or the two of them left. "Too religious."

"Christ Freak." That is all I heard from the two of them. One day at lunch my boss was at her desk so I asked him why they were treating me like that. He replied. "They are jealous of you." I had such a confused look on my face. "Why would they be jealous of me."

"I don't have anything."

"They have more things than I do." I just couldn't see it.

This went on for several months. I kept praying and couldn't figure out why they were doing this to me. Like I said I didn't have any idea. I even prayed for their help hoping maybe they would stop. On Saturdays I would watch these bible cartoons. It was good for me since I wasn't familiar with these bible stories. It was mostly for kids to learn stories like Daniel and the lion's den. It helped me learn these things as well I could memorize these stories and sing to the songs.

Later on God decided to take care of it for me. I was at work at night. A dog came in and I took him back and gave him a towel and water. He was scheduled to have surgery the next day. We closed up and I went to work the next morning.

I was working with the guy who called me "Too religious". He noticed the same dog I took in last night was there and he was to take care of him. "It says watch on his tag." He told me. I looked at the dog. "Oh that's the dog I took care of last night."

"He is harmless." (A watch on the tag means to be careful because the animal can bite.)

He still had doubts so I showed him. I went into the cage and the guy closed the door so he wouldn't get hurt. I took away the dog's water dish. The dog then jumped up and bit the dish. He ended up biting the other end of the water dish and I wasn't hurt at all. I came out of the cage with the water dish and told him. "See I told you he is okay."

He still had doubts, but went ahead and started taking care of the dog. I was working on some animals, but I could see him from where I was. Then I saw the dog jump on him and bite him. Before I could rush to help him another co-worker got there first and helped him out.

He went the medical place and got fixed up. A supervisor asked me to finish up for him. I said "Sure."

"No problem." They wanted to take the dog out. Gave him a shot to sedate him so they could do surgery. So another co-worker was ready to take the dog out. By now I was taking care of some other animals and I was directly across the dog's cage.

The other person who said I was a "Christ Freak" came by and was getting the dog out so the doctor could give him a shot was in the cage. The dog was jumping on him. He tried to keep him down, but lost. The dog bit him so bad he had to get out of the cage in a hurry and go to the medical place too.

By now my boss came over and posted a sign on the cage saying only vets were allowed to take care of the dog. The owner took him out with a couple of leashes attached to each other. I took care of the dog's cage while the owner was busy. Then the vet gave him a shot and put him in the cage.

The dog kept barking the whole time and never went to sleep. So they had to give the dog two more shots over thirty minutes apart. By now the dog wasn't asleep and kept barking. The vet finally called the owner to get the dog since they couldn't get him to sleep. I never did see that dog again and the co-workers quit calling me names. Since then I can really relate to the story of Daniel and the lion's den.

In case you are wondering God wasn't finished yet. Six months later the guy who said I was "too religious" ended up getting saved. Every time he had a question about religion who did he come to? Yep me. I had to help him since now he was a baby Christian. I enjoyed it.

Shopping Center

While I was working at the vet clinic, we were diagonally across from a shopping center. A guy entered the liquor store. Around his body and a dead man's switch when entered the liquor store. He quickly locked the front door, but forgot there was an exit door in the back. Figuring all of these people was trapped in the liquor store.

He wanted to see his ex-girlfriend and try to talk to her. Her current boyfriend was in there with her. As soon as they saw the explosives they ran out of the liquor store and try to warn as many people as possible. There was a bank next door with an ATM. Several stores were lined up on the other side of the liquor store. The owner of the liquor store tried to talk the bomber out of it.

The owner of the liquor store ran away from the bomber, he ran toward the back door like everyone escaped. The owner called the police and told them there was an attempted robbery in progress. The bomber was shooting at the cops. The cops never did shoot back at him. The place was surrounded. By now the other stores were evacuated.

As it turned out, the liquor in the store was like fuel for the fire. There was a massive explosion in the store and flames were literally going up in the air, landing everywhere, including the roofs of the store and the bank. All the money in the bank just added more fuel to the fire that was already going.

People in all the stores and banks were evacuated in time. Praise the Lord. The only person killed was the bomber which is what he was planning all along. No matter what happened he wasn't planning on leaving the store alive. Police later found a suicide note which explained it all.

The fire department and police arrived. The police had the area taped off with yellow tape on the sidewalks to keep people from getting too close. By four o'clock in the afternoon you could still see the flames and shopping center in smoke. We immediately had to go into lockdown.

Meaning that the whole place had to be locked. No one was allowed to go in or out of the building. This included staff, owners of the pets and the animals themselves. The employees were wondering what to tell the owners who were still supposed to come in for appointments.

The receptionists had to call the owners and let them reschedule an appointment. We weren't allowed to tell the pet owners why they couldn't come in. Just that we had to cancel the appointment. Then asked if they wanted to reschedule. Normally when we aren't that busy we let employees go home, but this wasn't the case. Nobody was allowed in or out till the locked down was lifted.

The staff was told to call back closer to the time to come in. Since we didn't know what was going to happen later. Surgeries went on like usual. Owners brought their animals in the night before or that morning before going to work. Other than the surgeries there weren't much to do.

Some of us wanted to go out and look at it. No one was allowed to. Nobody knew if there was going to be another explosion. Our safest route was to stay in. Another reason for the lockdown.

There were police cars parked on each side of the street to keep traffic from entering. If you wanted to leave they would let you do that. We didn't even know the lockdown was lifted till around five pm. A receptionist was able to come in and told us that there wasn't even a police car out there.

As soon as she entered we called employees to come in. Each section of the business couldn't leave till the replacement came in. The fire was still going on, but no threat of explosion was expected. So people were allowed to enter.

To this day, they never did fix the shopping center. You can drive by and see the damage. It makes you think about how you can go to work and not be home the same day. Are you prepared spiritually for it? Are you ready for when God calls you?

Hurricane Katrina

When I was living in New Orleans, there was a levee system all over the city. While living there, you were told not to worry about it. It has stayed up for years. Nothing will bring it down. Well a hurricane by the name of Katrina did.

By the time the Hurricane came I had already moved up to Maryland. But I remember the promise the government always told us while we were living there. Since the city is under sea level this place is protected. Why worry? It will never happen.

On August 29th of 2005 things changed. The hurricane came on shore and broke the levee. People drowned thinking the levees would keep them safe. People were literally flooded out of the city. Those who evacuated left their animals behind. They just came out of there off their roofs.

Those who were evacuated, the government helped them out, They had to relocate to another city. Some were heading toward our area. My boss agreed to help with the owners of the pets. Give them free boarding for the animals and help with some of the bills.

I talked to some of the owners. They were surprised that some people all the way in Maryland could understand what they were going through. I told them where I used to live. Of course hearing the same story. Those levees would never break. People can say they understand, but really don't till they have gone through it.

Being a red cross volunteer I knew how to help them too. Their animals were checked out and everything was fine. They took their pets home with them. Some horses were evacuated from New Orleans area and brought up to Maryland on a farm.

Things changed after six weeks. The animals were getting sick. The horses that were on the farm area all died. The owners who brought their pets here from New Orleans. All of them died. Pretty much days after each other. It was like an epidemic with the pets. Nobody could figure it out. Some of the owners even evacuated before the hurricane hit. So why their pets died wasn't making any sense.

The vet would talk to them, but afterwards they would talk to me. I don't know why. I am not a veterinarian. The only reason I can think of is that I am from the same area. That is why I asked how soon they left. They told me they got out as soon as they could, but traffic was so bad that it took forever to get out.

I found out the horses were lifted by helicopter, but they did get their legs wet this could be some foreign stuff on their legs. The owners said their animals didn't get wet. They drove up to Maryland, but anywhere they stopped and walked the animals could have had something. Especially with the way the rain and other particles were being transferred from the area.

Writing

I learned earlier that I do my best writing while listening to music. Whether it is the radio or even my CDs playing. While I was living in Maryland I noticed I would be playing Christmas music all year round and that is when I did my best writing.

Cynthia and I were big sci-fi fans. I always figured she was 100% more of a sci-fi fan than I was. I went to church on Wednesday nights and she would be watching Enterprise when it came on. Then record it for me and watch it again when I came home. So she was watching it twice as much than I was. Another reason I figured she was more of a sci-fi fan than I was.

She loved it so much she wanted me to write a script for it. I told her I would need a contact with the show to submit one. She would slow down the credits and I would see the names of the two who created the show. Sure enough it was one of the creators I knew from working on Star Trek: Deep Space 9. I had my contact. I really didn't want to do a script again. Especially since I was working so much I felt like I was too tired when I got home. I was planning on giving up on my writing. I can see where God was using her to get me to keep it up. It definitely worked.

I would be watching the show, taking notes and she would even give me ideas on what to write about. I wrote them down, but never used them. In December of 2001 she passed away unexpectedly so I stopped writing my project for the show and even quit watching the show. If I even saw ads for the show all I could do is think about Cynthia and the horrible experience of losing her all over again. Just reliving what happened to her, the church, my mom everything.

After doing the script for King of the Hill I got closure and went back to writing again and I did a script for Enterprise. I sent it in and did it based on the book of Revelation from the bible. I could tell God was just using me to accomplish what he wanted. I got it done in two weeks when after all I went through it should have taken months. No way in this world was I even writing it. I had a dream before started working on it. It ended being the opening for the script. Again I can see where God gives us signs even when we are dreaming.

After loosing Cynthia I needed some closure. I wasn't getting it from church since no one was helping me, so I needed to find another outlet. I ended up doing a project for King of the Hill. My mom and I watched that all the time since we were living in Texas when it came on and it is so true to life about the people in Texas.

It was mostly divided into two acts. Act one had to do with the death of Cynthia. Almost everything that was in the script was based on the funeral and what happened. I still can't believe that some of the stuff I wrote in there was true. Any normal person would not have acted like that or said those things.

I ended up having a real bad case of writer's block after working on the script after doing act one. I wanted to finish it, but I never could. It was like my memory was erased or something. I couldn't even write something by pencil it was so aggravating. I kept thinking how I am going to finish this and get some closure out of it. This is another one of those times you need to be patient and let God take care of it. He is in charge and knows what is best for us.

Sure enough that is what happened. Seventeen months later my aunt died from breast cancer. The next month my mom died from breast cancer. So in eighteen months I lost three relatives. All close to me and I was really feeling like something was my fault. No one to turn to. My family wasn't helping. My spiritual family of the church was doing nothing but spreading rumors and giving me more and more heartache to deal with.

There was no where to go to or anyone to get help from. So now I went back to my writing. I tried to finish the King of the Hill script and sure enough I did. The second act was about my mom. It just came out of me like the other one. I know I wasn't writing this at all. Someone else was doing it for me.

I ended up sending it in the production office in care of the guy who was the creator of the show. The next thing I knew is that I got an immediate request to sign a release form for them to read it. The person wanting to read it was Greg Daniels. I signed it off and he read it ASAP.

He replied with a gracious letter. Concerned about all the people I lost and what happened. It was a very moving letter from him about the whole ordeal I had to go through. He told me about how the best scripts come from our own experiences. Then he told me about a personal experience he went through and how it ended up on an episode of the show. We have been friends ever since. Today I always root for him when he is up for Emmy nominations. It is fun rooting for your friends.

When I moved to my apartment I ended up listening to Christmas music all the time. I would listen to a radio station that played Christmas music all the time. After the holidays were over I would play my Christmas CDs. I had a player that would do twenty-five CDs. All through the year I would hear the music. That would make it easier for me write and everything I wrote would just land on the paper showing that God was in control of my writing not me.

Sniper Shooting

In 2002 two guys started what is now known as the beltway sniper shootings. These took place in Washington D.C., Maryland and Virginia. It only lasted for three weeks, but seem like it lasted for months.

For a few weeks there my life here was actually turned upside down. I was working at the vet clinic in Maryland during this. When it first started on October 2, 2002 we were busy like usual at the vet clinic. Especially since people are out traveling. Like they do for the summer and they usually board their animals when they travel. The first murder took place in Maryland. These always get my attention, because I am wondering if it is near my area. Between this day and the next five people were killed or injured. News spread like wildfire.

Everyday they would be killing one person or injuring another. In reality it lasted twenty-one days. Each day felt like a week to us. It felt like twenty-one weeks to us. People were told if you needed to get gas to not stay in your car. Because you would be an easy target.

When they did that they became even more of a target. So the police ended up telling us to not to stand there. To move in a zigzag pattern while your car is getting filled up. This way you are moving and they will likely not shoot at a moving target. The snipers like it when the person is still.

If someone's car backfired, people would duck even inside of a workplace. Fearing that the sniper was shooting at them. When word got out about a white van everyone who owned one left theirs at home. If they were really worried they didn't drive it. Every white van that didn't have markings on it got stopped and searched. Whether you were using it for work or just travel.

Again like in Texas I was doing the weather reporting for my local area in Maryland. Since I reported it to a TV station in Washington D.C. I had connections there. People knew who was when I called in. I was friends with a lot of the reporters and others at the station.

When the shooting started at first it seemed like state thing. People were wondering what this guy had against Maryland people. When he ended up going into Washington D.C. then the Feds got involved. Then they started doing the same thing in Virginia. Parents were taking their kids out of school. They didn't bring them back or allow them to ride buses, etc. Pretty much what anyone would do.

One thing that the police were noticing is that they would always target gas stations that were near a highway. This way they could shoot at someone, drive off in a hurry. Go by highway or interstate and end up on the beltway. The beltway was in a circular highway where you can get off easily to just about anywhere. One reason they used it a lot and another reason it is called the beltway sniper shootings.

While I was at the vet clinic, there was a gas station across the street from us. We were also close to the highway. So according to Feds we were an easy target to get hit by the snipers.

One thing I was noticing was the TV station I reported for was having news anchor who mentioned things on TV. Here is one example: "So far they have only been targeting Maryland and D.C."

"Luckily they aren't hitting Virginia." The first thing I said. "You idiot."

"Now they are going to go to Virginia." Sure enough I was right. They were watching the same TV station I was.

If the anchor mentioned like they haven't targeted a kid yet. Guess what they did? Shot a thirteen year old boy. I was picking up on this really fast. Why other people weren't I still don't know? Toward the end he was reporting one county in Maryland and one in Virginia that they haven't struck yet. That was one I was living in.

Now they were forming a task force of police, FBI, ATF, Secret Service, Virginia DOT and Swat Teams. They decided to form this group right away, but I think they should have started it sooner. After a week they finally came up with a plan. A co- worker, Kelly, and I came into work early and there was a dark car parked where the vets parked. Right away we knew something was up. I spotted two guys in the front seat wearing an outfit that is all black. At this time no one knew what kind of car the snipers drove or what they even looked like. Neither one of us could hear what they were saying in the car.

So Kelly asked me. "What are they saying?" The guy in the passenger seat was talking to the driver. She knew I could lip read and wanted to know he was saying to the driver. "We've been spotted." I told her. "Oh hell!" Kelly said. So she quickly drove us to the front door. You should have seen how fast we ran into the building and locked the door.

Right away I knew something was going to be bad. My first instinct was they were going to rob us. (I guess I spent too much time in Vegas.) Kelly and I went into the building in a hurry. She went to start the equipment and I locked the door. Then I clocked in and there was a knock at the door. I went over to it and the guy who I was lip reading was at the door. I couldn't hear him and since it was dark the lights of the building was reflecting so I couldn't lip read off of him now.

He signaled for me to come toward him and I did. He didn't say anything and pointed to his leg. I looked and saw his gold badge. It was a detective. (Boy was I wrong on the robbery idea.) He wanted me to let him in. So I did.

The other guy showed up at the door and they were both detectives. Kelly came back and was asking. "Betty, why did you let them in?"

"They are detectives." I told her. The first cop asked me how I knew. "Your gold badge is a dead giveaway." I told him. His partner wanted to know how I knew it. He said. "We don't have time."

They ended up introducing themselves and showing us their identifications. "Why are you here?" Kelly asked. "We're with the special task force."

"Have you been keeping up with the sniper shootings?" He asked. "Yes." She answered. "We are here because you're business is a great target area for them." He told us. I haven't even thought of it, but it did make sense.

He ended up explaining to us how they shoot people at gas stations and use the highway to leave that they needed our help. "What do you need?" Kelly asked. "We need to set up a stakeout here." I was thinking like how are you going to do that? The dogs here would give them away.

He said they would need to put a SWAT team member on the roof of our building. One in the grass area lying down and facing the highway. He would have a small tripod and scope. "You won't be able to." I told them. The first cop asked me why. "The dogs will be barking so much everyone will know you are here."

"The guy on the roof won't have a chance." They began whispering to each other and the first guy started pointing to me.

"Show us where you are talking about?" The first guy asked. So I took him around the back way and show him where the trouble areas are going to be. While we were in the back the dogs started barking like crazy. He didn't realize there would be this many dogs back here. While we were walking around he was asking me questions like "How did you know I was a detective?" Plus other questions. I told him my minor in college was criminal justice. Then he relaxed and felt better about having me help him. He also wanted know what secret or hidden areas that I can get into. I showed him those.

Then I showed him the upstairs. They can get to the top and get out in a hurry. If they need to. The two of us came back downstairs. We met up with his partner and Kelly. Sure enough we were told not to walk the dogs out. They would have a guy at the hill near the highway lying in the grass. Plus one SWAT team member on the roof to cover him. It looked like a war over that one building. We all felt like we were trapped or something.

We had to call the owner and let them know what was going on. The SWAT team told us what to do when the owners came in. Plus what to do when people would come in with their pets for check ups. We had a list of what to say to them. The owners of the pets would ask us why a guy was on the roof. We couldn't tell them the truth. The staff could crack jokes so they would laugh and not ask any more questions.

We had a staff meeting going over this. Especially after the SWAT team talked to us. When the staff turned to me they said. "Betty."

"Just be yourself."

"No problem." I replied. Everyone started laughing like that was new for me. Yea right. Sure enough we followed their orders and the day went by fine for the owners. The employees? It was different story.

Everyone at the workplace would have to be verified when coming in. The owner had to give the SWAT team our names so they knew who was coming in. The customers they didn't need to know. If it was someone we didn't know we were to alert them. Everyone says their day goes by fast. For us it seem like it took forever for a day to go by because of what was going on.

With more of the shootings going on in other cities. The SWAT team had to leave, but they left us two cops to watch the building. The SWAT team members had to be where the latest shooting had occurred at. When no shootings were near our area, the cops would leave their car at the clinic.

They would take some of our candy and we told them to take as much as they wanted. Each day they would take more. At night they parked their car at the gas station. This way it would discourage anyone from shooting at us.

Even though all these shootings were going on I really wasn't worried about being shot. It didn't really hit me that anyone here was a target till the SWAT team showed up at work. Then I started noticing something. Again I went to the Elder Tom at church about it. Instead of him helping calming down about it or try to be supportive they just brushed me off again like usual. My mom was in Texas with not much time left to live so the church didn't care.

After a while the people got used to the police car being there and no one really paid much attention. There would be days that I had to walk home from work. I didn't have a ride home. I was worried that I could be an easy target. Since I walk through a school and a city park to get home. For me these were shortcuts or I would have to take the longer way to get home.

Just like living in Vegas I took shortcuts no matter where they were. This way I would cut my time in half. And I could get home sooner. Some people would sell t- shirts about the sniper shootings during this time. They thought it was funny so they would sell them. The t-shirts would have a bull's-eye on them in case the sniper wanted to shoot you. They were selling good. Some people thought they were funny and others didn't think so.

The night before the guys were caught, the news anchor name two counties they haven't shot people in yet. One was in the same county I was living in. I got ready for work while watching the TV. Sure enough the snipers were caught in the same county I live in. Praise the Lord. They were planning on going into the city and shooting people in the same city I live in on that day. I keep thanking God for them getting caught that day.

Mom's Cancer

My mom's cancer came back a few months after Cynthia had died. The cancer doctor said it was the stress of loosing her daughter that brought it back. There were tumors on the body scan that were all over. The technician said all these black spots were cancer. Not to count the kidneys because they were normal. My mom was surprised when she was counting them.

The first one I noticed was the one in her head. She didn't see it and neither the technician. I had to point it out to the two of them when I was the one with the bad vision. My mom then panicked. "There is one in my brain." Now I wished I never said anything. The doctor ended up confirmed it. Then they had to rush an MRI to find out how bad it was. I felt like first I lost my sister and now my mom. They told her she had six months left to live.

As soon as mom got home, she called up her sister and told her. We didn't hear anything from my aunt till a few months later. Her breast cancer came back also, but it was in a later stage than my mom's. They both had chemo and radiation.

Liz came to Maryland and took my mom back with her. Liz and her husband weren't working and had a big house to take care of her. So that made sense. I would have had to quit work or put her in a home. So this was the best for them.

When I knew my mom was dying Pastor Sean wanted me to talk to mom. I said I was doing that because I talked to her everyday on the phone. He said "No." I had a shocked look on my face. "You need to thank her for giving you life." It was quiet on the phone when I was having a surprised look on my face. "Hello." He said. "Are you serious?" I asked. "Yes."

"Haven't you ever heard of that before?"

"No." I replied. "Why don't you try it?" I was still surprised. "You actually want me to thank someone for giving me a life of where I've been abused by my dad and gone through this hell?" He was really quiet on the other end and didn't say anything. I was so mad at him that I ended up hanging up on him. He's crazy I kept thinking to myself.

My mom kept calling me at four o'clock every afternoon my time because back then I didn't have a rotating schedule. Once I did she quit calling. She told me she just wanted to hear my voice even though there wasn't much for me to say. If I did say anything to mom and it got back to Liz I would get yelled at later.

Again no one at the church was helpful. When my mom died Liz made arrangements for the body to be cremated and shipped to me. She kept yelling at me over the phone saying that I better make sure I pick it up and other stuff. When I did get the urn I went ahead and opened it. I saw my mom and burst out crying. Elder Tom was in the car when I did that. No support just yelling at me and telling me to quit crying again. I didn't need that now. I wanted to get out of the car ASAP again, but I couldn't since we were heading to the funeral then.

My mom always wanted to stay in Maryland. She really didn't want to go back to Texas. So I told her that after she died I would have buried in the same place Cynthia was buried. She liked that since she liked the cemetery and that it is the same one that Francis Scott Key is buried in.

Answer to Prayer

You know how people tell you that God answers prayers, but in his own time. Here is another example of how that is done. I kept praying in or about September of one year. I won't mention the year for now, but anyway it was near September. I kept praying to God that I wanted to grow more spiritually. I was praying this for four months or a little more.

In January of that following year, something happened. A girl, Carla, and I were in a car accident. We had just finished shopping and were waiting for the red light to change to green. All of the sudden the car behind us hit Carla's car in a hurry. Then another car sped off in a hurry. (It wasn't later we figured out the car that sped off was the original car that caused the three car accident and did a hit and run.)

The middle car that hit us caused Carla's car to move forward even though we were stopped. Carla didn't get moved very much since she had the back of the driver's side to position her well and the steering wheel to hold her in and to hang on to. Me? I was in the passenger seat getting thrown back and forth.

The guy in the middle car came over and asked if we are okay. At the time we thought he was the guy who drove fast and caused the accident. (We didn't realize till later there was another car involved) Well to make a long story short. After I got hurt the church accused me about lying about my injuries. Started another rampage against me and I was told not to testify in court over what happened. Since no one believed that I got injured, including Tom's wife. They were all going to tell their side of the story in court and leave me out to hang to dry in court. Even the ones who weren't there. It turned out the original driver settled out of court and no one had to testify. You can see that was God's work again.

The middle car driver told them later after court that he had a lot of injuries. He was surprised that nobody else got hurt after the accident. Finally Carla told him that I was injured and she was protected by the steering wheel. Of course I couldn't take it anymore and left the courthouse. While they all told the truth of what happened to each other and were planning on lying under oath in court.

There was the answer to my prayer. Now you need to leave this church and go somewhere else. I was wondering as they put me in the ambulance why God let this happen or caused it. Now it made perfect sense. He was answering my prayers. If I wanted to grow more spiritually like I asked I couldn't stay at this church. But how to leave was another question until God gives you the answer one way or another…

Escaping

Stacy and I were having dinner. We talked a bit and she then asked me. "How is church?" She knew how much I love singing and going to church. Stacy was familiar with the people there that she was right to ask me that. I couldn't say anything. So she repeated the question. I still couldn't say anything and began crying.

"What happened?" She asked. Again I couldn't even talk. I tried to say something and couldn't even get a word out. I cried more and didn't even know why I was. She had a disgusted look on her face. "What did they do to you?" She could tell I was being abused by them when I wasn't even seeing it.

Finally I broke down and told her the most recent thing that happened. About the car accident and how they were treating me from it. She told me quietly. "You have to get out of there now!" Urgently Stacy said. "I don't know how." I replied quietly while still crying. People were watching us since I was crying so much.

"Come on."

"Let's go." She said quietly. We got up and left. Stacy and I went to a quiet place and discussed what my options were going to be. "If you leave them they will track you down." She stated nicely. The look on her face was if I she didn't want to even tell me that. "How can they?" I replied. "They are just a church." I was sure nothing bad would happen. "No they aren't." She told me. "I have helped get a couple of people *out of there* already." I couldn't believe what she was saying. Stacy then told me the names of the two she already helped. "I don't know these people." I told her. "That is because they don't acknowledge them anymore." Stacy told me. I still couldn't believe what I was hearing. "If you ask the people at the church about them you won't get any good stories about them." I was starting to wonder who these church people were. Then she went on to tell me a story about each one that she helped.

"The same thing is going to happen to you if you leave them."

"They will do nothing but spread a bad rep about you."

"That's it?" I asked. She had a strange look on her face. As if how can I explain this to you. "That is the least they will do." She answered. "What else can they do?" I asked. She started to say something and then stopped. "What is it?" I asked getting concerned. "I'm not going to tell you."

"I don't want to worry you."

Horrible thoughts started going through my head. "What have I gotten mixed up with?" I couldn't believe this is a church. A church would never do anything like this. I was trapped in a corner with no place to get out of. A sanctuary is definitely not what I would call this.

I did go up to Elder Tom one day and asked about a girl that Stacy told me in a story. Tom replied he knew of the girl. He wouldn't say anything about her. "She used to be a member, but we had to let her go after what happened."

"What happened?" I asked. Tom never told me. He gave me a look as if don't mention that anymore. I got the same look on my dad's face a lot. Usually when he was mad and drinking too much. I doubt if they would leave it nicely like that with me.

Especially the way they kept hounding me afterwards. I kept going every week until Stacy and I could plan something. If something happened at church I was supposed to take it in and not say anything. I couldn't risk them finding out something. This way no one would suspect anything until one day...

Leaving Church

When I finally figured that I had to leave the church I knew I wasn't going to be able to do it by myself and I was going to need help. Especially since I can't drive. Stacy was like a sister to me and helped a lot. We got together at my place and helped write a letter to them. I wanted it to sound nice so maybe they would let me go and not be mad at me. Like I've been hearing so far. I didn't want the same thing that happened to them happen to me also.

I thanked them for helping me with the death of my sister and mom. Thanked them for helping me move and anything else I could think of. I didn't blame them for anything. Even though I felt like I should have. I didn't mention anything about the worship team like David told me not to. Anything they told me not to mention I didn't. Even though I felt like I was getting abused again.

It took us a few hours to write up the letter. I printed them up and mailed them off. I sent one to the church's affiliation that was higher up then the church. I ended up sending a copy to a former pastor. Who was their retired one from the church. Slowly I was being taken off the email prayer list. No more bulletins came in the mail. I was getting a bunch of nasty (putting it nicely) letters sent back to me. Including one from the retired pastor. He was yelling at me stating "I am getting sick and tired of hearing these complaints!" I don't know why he even said that. I never complained to anyone about anything in the letter. I was polite. So why he said that I couldn't understand.

Like I said I didn't want any of those problems like the other former members had with this church. Nice and being nice was all I could think of. Even to the point where I didn't reply to these people. Again I was trying to break it off from them as nicely as possible...

Being Stalked by Church

Sure enough after I left the test church I figured I was okay. Again I was wrong. They knew I would go to another church. Like I mentioned, Stacy was friends with a few churches and knew a lot of the churches around here. I knew there was a church near me where I worked. I walked over to see what kind of church it was.

They told me a few things about it. I wasn't sure if it was a church I wanted to become a member or not. When I got a hold of the secretary who was there, she asked for my name. I gave it to her and she had the weirdest look on her face. She asked me if I was a member of the church I just left. I was thinking how she knew that. I asked her "Why do you want to know?" She replied "They are trying to find you."

"You should go back to them." She said. "They want to talk to you." I had a shocked look on my face. "They are calling all the churches in your area." I was beginning to wonder who these people were. "They want you to come into their office and sit down with them." I was in so much shock. "What are their names?"

"Maybe I can call them." She gave me the names of Pastor Sean and Clark. Now I really was getting worried. "I have their numbers if you need them." She handed me a piece of paper with their names and phone numbers. I started crying and left. There was no way I was going to get away from these people. I knew it would never happen now. I felt like I was living in Vegas again. My life was spiraling downhill really fast. The difference this time I had no one to go to. Not even spiritual guidance to go to.

They would call my house and leave messages on my answering machine. Telling me I am in trouble and that the only way to solve this problem that I am in now is to come back to church. Plead guilty and suffer whatever punishment they felt was appropriate for me. As far as I knew I didn't do anything wrong. I would spend time crying over it.

There were so many messages on my phone that I was afraid to answer the phone. Every time the phone rang I would let it go to voice mail. Check it afterwards and try to listen to it. At that time you couldn't delete it till you heard the whole message. One of them were from Pastor Sean. "I know you are home."

"Answer it!"

"We need to talk." After a bit of silence. "Okay."

"You want to play that game."

"Fine."

"We can do it too." Than he hung up. I was paranoid to the point where I couldn't tell anyone. Not even my step-brother. I was even being told that my protection was gone. If I went to another church Satan would attack me. I would lose my job. I would have all sorts of problem. Like I said they prey on your weak spots and use it to their advantage. (I found out later this is referred to as spiritual blackmail)

Rethinking what I had done wrong and not knowing who to believe. God? The Pastors? The co-workers I was with didn't even know what was going on. I would have a system by the phone company where I could block their numbers. It helped some so I wouldn't get their calls anymore. Then the letters began coming in the mail. I would receive letters after letters telling me I can't go to another church. Usually you are supposed to do a letter of transfer when you change churches. They made sure that wouldn't happen. If I did a letter of transfer to another church they would call the new church and mock me (putting it nicely). To the point where the new church wouldn't take me in. The new church wouldn't even let me join until the Maryland church got me back. This way they would ensure their members wouldn't leave or no one would believe them.

The other members who Stacy has helped never went to another church. The families are either mad at churches. Or they feel abandoned by churches and God for what has happened.

Considering that when I was there, they were listed as pastors, got paid and were never there anyway I guess it doesn't make much difference. I don't think I'll ever get a letter transfer done no matter where I go to. They have pretty much ruined it for me. Again some people take things for granted and don't know the little things do matter.

Virginia

On December 9, 2003, there was an earthquake near Richmond Virginia. It was a four point five magnitudes on the scale. There is a fault called the Virginia Seismic Zone near Richmond. So there have been several earthquakes along the fault line. From as early as 1774 to 2010.

There was a smaller one that occurred the day before. Like usual no one expected a bigger one to take place the day afterwards. Nor did they expect to have the same effect or be worse the next day when...

Maryland Earthquake

I was home that day. December 9, 2003, I was busy working at my computer. The windows out to the front door were open. I had three different wind chimes outside. Each one would play a different song when the wind came by.

This time it was different. Chip and Ivan ran up to the window really fast. I took it to mean an animal was outside. We would feed the squirrels and other animals so Chip and Ivan can watch something. Chip would let me know when a squirrel came up to the house. Like "look mommy a dale is outside." So I would have to stop and look outside.

My wind chimes were moving, but they weren't playing a song. The movement of the earthquake caused them to sound like a "pounding" noise. All of them were doing it. Some people in Maryland never heard or felt something. All three of us were at the front windows looking out. Chip kept meowing at me as if I should go do something.

I knew something was wrong, but not what. I called up the weatherman that I report to on the TV station. I told him about the wind and other things that were going on. He told me it wasn't anything.

He also said he was busy because of the earthquake in Virginia. "It can be felt up here can't it?" I asked him. He was very persistent about his no answer. After the noise stopped I wanted to check on it some more. I turned on the TV and there was the meteorologist I spoke to on the phone. He was mentioning things about the quake in Virginia. Now he was stating that several weather observers were reporting feeling it as far as twenty miles north of where I live.

All I could think of was that isn't what he told me on the phone. The other people who didn't notice anything were the ones who had their windows closed. At the vet clinic no one noticed anything, but the animals sure did.

They were wondering why the dogs were barking for twenty minutes. Plus the cats were wanting out of the cages. I told them on the phone about the earthquake. I could hear a receptionist telling people. "Hey Betty said there was an earthquake."

"Oh that explains it." Another receptionist stated.

Where I live no one got hurt. Nor did anything in the houses get broken. If I had my windows closed I doubt if I would have even noticed anything. The quake was later reported as far north as Pennsylvania. As far west into West Virginia and all the way east into the District of Columbia.

The Church of Refuge

After I left the test church I wanted to get into a church again. But I didn't know where to go to. Like I said earlier they were already tracking me. By walking distance of home and work. Not driving since they knew I couldn't drive. Stacy knew of a good one to go to. She told me I would have to change religions. I've done that before so that wasn't a problem for me.

It was in another city so maybe that helped. When I decided to join this one they asked me if I had a letter of transfer to do. I was surprised but started thinking I can't do that because of what the previous church said. I ended up saying "No." thinking that now I can't join since I don't have a letter of transfer to do. Hoping and praying that I could join without the test church finding out.

They told me not to worry. Pastor Adam could tell I was concerned about that. He reassured me that I could join by affirming my faith. So I wouldn't need to do a letter of transfer. "Thank God" I kept saying. This way the test wouldn't know where I was. But God was telling me something different.

I kept having a weird dream. I would dream every night where I was in a checkout line at Wal-Mart. Pastor Adam was in front of me. Not knowing I was behind him. Pastor Sean was behind me and I couldn't see him. Pastor Sean would say to me "Betty."

"Where have you been?" I would have a paranoid look on my face. Hoping it wasn't him. "We have been looking for you." Pastor Sean would tell me.

Pastor Adam would see me standing there and ask. "Who is your friend Betty." I couldn't say who this guy was behind me. Nor did I want either one of them finding out that each one was my pastor. I didn't know what to say or who to answer. Pastor Adam would introduce himself and the name of the church he would work at. Pastor Sean would know the name of the new church I went to. I would panic, Pastor Sean would give me the weirdest look. After this is when I would wake up.

I kept having that same dream every night till finally I had to tell Pastor Adam why I left the test church. I told him "If you don't want me to join or take away my membership and kick me out I wouldn't blame you and I could find another church to go join I guess." There was some silence from him. I couldn't understand the look he had on his face. I figured this new church would after all the stuff I went through. Plus the way the test church treated me. That all churches were like the test church. I was surprised when Pastor Adam told me "I can't find any fault in you." I was so surprised and shocked. "You can stay if you want." He told me. Again I thought I was hearing things. I said "Yes." Really fast and excitingly. "Finally someone believes me." I thought to myself. I finally felt spiritually accepted for once in years.

Once I finally had this conversation with Pastor Adams the dreams stopped. I can see God was telling me to talk to someone about it. Believe me he gives you hints. You just need to be able to figure out when he is telling you something.

The refuge church was smaller than the test church. They only had fifty congregation members per service. They had services on Saturday nights; Sunday morning they had two, and a Sunday school between the two. They had a building, offices, etc. Unlike the test church.

The test church barely had an office. The secretary was in the hallway. No office for her, They had to rent out a place for their service. Pastor Sean and Clark were getting paid whether they were there or not. They also got paid when they would preach at another church. Pastor Sean had a cheap car. It makes me wonder where they pocketed all this money they were getting. Not much was going into their "building fund" but they would say they weren't getting much in their budget they got paid if they were there or not. I hardly ever saw them the whole time I went to church there.

We never did have a church directory. Never knew where the staff lived. They could have been putting the money into their houses and no one would know. If it wasn't for their homes where was it going?

Patch Adams

If you have already seen Patch Adams then this will seem familiar to you. I saw the movie, but didn't know it was based on a true story. After I moved to Maryland then I knew it was true.

Dr. Patch Adams runs a clinic in West Virginia. The free clinic is named Gesundheit Institute. It is a German word which means "Good Health". Since it is a free clinic he goes around places to raise money for it. Mostly to colleges and other places to do stand up comedy. He then gets donations to entertain people.

One of the colleges near where I lived is where he would come by and do his stand up comedy. Believe me he is good. He could have a career as a stand up comedian. Or even go into acting like a lot of stand up comedians do. But you can see where God has had other plans for him and he has defiantly gone down the path that our Lord wants him to.

If he finds people at the colleges majoring in medicine he tells them about his clinic and hopefully gets people to help him in the clinic. He is later mentioned in the local paper saying he was here yesterday and there is a photo of him. He did that every year I was living in Maryland. He is just as funny and smart as the character Robin Williams played in the movie. God bless him and his work. You can tell he is doing work for the Lord.

Stacy

The girl who helped me get out of the test church and I ended up started a bible study group for women. It worked out good. We met at her house so the people in my previous church wouldn't be looking for me. We had it on Wednesday nights. There were at least five to ten women who came we worked on two different types of books and had fun doing it.

She would also take to a church in West Virginia. As soon at you went pass into the state line things and people were different. It was even smaller than the church I went to in Texas. It was traveling back in time going to West Virginia. They would meet for service on Wednesday nights. Stacy already knew the pastor and his family so I got to meet them.

I got invited to go to Georgia and see my niece graduate from high school. So Stacy and I came down to Georgia by bus. We stayed at Mary's house and watch her daughter graduate.

We would take trips to Ocean City and Rhode Island. We even went to Amish area in Pennsylvania and bought some stuff at a store. Boy did we get stared at being in there. You would have thought we were from another planet. The mother and daughter were speaking so softly I couldn't hear what they were saying.

She seemed to be a bit paranoid. If we went into a restaurant and there would be a couple speaking Spanish. Stacy would want me to hear what they were saying. She was already overweight and weighed over three hundred pounds. So she assumed they were talking about her. So I had to ease drop on the Spanish couple's conversation. I didn't want to, but Stacy would keep it up until I did. I listened in and they were talking about the weather.

I told her they were talking about the weather. "No they aren't."

"They are talking about me." Stacy told me. "Do you want to ask them?" I told her. "I don't speak Spanish." She told me angrily. "I know." I told her. "I bet you they speak English too." Stacy told me. "Let's just drop it." I told her. She started saying hard. "Good."

"I don't like ease dropping anyway." I told her.

One Wednesday night we were having a women's bible study. The five of us were working on a book by Joyce Meyer. In the workbook there were some questions about someone who was robbing your joy. You had to put down the name of the person as the answer for the question. I noticed that every time I was answering the question, Stacy's name kept popping up and I was writing it down. That was another sign from God that she was doing something to me and I wasn't picking up on it. When I was writing her name down it finally clicked.

Refuge Worship Team

This one was different. Now I knew I sang soprano and these people didn't mind. Like the other one I had to try out first. That went well and I was in. I was the only soprano in the group but apparently it worked out. We had microphones with cords and we were told by Pastor Adam to take them off the stands and bring them as close to our face so people could hear us. I did what they said.

Apparently something was different with me. They didn't know I could project my voice. As soon as I did Pastor Adam wanted us to stop. I had to bring mine down halfway since I was coming in too loud for the speakers.

The pages were labeled with one letter per word. For example the note could be a "D" and that would be the only letter above the word we were singing. I didn't know anything about the notes so I just ignored it. One time Pastor Adam was telling us we were singing a "D". Apparently I was the only one not singing it. I didn't have any idea what he was even talking about. He ended up just telling me to bring the note down a little.

There were six of us on the team. Three guys playing electric guitars, one lady is playing a piano and the rest of us just singing. A few times the people playing the instruments were gone so the rest of us had to sing a cappella. People told us quite a bit we sounded good. A lot of times I could never tell. We practiced an hour before the service.

They had a trap set there that was hardly being used. One time there was a junior high school kid playing it. He ended up drowning everyone out. Since I had some time to kill before the service, one guy was practicing a song with his guitar. I would keep up with him while playing the trap set. He told me I was doing a good job. I told him I couldn't do it since I had no music talent whatsoever. He told me to keep it up on playing the trap set and start doing it when I was off. This was the first time I played any instrument since my mom was trying to teach me to play the piano.

Sure enough I ended up doing the trap set when I was off from the vet clinic. Later on I couldn't unless they let me off on Sundays. They were scheduling me from Saturdays to Wednesdays so I couldn't go to church at all.

Mission Trips

This is the first time I had ever heard of someone from the church going on a mission trip. At this church it was only for the kids and a few adults that were allowed to go somewhere and preach the gospel to people.

Once I heard that a church even allowed their members to do that. I kept wishing they had one for adults. I could see myself speaking to others in different languages. It would make so much sense why God wanted me to learn all these different languages such as: German, Spanish, Danish, Dutch and even sign language.

But like I mentioned there wasn't one for me to go to or an opportunity to come up. So I never did think of it again and kept busy with work.

2005

I was doing some assistant editing and head writing for an online magazine. Nothing unusual for that. I ended up traveling to Indianapolis. I was working at the vet clinic so I really didn't think much of this.

But people were coming up to me asking me about work with showbiz. I couldn't understand it. I used my pen name when I talk about work. Plus I used my pen name how would someone know about me with my real name.

I ran into some former co-workers with the production company. We started out having a blast and reliving the fun stuff about work. I had to take notes about stuff for the article. At first I would introduce myself under my pen name. So the actors and other people didn't recognize me. As soon as someone referred to me as my real name. It was like walking into another room

Now instead of being someone who was doing an article, I was recognized as a writer for a series. I liked it better when people didn't know. Another reason I like writing. Your name is on TV, but no one recognizes you. No photo required. I could live next door to you and you wouldn't know it.

Some of these people have big mouths. I have a couple of ideas who it was, but I won't say anything. In one way it was fun spending time talking about work again. But then the fans would be listening in on our conversations. It is hard to explain when you can be on both sides of the fence. If I don't know these people I could be asking why they don't tell us more. Being in the business I wonder why these people want to listen in.

Sometime later I ended up learning I have to give up the fan part. It doesn't work anymore. It was giving me emotional problems and I was loosing so much trust in people I thought I could trust. Now I know I can only stay on one side of showbiz ness. I can't go back to being a fan of certain shows. I have to stay on the celebrity side of the business. I have to learn to trust people again. Sometimes fans can get too dangerous.

I was supposed to be at a dinner I paid for. This was before they figured out who I was. I paid for the dinner and never showed up. I was getting too sick to even manage to eat. I even ended up staying in my hotel room for over eighteen hours. I slept so much that I never felt like this before. I even had a hard time explaining it to my doctor when I got home. After I got home it hit me worse than it ever did...

Almost Dying

The very first symptom I could tell I was having been when I became a vegetarian. I didn't see it as a problem, but I was having a few symptoms. I told the doctor about it and he said there isn't anything wrong with it and gave me some meds for the other symptoms

I was having. The meds worked, but I was still a vegetarian. Until something else happened.

I was getting sick in October of 2005 and didn't even realize it. At least a few of my friends picked up on it. This is why they are referred to as my step-family. My normal family didn't have much to do with me as you have noticed by now. They are more than friends to the point they act more like family. So I call them my step family.

I was having symptoms to the point to where I wasn't eating. I went from having a vegetarian type of diet to a vegan. I wasn't even drinking soy milk which is okay for vegans. I was pretty much just on a bread diet and eating fruit by the time they saw these symptoms. Some were like flu like symptoms. I would just not eat, have diarrhea and some other type of symptoms. I ended up loosing five pounds everyday. By the time I went to the doctor I had lost twenty-five pounds in five days. A friend of mine made a bet with me. I told him how excited I was that I lost twenty pounds in four days. He said to me. "I'll make a bet with you."

"Sure." I answered. "If you loose five more pounds you have to go to the doctor." I said "Sure." Thinking what are the chances of that happening. I told him this was a freak thing and that it was great I was loosing this weight and nothing was wrong. He was right and I was wrong.

I lost five more pounds and ended up going to the doctor. When the doctor came in and asked me what was wrong I said "I lost a bet." He had a shocked look on his face and asked me what happened. I told him and he agreed with my friend. He said it is a good thing I lost the bet. He asked me if I was trying to loose weight I said "No." Then he said it was his job to find out why.

Sure enough I ended up loosing forty-five pounds in nine days. The doctor wanted to get me in to see specialists. He would even put me down as an emergency case. But since I was classified as a new patient some of these doctors wouldn't see me until a month later.

I was living in my apartment by myself. I didn't have an appetite so I didn't eat anything. I was told back in Texas by doctors if you aren't hungry don't eat anything. So I followed that rule. During this time it was the wrong thing to do.

It got so bad that I was getting weaker. I ended up in the emergency room three times for dehydration. The last time was twenty-four hours before I couldn't go to work. I was literally bed ridden. Too dizzy to get out of bed and too weak. The only time I got out bed was to go to the bathroom and take my meds. Why no one had me put in the hospital I still don't know.

On the head of part of the bed frame, are some metal bars. They go in a circular pattern and cross over. I was so weak that I would use them to literally pull myself out of bed. I was getting weaker and weaker. My cats were just trying to eat so they try to get me out of bed. Chip was even resorting to biting me to get me come out of bed and feed them. I am sure that was God's way of telling me to get out of bed.

I did get my energy back after a week. I didn't eat much, but I made it a priority to go to work. I was told my doctor's office that if I would eat something I would get rid of the dizziness and my strength would come back. So I did eat a little. To this day I make sure I eat a little instead of nothing.

Finally it was in January of 2006 that I was sent to a GI doctor. He put me on some meds that actually got my appetite back once a day. Around lunch time I would be hungry. It worked for a while until August of 2006. It started up again. It was over a weekend. I was having the same symptoms again. I lost fifteen pounds in three days. I told the nurse on call what I was having. I told her I had an appointment to see a different GI doctor for a second opinion on September eighteenth of this year. She told me I wouldn't even make it till then. I had about twenty days left to live. I had to call the new doctor and tell him it was an emergency. This doctor told me to get in this week. I did that I got see on that Thursday. All the tests that took months to do with the other specialists got done in forty-eight hours this time.

They really worked to get it done ASAP. I don't know how that happened. So in the end I ended up loosing ninety-one pounds in a short time. I can still feel the effects from all of this. I never did get my appetite back and there are some friends of mine who actually "nag" me to eat something. Otherwise I would go a whole day or even longer without eating something.

I don't even think about it. I will remember at times to eat something because my meds will require me to eat something, but if I do it is something small like a bag of chips or a small snack bar. Peter will even ask me if I am with a friend. If so I have to hand the phone to him and Peter will ask him "What is Betty eating?" My friend will tell Peter what he sees on my plate. Then Peter will have to remind me to eat everything. If I don't he nags me later. Peter even has both of our lines memorized on the phone. "Did you buy groceries?"

"No!" I start laughing when he does that. "Why not?"

"I'm not hungry."

Sometimes this gets really embarrassing, but he is just trying to make sure I am not getting sick to where I end up loosing all that weight in a hurry like I did before. I had auras during this, but I can see God's hand working in this since I was so close to dying I should have had repetitive grand mals from all of this. He kept that from happening.

I already made peace with God about dying and going to heaven. Every time I have another Christmas or birthday all I think of is this my first (or whatever number it is) Christmas or birthday that I wasn't supposed to be here and I should have died ages ago.

People shouldn't be thinking this when these important events come up, but I still wonder why he is keeping me around. Peter thinks it is so I can do something. Then when it happens he comes up with another idea, because I have already done it. I probably won't find out till later.

Stalking

This really begins with Stacy after she helped me escaped from the test church. Like I said earlier if she didn't get me out of there I would have still been there. I would have not realized that it was that bad.

In that sense I'm still grateful for her helping me. I would have never found refuge or know what a sanctuary really is.

After that we became good friends. If strangers saw us having dinner at a restaurant they would assume we were sisters. She was quick to answer "No."

"We're just friends." The employee would have a surprised look on her face. The employee was expecting us to say yes to the question. That is how good our friendship was. Stacy would always offer to take me to stores and other places on my day off from work. I would always pack enough meds to last me for the rest of the day since I didn't know how long we would be out. I was on my seizure meds and meds for my raynauds at the time.

One day we went shopping and it was getting toward dinner time. We usually went out for dinner. Stacy called her mom on the phone and asked her to take care of the dogs because she was going home. Stacy was living with her mom so I couldn't see what she meant. I just guessed she was referring to being home after dinner. I asked her. "Where are we going?"

"We'll be home soon." She replied so I didn't think anything about it. The next thing I knew it we were driving in a different direction. "Where are we going?" I asked again. "Home." She replied.

Finally we were on a highway. I never had seen this before. I was watching the traffic. She wouldn't say where we were going. I was even thinking about jumping out of the car. When I looked at the speedometer she would speed up and blocked my view so I couldn't read it. When I was looking around to see where I could jump out she would drive the car to where I couldn't jump out. Get close to a car or do something else. I was literally trapped in the car and couldn't get out. I didn't know where we were or where we were going.

I finally started asking more questions. Stacy would then turn up the music or ignore me. I felt like I was literally being kidnapped. When I tell people this, they say "You weren't kidnapped."

"Nobody wanted money for you."

"So you weren't kidnapped." Maybe not, but I sure felt like it. I couldn't tell people where I was. I didn't know where we were going since I don't drive. The place didn't look familiar. Even the street that we ended up on didn't have a street sign.

It was like I was in a town with no one around. People were gone. The reception on my cell phone was horrible. If I called the police what was I supposed to tell them? Where I was? I couldn't tell them the name of the street. I didn't even know what town I was in. For some reason people didn't believe me.

I had enough of my seizure meds to last me through that night. But not past that. Since I couldn't get a hold of anyone, I kept trying to tell Stacy I need to go home. It was getting cold and I wasn't home to put the heat on for my two cats Chip and Ivan. She would let me call Peter and let him know that cats needed help. According to her rules, I wasn't allowed to tell him or anyone else where I was. I didn't know where I was nor did I even know what to tell him.

Again I felt like I was being kidnapped or held hostage. I called Peter and asked him to help me out. He agreed and asked me where I was. I told him I was with a friend. Stacy was watching me and listening to what I was saying. He asked me, "What is wrong?" I quickly answered. "Nothing." He said "Okay." Surprisingly, but didn't think anything of it. I wanted so much to tell him what was going on, but still where was I supposed to tell him I was?

Stacy kept me there for the weekend. Each day I would beg her to take me home. I even told her I was out of my seizure meds and that I would have one if I didn't get them. She didn't care. She just wanted me to stay there. Didn't care if anything happened to me. If Stacy told me what she was planning I probably would have gone and taken enough meds, but without telling me. She knew there was a chance I would say no, but didn't want to take the chance. It was too important to her. Whatever her plans were.

Plus I still had to be back at work Monday. Apparently that didn't bother her either. As long as I was there with her she didn't care. I figured out later Stacy was a controlling type of person. This explains why she got me out of the test church. She wanted to control me rather than have the church do it.

Finally Sunday she gave in and took me home. I was crying so much that she gave in. I still don't think it was the meds that made her take me home. She could see how much it was bothering me. I had to wear the same clothes for three days, not being able to take a bath or anything for three days. You can tell God was in control of that one. I should have had seizures the whole weekend. Especially after twenty-four hours. Once I got home I wasn't going to go through that again. So I did whatever I could to get rid of her. I blocked her number on the phone like I did with the others from the test church.

I ended up getting a new number since I knew she would be trying to call again. I had to make it an unlisted number so Stacy wouldn't find it. She knew I would tell the members at the refuge church about it. Plus my sister Mary. So she would call the refuge church members. Pretending that my sister in Georgia was trying to find me. That my sister needed my phone number. Stacy couldn't even remember Mary's name. Luckily they didn't tell her. Another sign that God is in control. Praise the Lord. The church members called me after wards. I found out then I was doing the restraining order on Stacy. That it is against the law for her to try to use another person to find or get information on you.

There was a girl who already had a restraining on Stacy. So now I would have been the second one. Stacy was determined to keep me from getting one done on her. Stacy wasn't going to let that happen. Because this would give her a record.

I had a copy of the restraining order put at the vet clinic. Where I worked at a photo of her so they would see her as soon as she came in. They would stop her as soon as they saw her. The apartment landlord had the same thing. So what does Stacy do? Comes to my place at night, with her kid and has him watch for me. This was her idea of thinking that I would come home the same way and she could catch me.

Stacy was right in one way. I did come home the same way every day. I would recognize her van, car or whatever vehicle she was using. She didn't know about my past. Like how I was able to get around cops and escape unseen. I used the same technique on her. Showing how God takes a bad situation and uses it for good later. I ended up getting into my apartment without her seeing me.

She later started thinking I was in the apartment. She might have called work. Found out that I had left so sure enough I was home. Stacy knew I couldn't have been anywhere else. I had the blinds down so she couldn't look in. Her kid came by first knocking. When I didn't answer he gave up. Her? She was more persistent. Stacy knocked and kept calling for me outside the door. She didn't have my phone number so Stacy would yell for me through the door.

She did that for several hours. I could hear Stacy asking her kid. "Are you sure Betty is home?"

"I don't know." Stacy's kid answered. I wished now I called the cops. I was trying to get Stacy to leave. Plus there was no way I wanted her know I was there. Then she would give up and not come back. After another hour Stacy finally left.

She ended up coming to the apartment complex again. Parked across from my place. This time her car was in front of my apartment. She was determined to find me when I got home. There was no way Stacy was going to miss me. Of course I saw her car before she saw me. I already knew she was there. I fooled her again. I got into my apartment without her knowing it. From using my old tricks of living in Vegas. God is good. Like I said earlier Stacy is a control freak and doesn't want people not doing what she wants. Stacy even has so much control over her kid. He has a compulsive cleaning disorder. His bedroom is even cleaner than hotels. That is how bad it is and how much he is suffering from her abuse. This is why she was so eager to get me out of test church. It was either the church having control over me or her.

Since she lived outside the city and in a smaller town the sheriff would be the ones to deliver the restraining order. They only day they did that was on Mondays. So she would stay out of the county on Mondays. Come back home on Tuesdays. This way she avoided the sheriff. Stacy would stay at the same home where she kidnapped me. I even told the sheriff to go wait till Tuesdays. This way they could serve her the papers. They said they only did it on Mondays. Of course they never did serve her the papers. Because of this I would go to court on Mondays. Stacy was never served so I have to come back to court each Monday morning. Find out the same thing every week. After a couple of Mondays I gave up. She won and there was nothing I could do. It was either do this every week and loose time from work. Or give up on this and continue to have a job.

I can see now where God was having me do these things in Vegas to use them now to save my life from people like Stacy and the test church. When I was doing these things it sure didn't make sense, but it does now.

As soon as she was able to beat the restraining order and there was nothing else I could do. I can see God's hand working in here again. Some things happened within a month's time. It was moving so fast I didn't even have a chance to think about it. I was loosing my apartment and some other things. I had to be moved out within a month's time.

Where was I going to go? Mary offered me to come and live with her until I could get my own place. The first thing I thought of was now I really was going to be home. I already knew where I was going to be going to church. Since I decided that months ago. I thought I would be with my physical family. Everything would work out just perfectly. Like I told Mary on the phone. "I'm coming home."

*GEORGIA*

Okay this is getting bizarre. First Wayne Newton, George W. Bush now I have to contend with Willie Nelson coming down to this state after I moved here. What is it with everyone? This is just too weird even for me. If I move to another state someone else would probably be coming there too. It's a good thing I'm not one worry about it and laugh at it.

Weather Reporting

Since a lot of TV stations get their weather information from local schools and other places I had to start going through another area to do my weather reporting. This one is through the internet. The only problem is that when we have a storm, the power goes out, then I can't report it.

The information is gathered and sent off to the COCORAHS. This stands for Community Collaborative Rain, Hail and Snow Network. They are located in Colorado. I keep giving my info once a day. I try calling into a local TV to report things more urgent like snow totals or severe weather. When the power is out I can't get to my computer to update them.

Since I haven't been here long. We had a bad flooding. It would say on the form how the rain is severe. For example if this is normal or something you only see in a blue moon. I couldn't say either way since I have just moved.

On January 7, 2009 it turned out to be different. Streets were flooded to the point where huge rocks that were stable. Were moved into the streets. Roads that should have been closed weren't because it happened too fast.

It turned out it was something that hasn't happed in ages. Like I said I was new here so I didn't even know. I guess some things you learn the hard way.

Chip & Ivan

When I moved from Maryland to Georgia I brought my two cats with me. Chip and Ivan. To me they are two of my kids and I wasn't going to leave them. Especially when they have helped me and God has used them so much.

I moved into my sister's house and brought them with me. I ended up having them inside for several reasons. Since they were declawed they were more vulnerable to attacks from other animals. They couldn't climb trees.

Finally, I wasn't allowed to have them inside because of the allergies. So I didn't have a choice. One by one they started disappearing. There we dogs that are loose in the area and end up finding the cats. I would see one at the back door wanting in and I couldn't let them in.

I tried tracking them down from the microchip that was planted in them. No one called and weeks turned into months. I finally gave up and assumed they were dead. There was no way they could have survived from the dogs and no weapon for them. I saw chip one night and the next night was Ivan. Then they were gone.

Sanctuary Church

The first time I came to this church was when my niece was graduating from high school. Mary wanted me to see the church she goes to. Plus visit it to see a different church. At first it seemed like a nice church. I couldn't get over the size of the church. The monitors were good for a person like me who has bad vision. What surprised me was when the choir director showed up on the stage. He was telling the congregation to stand up for the hymn. I didn't have a problem with that. But I never seen one conduct the congregation during a song. They usually conduct the choir. Right away I was saying to myself. "This is definitely not a normal church."

After I got back home, for some reason I kept thinking about this church. I would say to myself. "This is a good church to go to." Then later I would say again "No they are too crazy." I kept debating about it. I couldn't understand why when I was living in Maryland at the time. Finally after a month I decided. "Well if I had to move to this place that is definitely the church I would be going to." Someone had the same idea in mind.

Thirteen months later I became a member of this church. Because of the way the test church in Maryland was. I can never do a letter of transfer to any church I join anymore. This is one place where you feel like family. I can go into a place and get a hug. A lot of places even churches would just say hello. Maybe smile at you. And that would be the end of it. But never even offer a hug. Even if I begged for one the other churches would act like I was crazy. They would give me looks like "Have you been drinking?"

"What is wrong with you?" or just walk away.

When someone is having what is known as a "bad" day, believe me they need something or someone. Especially in a spiritual sense. Not people who give out bad looks or walks away. I know any counselor can say the same thing. But being able to do it without being told to. Even just offering is a big step. There are people today who would rather just walk away. And think it is an embarrassment. I even know some people who think giving out a hug is a chore. Especially when the person needing it or is begging for one.

I know I am being treated better here spiritually than any other church I have gone to. But after what I have been through it is harder to get it out or over it. I feel different somehow. I know I'm not being persecuted for religious beliefs. After all that has happened. It is hard to shake it off and is taking longer than expected.

People here want me to join an activity or get involved in something. I have dropped out of activities that I am still feeling insecure about. People tell me I did a great job on something. I think to myself "Who are you?" and "Are you sure you have the right person?"

In some ways I still feel like I am being persecuted for my religious beliefs. Because they aren't yelling at me. Not calling me names or doing something mean to me. That is all I had to deal with at church. So why are they being nice to me?

Ask someone what a sanctuary is they will tell you what part of the church it is located. They will even point to it. Most churches have it near or where the alter is located. For me? A sanctuary is a place where prisoners or fugitives are entitled to immunity from arrest, execution and can get it. Even today you can have it. Just a lot of people don't know it exists today just from abuse. It is there you just have to find it. Fortunately. I have found it here.

Awanas

Now that I go to the Sanctuary Church they have a program that they have for kids called Awanas. Approved Workmen Are Not Ashamed is what the letters stand for. It is used to teach the word of God to kids. When I joined up with them. They were starting a new group for the two year olds called puggles. I figured if I was going to help out that would probably the only group I could help out. Since the other kids already know their bible verses. I have hardly looked at a bible. The next group would be learning bible verses. I don't know bible verses like these kids do. I felt like a beginner with these things. They would recite things that I never heard of. Where in the puggles group I can help them from being ashamed like I've been all my life. Fortunately these kids have loving families.

When I was living in Virginia, my sister went to a non-denominational church. Since it was on a Naval Base. Cynthia would teach a Sunday school class that took place the same time as the church service. I didn't really learn anything there. I would just watch the kids. Kind of like babysitting. Sort of like making sure the kids didn't eat the paste for example. But here it is so different.

I also didn't know how I would be able to do this. Subconsciously I knew I was from an abusive home. the majority of the time something like this gets passed down from generation to generation. So if I was abused it would more likely be that I would abuse my own kids. Again it shows where God is in control. I never did nor have I ever hurt anyone being in this group. We give them a time out and that is as far as I've gone. Maybe God is showing me that I can have fun with kids and not have to worry about that happening. I was even being tested for my first year of this, but having to teach some kids of the parents who work there. Now there is a challenge.

Sure enough that is what has been happening. I've been enjoying being around the kids. I've noticed them smiling and wanting my company as much as I want theirs. They are not afraid of adults like I've been all my life. They have such a trusting spirit where mine never really developed. Sometimes I feel like my childhood was taken away from and now I'm just getting it back. I love teaching these kids about all things that have to do with God.

These kids get to learn about God and Jesus and don't have families who abuse them. When I tell Peter about what we taught them. I have to keep explaining to him that I'm working with the two year old group. He then says "Working with someone with your own age group."

"Of course." I reply. "Good you can relate to them." I have to agree with him. I've been involved in this group since they started and I don't think I can be in another group. I help them out in so many ways we are now teaching them sign language to the two year olds.

I've noticed that the kids here really like me and I've stopped feeling strange being around kids and enjoy it now. I don't worry about hurting them since that is another fear that has left me too along with the others. I look forward to coming in and helping out and I feel they enjoy being around me too.

Fighting

One thing I've noticed is after going through all these "trials" or "troubles" or whatever you want to call them. Is that they make you stronger, physically, emotionally and spiritually.

It shouldn't get to a point to where you are fighting within a family, church or business. But sometimes it can't be avoided. You try your best to just stay out of the way and just watch from the sidelines. Sure enough something happens. It can't be avoided and then what happens? You are in the arena, getting beaten up in one of these areas and you don't even know what happened. Or how you got there for that matter.

I've have gone through things where it is too traumatic that I forget about something, almost like PTSD. Then God fixes it so that I remember it. When it is time for me to be strong enough. In one of these areas or all three and I can handle it.

The one time you really do need a family you may not have a physical one to go to. What do you do? You find yourself another one. Some people are so close, that you will even mistake them for a family. When they tell you they are just friends. Then there are others that you can tell they aren't related. But are so strong that you can see a type of bondage between them. That is stronger than anything you can think of or comprehend. Like for example a...

## Spiritual Family

This is one place where I really feel like I have a family. People are so supportive. If I call someone and tell them I am going to the doctor, for example. They offer to pick me up. I am in so much shock you can see it in my face. I tell them I don't need one since I am taking the bus. But they still offer to give me a ride or say call me if you need a ride.

The bus driver even offers to buy me a soda. When we just talk on the bus. My real family would never do that or be this nice to me. People you would normally think of as strangers are really your friends. People you think of as your friends are really your family it is so different.

Your biological family are more the strangers in your life. In Mark 3:24-25 It says: 24 A nation whose people fight each other won't last very long. 25And a family that fights won't last long either.

Explaining that a true family whether spiritual or biological shouldn't be divided. Like one in Maryland and Nevada was for me. My spiritual family in Georgia is no way divided. Even more united and stronger than any family I have ever seen in my whole life. Praise the Lord. I thank God to bless each and every one of them. I doubt they even know how much of a blessing they are to me.

## Choir

I joined the church right away, but I wasn't allowed to join the choir until the first practice they had. They have practices on Wednesday nights. This Wednesday it was right after the fourth of July weekend so there wasn't any practice so I had to wait. For me it felt like an eternity. I am the type of person who can't sit back and do nothing. This is why when I got kicked off the Worship team in the Maryland test church. It was a big blow to me physically, emotionally and spiritually. Again I felt like I was being punished for not doing anything wrong. So as soon they had practice I jumped into the choir box and began practice. It felt good being in the choir again after a two week off from moving from Maryland to Georgia.

When I came to practice the Choir director, Lenny, asked me what I sing. I told him soprano. Not even knowing there was a difference with this section. So I was automatically put in with the second soprano area. I didn't have a problem with that and sang. Shortly after the first practice one of the girls next to me was wondering what I was doing. Of course I didn't know what they were doing or what was going on. I got assigned my robe, etc., and then I found out why they were giving me looks.

At the second practice they told me. "Why are you singing down here?" I couldn't figure out what the problem was. "I sing soprano." I told them. "I know. So do I, but you need to be in the upper part." Someone else stated. I had a confused look on my face. "Why? Am I singing that badly?" I asked one of them. "No you sing first soprano."

"We are second soprano." Man now I was really confused. "There's a difference?" I asked her.

"Yes."

"You are hitting the higher notes."

"Go ask the choir director." Still confused I went down there in between songs. That we were singing and told Lenny "I need to be moved."

"Why?"

"Is something wrong?" He asked. I bet he was worried I was already having problems when I just got there. "No. I sing first soprano." He had the weirdest look on his face.

"Okay sing it." Now I was convinced something was wrong. So I sang a song to him just a short part. Sang the higher notes like the girl told me to do. Plus I projected my voice like I've been doing it and not even knowing it. Sure enough he had the biggest smile on his face and agreed. He pointed to the back area. "You're in the back." Okay now I'm really in trouble I thought. I moved to the back row. With the other first sopranos who also project their voices too. At least now I know where my classification is even though it took years to find out.

Sure enough as soon as I was in this choir I noticed a big difference. People were actually helping me. I could ask questions and they answered them. If I didn't know anything about music that the director was talking about a person near me would show me what the signature on a page looked like. Even mark it for me so I can next time remember what it is. Now I know what to do if I saw it again. One would ask me what notes I sang. I didn't know what to say or even what she was talking about. I showed her in the book and said I sing from here to here. Again I didn't know anything about music. I couldn't even say what octave they were or what even the notes were.

I've been in other choirs and worship teams. We would have prayer at practices but not before a performance. This is the only one I've been to where we would have a prayer before a concert/special we do. It is so uplifting to give it all to God before we leave the room. And then head out to the sanctuary. Why the others don't do it when they should. God is really in control and it shows. I believe others should follow this example.

I still feel insecure at times about my singing here. Especially compared to the other places. I don't know if it is because I'm in a choir. Or because I'm not on a worship team. The other one I was in. There were eight people if you include the musicians. Four if you don't. There were six in the other worship team. Now I'm in a choir that has at least seventy people. A big difference compared to the others. I've never been in one that was over fifteen people.

It would seem easier if you think about it. Since if I mess up who would even notice? But it doesn't feel like it. It feels more like people will notice it more. If they were spiritually abusing me in the choir, I would feel different. Like it was something I was used to. Since they are not spiritually abusing me, I feel different. Like an insecure person.

This shows how much abuse I've had in the different churches. I've mentioned earlier that getting a compliment is something I'm not used to. Being around a non- abusive person is something new to me. I've been here at this church for a few years now. But someone actually being nice to me is not normal. It's like I want to hide in a shell or something similar. I hide it inside of me so well. That people in the church don't even notice it. Until it burst out of me to the point where I can't do anything about it and I end up crying. Again I put my hand up to my face and hide it. They don't notice I am trying to stop it and think I am trying to stop a sneeze.

Which is part of the abuse I've had all my life and having a hard time getting rid of it. The insecurity of church is definitely the spiritual abuse from the previous churches I went to. They have it drilled in me. That if I try to accomplish something that isn't part of their approval. That in no way would God approve it. Again showing how much worse spiritual abuse can be.

Fortunately, this choir has so understood about the abuse. They are so used to seeing people getting attacked spiritually themselves. That they are supportive in helping me. I've been getting help with things I never felt comfortable about. I don't even tell my family (biological) or anyone for that matter and get the support I need.

If I have to get up and leave for a reason. They have another choir member check on me and make sure I am okay. Never seen that before at any church. I had surgery shortly after joining this choir and received flowers. Again nothing I have ever seen before. Makes you wonder why is this one different?

Spiritual Attacks

It took me awhile; I have found my sanctuary home here. I know that this is where God wants me to be. Everything I known all my life is different compared to before. Things have slowly begun to be different for me. I would do things here that I never dreamed about. Or have a chance to do. One thing they do here is go on a mission trip for example.

If and when you do something that God has called you to do. Someone isn't going to like it. I'm sure everyone knows who I am talking about. You have heard ministers preach about being in God's army. Believe me Satan has an army of his own too. He has them attack you where you are most vulnerable.

One example would be when I go on a mission trip. He knows what is going to happen. Maybe God knows someone will get saved. So Satan knows you will help save a soul. Nope. He doesn't like that. So he will use whatever means he can to keep you from going. Like, causing you to get sick. This way you are ill and now will cancel being on the trip. You don't go, the person doesn't get saved, and he wins.

Another example would be what I went through. Kids who have been abused are easy targets for him. How many times did I say I was mad at God for something? Right there Satan is winning from what I went through. This would be one good way to help Satan with his tricks. Trying to kill myself? He wins again. Each time God had to really work at it to stop me from doing something. Again God knows what I'll do in the future that he has planned for me. Something Satan doesn't like.

The alcoholism that my family has gone through from one generation to another gets passed down along with the abuse. Again showing how much Satan has control over this family. Some could say that they were worshiping the bottle more than God. As I mentioned earlier my dad quit going to church and was more dependant on booze than God. I can name people in my family who have passed away from something that has to do with alcohol.

In Exodus 20:5-6 it says: 5 You must not worship or serve any idol, because I, the LORD your God, am a jealous God. If you hate me, I will punish your children, and even your grandchildren and great-grandchildren. 6 But I show kindness to thousands who love me and obey my commands.

When this happens it feels like we would be easy targets. For spiritual attacks and wouldn't fight. As I mentioned earlier, because of all the things I went through. I am more of a fighter than I used to. Physically, emotionally and even spiritually. So now if Satan wants to attack me he has to use more things to accomplish his goal.

Believe me he does. I was living in Maryland and doing a review of a movie called "The Passion of Christ". My church wanted me to write one up for their newsletter. They liked it and printed it up. At the time I was writing it up, I was having all sorts of problems with my computer. What better way for him to attack you? Then while you are doing something good that will help other people?

Even while writing this book I am getting attacked spiritually by him. You can see how I am getting upset and changing what happens to me. And then after I become stronger spiritually from it that what I am writing becomes stronger.

I can post somewhere that I am feeling bad or not well. Then people tell me that I am spiritually being attacked or abused at the time I write the post. They offer support to help me from it. It wouldn't even have to be people from my church. There are people from work who can tell I am being spiritually attacked.

God does give you the strength to handle this situation. But you have to let him in and help you. One thing I have been told a million times is to pray. It doesn't matter what the situation is. If you want something, you have to pray about it. God won't hand it out to you on a silver platter. Just like a job. You get the paycheck, but before you get the money you have to do the work. Right? Same thing applies here. If you want the reward you have to work for it. Believe me it won't be easy as saying a child's prayer and expect a million dollars in return.

When I was first hearing there was a God that rewards you, that is the first thing I did. Pray and expect a new car. I wasn't old enough to drive yet, but who cares, right? Wrong! He only gives you what you need. If you need to get stronger spiritually you have to go through trials. What happened when I wanted to grow spiritually? I ended up going through trials, more abuse and then leaving the test church. No way was I going to grow more by staying in that church.

Just like you need food to eat and water to drink. You need to replenish your spirit by reading the bible. That is the spiritual food your spirit needs. Going to church helps too. You are listening to the sermon and getting the word through another method. When you are in church service, how many times do they pray? Did you count? Because they know how important it is to pray. This is why they do it so much in one hour.

When you loose your car keys do you pray? Try it. If you ask God to help you find your car keys for example He will tell you. Maybe he will tell you something. One time I was having trouble finding something. I looked all over and couldn't find it. I prayed several times and didn't find it. I ended up going into an elevator and the two of us were discussing it. The other person told me maybe it is in your coat pocket. Sure enough where was it? In my coat pocket, and that is just one example.

He used the other person, but he was still communicating. You need to communicate back. He is eager to talk to you why aren't you talking to Him? If you are already talking to him, is it enough? Or do you need to talk more? Are you sure it is enough? Maybe your relationship with him needs to grow more? Remember how your relationship with your parents grew from when you were a kid to now? Same thing. Your relationship with God needs to grow also. It is a two way street. The less you let it grow the more likely Satan will intervene. You definitely don't want that.

Again you will have attacks from Satan. He doesn't want you to win this war. The battle has been going on for years and will continue on after I am gone. So he will try to conquer you for your most prized procession. Your soul. You might think it is not valuable. But if it isn't why is there a battle going on for it? God gives you the choice to make your decision. Satan doesn't and tries every mean thing he can think of to win. Each one of these attacks causes you to go in one way or the other.

Let's try another example. I was in this situation with this book. I was driving down the road. There is an intersection. I have two choices. Turn left or turn right. Both of these ways are my choices from God. I have a free will to go to go either direction. If I turned left I was going to do this book. If I turned right I wouldn't do the book. See the free will? Either way it had something to do with the decision of doing this book. I know what some people are thinking. I could have gone straight ahead. That is true. Any intersection would have a straight ahead sign. If I had stayed at the test church more likely I would have gone that way.

But since I have grown spiritually I don't see the road ahead. It is like an intersection, where you see a fence. The sign up ahead says turn left or right. If I go ahead it will not be a smooth road and a terrible ride you don't even want to go. God gives you warnings and signs. Do you see them?

Both have to do with spending eternity in one place or another. The choice is yours. Give in or fight. Each battle you win over Satan is a reward for you physically, mentally, emotionally and *spiritually*. It also shows you which way the road is turning. Just like I didn't see the road up ahead. The question is each battle that you win will cost you. Which side of the battle are you winning on?

## Writing

Now that I'm writing here instead of Maryland. I found a radio station that plays Christian music all the time. So that helps me while I am trying to write my projects. I've noticed when a song comes on the radio that I can sign to I stop whatever project I'm working on and sign with it.

I always pray before I start a project for that day. When I was working for a company, there was one project I was working on. I didn't come up with it, but I was assigned to develop it. Religiously it was not what I wanted to work on. Too dark, had to do with devilish type characters and other evil things that I don't even want to put in here, but you can figure it out.

I kept wondering why God would want me to work on this project. Religiously it was not what I felt God wanted me to do. I worked on it and then it dawned on me. If someone else had worked on it. the project would have been dark, scary, and just as evil as it should have been. Since I was developing it, the project came out like a light comedy/drama. Plus in one scene I had the evil type of characters actually kneeling on the ground and praising God for being alive. Now I can see why God wanted me working on this project. It makes so much sense now. Not to mention God is in control again.

I ended up doing a documentary on a famous person and I noticed I was adding a lot more religious part of the person's life. If someone else was doing this project there would be less of the religious part. You would have never known how religious the person was. It is never mentioned in stories. You would just see a normal documentary.

Again any documentary I would write about would show more about the religion than another documentary. No matter if it was about one person or the whole country. People leave that out in almost anything you watch or read anymore. Why? Because they feel it is a controversial subject. Always thinking separation of church and state means one thing. When really it means something else. It is a part of history. Why leave it out?

## Concert Band

Now I was actually doing what I wanted all my life. Be a percussionist. I started out doing a bass drum. They were having a beginning band so I figure that is what I needed. Especially since I never played anything but a trap set in Maryland. I still didn't have any knowledge about time, notes or anything. So I figured I better start from the beginning. Then try to get caught up like the people in the concert band were. If I was lucky I could learn really fast. And hopefully jump in to how well my relatives and friends were.

I was constantly being told by some people that they were better players than me. I would never be as good at they are. It reminded me of my mom again. They would take me to and from practice. It got so bad hearing it on each way to and from practice. I finally quit riding with them. I was able to recite back to them word for word. Everything they would tell me. I finally was able to catch a ride with someone else. Who was also a band member. We both became best friends since then. Another sign from God.

One person in the band asked me if I wanted to play another instrument instead of percussions. Like a clarinet for example. I had the weirdest look on my face and told her "I am not putting anything in my mouth."

"Spoken like a true percussionist." The band conductor replied. The girl then asked if I could play a flute. "That is just near your mouth not in it." She told me. I looked at her again and replied. "That is still too close for me."

I've heard this during some of my practices that we would have on Monday nights. "I believe any person can have the ability to play an instrument of any kind." The concert band director has said several times. I was so surprised when I first heard it. He is right in a lot of ways. I wish my mom had told me the same thing instead of what she would say to me. You don't know what someone can accomplish if they aren't given a chance. Personally I don't know if talent is needed for playing an instrument. But I must be doing something right and not know it.

Sometimes my friends would have to answer my questions. I would have about playing an instrument in my section. Or music all together. Even explain what the conductor just said was a compliment. I don't have the faintest idea that what he was saying was a compliment. People assume you already know this stuff. If you were in band in school you would know this stuff. People like me never did and are learning.

Sometimes I wonder if I had been able to build on my music skill when I was younger instead of them getting brushed off like they did. Maybe I could have been a professional musician. Or been respected different. I guess we'll never know about some of these things. Maybe my self esteem would have been better. I guess maybe I'm not supposed to know.

Orchestra

When I started joining the orchestra, I was playing percussions just like in the band. The only difference is that I'm playing the cymbal and auxiliary pieces. I still didn't know how to read notes so I couldn't do the orchestra bells yet. (some people refer them as the xylophone) You definitely need to know how to read notes for that instrument.

When I started playing the orchestra bells, I was labeling them. Black letters on white papers. When my vision got worse, I had to label them in different colors. This way I can tell the different octaves. Now, I've gotten to the point where I don't need them labeled anymore. Since I know where the keys are on the bells.

Because of my cataracts, the lights are making it difficult for me to see the music. One guy recommended I listen to the beat. For the past three weeks it is becoming harder and harder for me to see the music. The papers look blank to me when everyone else sees notes and times. I have been listening to the music when we practice and memorizing where the octaves are. Then I listen to the different notes and play them. It is getting difficult I noticed to keep up when we change from a four/four time to a three/four time for example.

When he tells me I am supposed to play the cymbals. I place them next to my left ear. This way I can crash them as loud as the conductor wants me to. It won't bother me at all. They are right next to my deaf ear. Showing again how God takes something bad and uses it for good.

Sometimes I can see the conductor cueing me in to do something like a cymbal crash and other times I can't. It is as if my vision is fluctuating again. Just like it used to before they gave me glaucoma drops.

## Counseling

One thing I had to go to counseling was for my physical abuse and the other abuses I went through instead of the rape. I had already forgiven my dad for the abuse he put me through. But there is the trauma part you have to go through and talk to someone for one thing.

You have to work it out. Not just talk to someone but get it out of your system sort to speak. This type of counseling was different than the counseling I did in Maryland for the rape. For one thing they would have me not do homework for the counseling part of it. They would add a religious point of view for the abuse I went through.

I am used to a minister to tell you "You need to come into my office and we will talk about it." Then you come in at a certain time and talk about it. I heard this over the phone from my minister. "Let me go get that phone number for you." I could tell now I'm in the twenty-first century. "Okay what is wrong with this picture?" I thought to myself. Modern type of counseling I guess. Last century I would have never heard of that. Of course that was what? Twenty years ago? Obviously this made a big difference. Welcome to the twenty-first century everyone.

Hand Bell Choir

After joining this church my sister was asking me if I want to join the bell choir. I had the weirdest look on my face. "They have one?" I asked. "Yes."

"Of course." She stated. I never saw it so I was wondering where it was. Mary took me to their practice session. I ended up joining it right away. Since I've wanting to do this since I was a little kid.

Like I mentioned back in Vegas. They had a hand bell choir there. But I left before I was old enough to play. Again here is an example of God listening to me. I was able to move to a church where I feel secure. Plus do something I always wanted. Even if I was not able to play an instrument I wanted to play hand bells. It has been like a passion for me. I know my mom would be proud of me doing this.

After seeing the way they play their bells. I knew I would never be able to do the higher bells. Because they play so many of them at one time. Plus my vision isn't that good to keep up with them. So I took a lower section of the bells.

The director has been teaching us music reading. Pretty much what anyone in band already knows. It has been helping me a lot. Since I never had band and I'm still learning this stuff. Of course some people take this for granted. Thinking that everyone knows this. Just because you play an instrument. I've been absorbing it like a sponge takes to water. God has been teaching me through him.

Some people don't show up and don't let the handbell director know they aren't coming. One friend told me if I didn't come or let him know. That he would have a legitimate excuse for killing me and would be acceptable. Peter told me it would be two for the price of one. The handbell director could kill me and choir director could officiate at my own funeral. This is definitely a family. Showing that you are wanted and needed. Now doesn't this show love?

Vision Loss Again

In June of last year, I lost so much distance vision and nearsightedness, to the point where I had to be moved in choir. I originally was in the back row of the choir. I figured I wouldn't be able to do this stuff. Being so far in the back if the choir director wanted to signal for us to stop singing. I would never be able to see him. It was bothering me so much. In choir, hand bell choir, and orchestra. I thought my only option was to quit all these things I loved. Since I was having trouble seeing and reading these pages.

Nope they weren't going to let that happen. I should have seen that coming. The orchestra director gave me color stickers to use on the pages so I can see when I switch instruments on the hymns. I use color pencils to show when I need to change on the time. On the orchestra bells I already had the notes written, but now I use colored ones so I can see the different octaves. I highlight my notes on the hand bell books.

In choir I got moved down from the back to the second row. So now I can see what the choir director is doing. I still use the practice CDs they give us so I have the words memorized. When they give us books to look at. I highlight the higher notes so I can see when I need to go to the higher octaves. I have them memorized and can see what Lenny is doing. Since I've been moved down closer to him. You can see how much they go out of their way to help someone.

Several months later my cataracts grew in a hurry. Within three weeks they grew a lot faster than what is normal for this to happen. I have polarized cataracts so they are reacting to the lights in the sanctuary and other places. Things and even people look blurry and are in a shade of a color.

When someone has cataracts they are usually in the center. This creates problems. But the average person has per ferial vision so they can still see some. All of my per ferial vision is gone. Like one friend stated it is a double whammy for me. Even though it is a temporary ordeal. I am pretty much going totally blind until they remove the cataracts. Until the surgery is done I have to find a new way of singing in the choir. Trying to play in the orchestra and play in the hand bells. All three of these require vision.

I don't see it as a bad situation. Just another trial or challenge from God. If we do a song I already know. Then it is not a problem. In orchestra we were doing a new song. I kept messing up since I can't see the music. What did I do?

The drummer next to me was keeping beat. So I followed him. In hand bells when it is a new song. The director will help guide me since I am sight reading.

Vacation Bible School

The first year I volunteered to do vacation bible school I didn't know what was involved. I was able to get a ride with someone. Since I did work with the puggle group all the kids I knew were in with the three year olds. So it makes sense they would have I work with them. The only problem I had was that the kids would bring their friends with them. It is good that they did that, but not good for someone with vision problems. So when I was in charge of a few kids ended up being in charge of too many for me to handle. If I did this again next year I wouldn't be able to handle the kids. Sure enough my answer was in front of me. The music department.

The following year I was working in the music department with the vbs. Now I know this is definitely my section. They teach the kids some dance moves to the songs and some sign language. Two things I already know and do at home. I've been practicing sign language at home everyday with religious music. The only difference is that no one knew it at the time. Again keeping things hidden.

The third year things were different. They are teaching these kids grade one of sign language. This makes sense since they don't know sign language. But then they would do grade two in sign language in another song. The people in the church didn't notice it. This of course confuse even the adults. So I would comment on the videos. Like, "You are confusing the kids when you play number three and number five since they are doing the same word two different ways." Strange how the church staff pick up on what I know.

The people who were on the mission trip this year. Were introduced to me doing sign language twice. They saw me do it two different songs and finally picked up on the fact that I have a hearing problem. Man they are quick. We would be schedule a certain time during the night to have dinner.

One year they must have picked up the fact that I don't eat much. So I had one minister sitting on my left and another sitting on the right side of me. If I had a little bit of food on my plate they would take some off of theirs. Then take some of their food and put it on my plate. Not asking if I wanted more food. But keeping an eye on how much I was eating. I keep wondering if it is a good sign or bad sign. That I had a minister on each side of me. Hum... still wondering about that one.

This is something I look forward to every year. Especially when I can teach someone else another language. Plus I feel like I am exulting God when I do a song in sign language.

Mission Trips

I've been on a few mission trips. Each time I go I end up learning something different when I come back than when I left. I help out in some area that I am familiar with. I usually end up working in the construction area after building three houses back in Texas.

I usually end up being the only girl in this area. Usually it is jut the men working on these projects. Some of them would tease me about being a girl. Plus joke about how they have to teach me something I already know. I end up saying something like. "You want me to go work with the girls then?" Of course I'm laughing. They have a panic look on their faces.

"No. You're staying here." Even the mission trip leader already knows which section I'm working on. If I wanted to work in another area I think he would have me checked out. To see if I'm okay.

I've been able to help out in places where I used to live. Slowly this church has been learning where I used to live. Wait till they read this. Sometimes people hear that an area has been hit by a disaster. When they never realize how many people have been affected. You don't know if the guy sitting next to you in church, used to live there. Or how they have relatives over in the same area. It really feels good to help someone. Just like the Red Cross work I did. You and everyone else benefits.

I grow more spiritually after hearing testimonies from people. There are a couple of things we can use to help us with reaching the word out to people one is a FAITH outline or the ABC's. Here they are:

F= Forgiveness We cannot have heaven and eternal life without God's forgiveness. "In Him (meaning "Jesus") we have redemption through His blood, the forgiveness of sin".

A= Available God's forgiveness is available, and it's available to all people. "For God so loved the world that He gave His only begotten Son...." But, it is not automatic. "Not everyone who says unto Me 'Lord, Lord' shall enter the kingdom of heaven".

I= Impossible It is impossible for God to allow sin into heaven. God is love. "For God so loved the world..." But He is also just. "For His judgment is without mercy." And we are all sinners. "For all have sinned, and fall short of the glory of God."

T= Turn To "turn" is to "repent". We must turn from something, and that something is "sin" and "self". "Unless you repent, you will all likewise perish." And, we must turn to someone, and that "Someone" is Jesus. "Jesus died for our sins according to the Scriptures, He was buried, and He arose again the third day according to the Scriptures."

"If you confess with your mouth 'Jesus is Lord', and you believe in your heart that God has raised Him from the dead, you will be saved."

H= Heaven Heaven is eternal life. Heaven is "here". "I have come that you might have life, and that you might have it more abundantly." Heaven is also "hereafter". "If I go and prepare a place for you, I will come again and receive you unto Myself; so that where I am there you may be also."

A = Acceptance "Accepting" that Jesus Christ is your savior. He is the one you need in your life. He is here and willing to comfort you in your life. "Admitting" he is the one who will help you.

B = Believe "Believe" that he can help you and save you from your sins. "Because" you are and sinner. The only way to get to Heaven is through your "Brother" Jesus Christ.

C = Confessing "Confessing" that Jesus "Christ" is your Savior. That you need him in your life. That without him you will not be able to get into Heaven.

Listening to the people we have helped and having a sermon in the evening. You come back home a different person than when you left. Makes me wonder why more churches don't do it. It benefits the people who go and those we help. It's a win/win situation. Those we help of course. The church that sent for us. Our church that allowed us to go. And especially us for how much we have grown spiritually by being able to help someone.

## Signing

I didn't learn sign language till I went to the Chris Cole Rehab Center for the Blind in Austin Texas. They had a few people there who were blind and deaf. It was the first time I learned how to do some words in sign language instead of just doing the alphabet.

I was so excited about communicating in another language that we only learned a little. Once the people who were deaf and blind left the rehab center they stopped teaching us the signing.

I ended up teaching myself the rest. I wasn't sure how or well I was doing till there came to the point that I got tested by God. I was doing some volunteer work with the red cross and came across some deaf people. We would sign for a while. They would sign like to me a hundred words per minute. I had to quickly learn how to sign the words "slow down".

Because of my vision problems I had a hard time seeing what they were signing. I still have to sign slow down sometimes. When I am challenged to communicate with a deaf person. I saw a girl who was a professional sign language interpreter. Signing to a song at the test church in Maryland. Then I finally saw what I can do with the sign language I know. I began practicing my signing by doing it with a song in the mornings.

I also use it to see if I am wake enough in the mornings. If I mess up I need more coffee. I love being able to do it with music since I am at a slower pace with the signing. Plus I get to dance to religious music. I end up expressing God's word in another language and exalt him like it says to in the bible. Another reason I help out in the music department of the Vacation Bible School. I've also do it on mission trips to entertain people.

The last time I had a complex partial seizure I was unable to talk. The area that was affected in my brain was the section that controls your speech. I felt so much like I had tape over my mouth. I could see, hear and look at people when they were talking. I just couldn't speak back.

I was able to move my hands and tried sign language. Unfortunately the staff couldn't even figure out what I was doing. Finally someone figured out I was communicating. They didn't know it was sign language. But asked me if I could hear them. I ended up moving my right hand up and down like a person does their head. Finally they understood. They told me I would be alright and someone signed the letters O…K… so I knew they understood. Praise the Lord.

Right after they understood me God gave me my voice back. I made a noise like someone was just able to breathe after not breathing for a while. I finally could talk again. So when you learn something you should keep it up. You never know when you will need it again.

I've also begun doing it at the local nursing home. I spend thirty minutes doing sign language to religious music. The people seem to like it. After I'm finished they tell me things about it. I've been doing it every other month so far. Nobody wants me to quit yet.

Today when I walk around somewhere and I hear a song on the radio I have to stop what I am doing take a break and do some signing. I feel like I have to sign it. When I go to church on Wednesday nights I hear the music from the building next door. If it is one I sign to at home I just start signing to it. So while I am walking and not even realize it. I am doing it till I get to the door and then find out I can't open the door. Because both of my hands are being used for God's glory.

### Neighbors

I now live in an apartment complex that is for people who are sixty-two years old and or disabled. Since I am disabled I was able to get in. (I am not old enough) The neighbors here are different. People here really do try to help each other.

They have a worship group that meets on Tuesday mornings. A minister from a local church comes by and gives a sermon. There is usually one denominational a different week. So all religions are represented.

People here when they hear someone is sick try to help each other. Even when I can't get out they will lend me something since they know I can't get to the store. I can't drive, but even help out as much as possible. They seem to like it when I do songs in sign language, tell stories and just passing out stuff for them. Everyone contributes in one way or another.

Any of the other places I have lived in they were never like that. When I was living in the apartment complex in Frederick. No one offered to help me. No one knew who I was. All they knew about me was which building I lived in. They would refer to me as the vet girl.

If one of their pets was sick. They would come over and grab me. Wanting me to take care of their pet. Like I was a licensed veterinarian. Who cares if you need a ride? What my name was? I'm just the girl who works at a vet clinic.

Like I said it is so different here. I am not used to it. People offering to help one another. I feel like I've landed on another planet or something. Some of the church's homebound members live here. So I was on the committee at church. Doesn't bother me a bit. I live here anyway. So it makes sense to me.

Entertaining

One thing I've noticed all my life is that in one way or another God wanted me to entertain people. Through dancing, roller skating, singing, signing, playing instruments, hand bells, writing for television or even just cracking jokes. It all ads up to being the same thing, entertaining.

Through the years I've even developed a smart-alecky personality where even just making a remark is funny and gets people to laugh. Some people have told me it's not the right thing to do. The majority of people like it because it makes them laugh. If God didn't want us laughing he wouldn't given us this gift.

In my writing it seems the best kind of writing I do is comedy and stories that exalt God and uplifts him. I always feel better when I do His work. The majority of the time people ask me how you wrote this. I answer I didn't write it, God did. Believe it is the truth even the title for this book wasn't my idea.

As you read previously he uses me in everything. I can see why people like to go into the entertainment industry. They really have a gift for it and like to spread it around. Why people think of them as idols I haven't figured out yet. Even today I can't tell some people what kind of work I do because they say mean things about my work. When I just do what God wants me to do.

My biological family is like that too. They would rather tell people I'm unemployed. Or I just sit around and watch TV all day. If that was the case how could have written this book?

I always feel better entertaining. I help others feel better and I feel better. So for me it is a win/win situation. Another reason I do so many things in church. People assume I am a workaholic. When I'm not a workaholic. If you were to categorize all the stuff I do as entertainment it makes sense now. Why I do so many things. Even the concert band is entertaining too.

I'll ask for prayer requests for friends of mine that work in the same business that I do. (showbiz) Some people don't want to do it and others do. As the saying goes. "You can't please everyone." I just wish they would feel the same about showbiz people as normal people. Or like the book says. I guess it depends on how you are raised up.

Ministry

When you see the word minister what do you think of? Someone who is ministering to others, right? Like the minister who gave out the sermon last week, right? Believe me you can attend a church and there can be one minister. Like the one I just mentioned. Or you could have a hundred. How do you ask? You can have a minister who works at your church and maybe an associate. But believe me there are more.

Some churches are so big that they have ministers that specialize in one area. Like the office area of the church for example. I could list them all, but you would need another book for that. But now you have the general idea.

In the dictionary you will find a list of definitions for a minister. One that comes to my mind is the one that specifies someone who is attending the need of others. Okay your minister does that. I'm sure you can think of how many times the minister was there when you needed help. Physically, emotionally, spiritually and so on till you have listed them all.

What about you? How many times have you heard that you are part of God's army? I've heard that so many times I even have an automatic response for it. The ministers are the generals and I am a lonely private stuck in the back who can't do anything. I can even list a hundred excuses why I can't even do anything.

Believe me there is still one that hasn't been covered in here that ministers are always talking about and no one does it. The definition is the one I stated earlier, to attend to the needs of others. Another thought that comes to mind is healthcare. Doctors, nurses and so on attend to others. There you go they are a minister through another source, but they are still ministering.

Okay, now that you are getting the idea, lets try another one. What about the choir members? Are they doing a ministry service? If you said yes, you are getting the idea. If you said no, I suggest you look it up in the dictionary for yourself. Under the word "Ministry".

What about the people who welcome you in their church? The ushers? That person who volunteered to open the door for you? How about the one who handed you a bulletin? Getting the idea?

Okay next. What about the job you did today? Did you answer the phone at work? Connected the person who was calling to the right department? There you go. You are doing a ministry and didn't even know it. God puts people in different needs everyday. Whatever you are good for and people are just not seeing it.

The more you do a ministry, the better you get at it and the more you feel better about it. You grow spiritually, get better at it and then advance up. Like a military person getting a promotion. The only way you will know what kind of job or military position you are qualified is to ask God. He knows what you are good at. You can ask him and he'll tell you. As you can tell from reading this, he knows how to get a hold of you. You just have to listen. I'll even tell him I don't know how I can get through a day without him.

As you have read earlier, everything I was abused about God has taken that and has made me minister to someone through that. I was told I don't have anything to do with music and what am I doing now? Abused as a kid and now I help out with kids. Took breaking into cars and used it to get away from a stalker. Can't hear? Now I entertain with sign language. The list goes on and on. He takes things with you and turns them around to where they are helping you and others. Have insecurity? Believe me he takes care of that. No matter what your problem is.

So when the next time comes around and the minister says "We have a ministry that is ready to be filled." or "What kind of ministry are you doing for the church?" What are you going to say? You should be able to answer right away with a list of what you are doing. I've already gone through so many things and I know I am doing God's will. Now here is my question to you. What is His will for you?

# COUNSELING

Even today it is still hard for me to take compliments from time to time. I'll have someone tell me I did a great job on doing something. I have to get someone else tell me if it was a compliment or not. Then they tell me it is and to take it as one.

I've even been told "good girl" or "you did a great job." All I keep thinking "I wish my dad or even someone in my biological family had said that to me." Of course they never did. Peter will end up saying they (referring to my church) *"They are your family now."*

*"You've got to think of them as your family."*

He's right you know. If you look back at what I've been writing. I've mentioned that strangers are more like my friends. My friends are more like family. Then my family is more like strangers. People will tell you it shouldn't be like that. I've had to finally accept it and move on.

I keep forgetting that my spiritual family is my family now. We did a concert at church and I was told I did good. I finally said "Thanks" to the person for the compliment. It shouldn't have taken me forty some years to finally learn to do that. Kids learn to do that at an early age. Again people don't realize what they have and take for granted.

People aren't supposed to be suppressing it when it comes to emotions. Society has done too much telling everyone to stop crying. Everyone should let it out. God didn't create all these emotions to keep bottled up and giving you ulcers. Counselors and other people will tell you it is better letting it out and showing emotions. Too many times men are told to suppress it when they shouldn't. Then they have higher blood pressure and other medical problems.

My dad kept holding it in so much till he got to the point that he took it out on us. If anything should be read is let it out. God didn't tell you hold it all in. That is man telling you. Children don't have a problem letting it out. How many times have we've been told to be a child of God. Believe me this applies to more than one way. Who are you listening to? God or man?

I am posting scriptures that I found through counseling that has helped me for my issues. Maybe it will help someone else. I used the New Century Version since I feel those who aren't familiar with the bible will understand or relate to it better. Plus I will be posting notes to help someone understand it better. They will be listed by subject such as faith. Under that will be the book like John. Followed by the chapter number 3. Next are the verses such as 16. If more than it will be followed by a – and then more numbers. Here is an example:

Faith

John 3:16
"God loved the world so much that he gave his one and only Son so whoever believes in him may not be lost, but have eternal life."
If you think you are the only one who has gone through physical abuse, I wouldn't be surprised if you meet someone else who has gone through the same thing. There are even support groups for people who have gone through that. There is usually one person people tend to forget who has gone through physical abuse. I'm talking about Jesus.
If you think about the day when he got the thirty-nine lashes just for not talking very much or being quiet. Wouldn't you call that abuse? This would qualify for not just physical, but emotional.
He was put to death for defending God's word and preaching it. He was being mocked by other religious people so that would be spiritual abuse. If you think about it. How many times are we willing to be persecuted for telling something about God? Just like when I was getting persecuted at work.
On the sexual abuse, for me, I trusted a teacher that everyone should be able to trust. Jesus trusted everyone. What happened to him? They went against him and abused him. Loosing their trust. Sounds to me like what I went through. Think about it?
This way God already knows what kind of abuse you are going through since he has already gone through the same thing. I certainly can't say God hasn't gone through the same thing. When in reality he

has. Not to mention that this is showing just a few examples. I bet I can find more. I'm sure everyone can think of more.

It makes you feel better when you talk to someone who has gone through the same thing. If you read these passages I have posted, hopefully they will help you. They have helped me a great deal. I hope they help someone who reads them. You will see you are not the only one who has gone through the same thing. But there are others. They went through it long before you were born. Unfortunately there will be others to follow me. Unless we can break the cycle of abuse. No matter what kind it is.

Alcoholism

Ephesians 5:15-18

15 So be very careful how you live. Do not live like those who are not wise, but live wisely. 16 Use every chance you have for doing good, because these are evil times. 17 So do not be foolish but learn what the Lord wants you to do. 18 Do not be drunk with wine, which will ruin you, but be filled with the Spirit.

Note: Even though it says wine. It is referring to any type of alcohol. God didn't create things to be abused. I doesn't matter what it is, alcohol, sex, or anything. Nothing is to be abused.

Leviticus 10:8-11

8 Then the LORD said to Aaron, 9 "You and your sons must not drink wine or beer when you go into the Meeting Tent. If you do, you will die. This law will continue from now on. 10 You must keep what is holy separate from what is not holy; you must keep what is clean separate from what is unclean. 11 You must teach the people all the laws that the LORD gave them through Moses."

Note: In other words you shouldn't be drinking in church, public and other places where people can even see you drunk. It is a sin along with other things. Too many bad things happen when alcohol is involved.

Anger

Proverbs 16:27-30

27 Useless people make evil plans, and their words are like burning fire. 28 A useless person causes trouble, and a gossip ruins friendships. 29 Cruel people trick their neighbors and lead them to do wrong. 30 Someone who winks is planning evil, and the one who grins is planning something wrong.

Note: If you remember when I mentioned the California trip. My dad was sitting next to me and drunk. He winked at me and was acting strange to me. Being so plastered he hugged me and it seemed weird. Later on when he drank he sang, spilled beer on me. He ended up passing out in the car. These last passages explain it all and he wasn't even angry. This applies to people who are easily angered. Which he was all the time from the drinking.

Proverbs 22:24-25

24 Don't make friends with quick-tempered people or spend time with those who have bad tempers. 25 If you do, you will be like them. Then you will be in real danger.

Note: This applies to people who are with wife beaters and child abusers. They get caught up with the anger. Then they are trapped and can't get out. If they don't get out then they end up being part of the chain of abuse also. The same would apply to alcoholics and others. Cynthia married a wife abuser after being abused by our dad. The cycle continues till someone stops it.

Child Abuse

Ephesians 6:1-4

1 Children, obey your parents as the Lord wants, because it is the right thing to do. 2 The command says, "Honor your father and mother." This is the first command that has a promise with it – 3 "Then everything will be well with you, and you will have a long life on the earth." 4 Fathers do not make your children angry, but raise them with the training and teaching of the Lord.

Note: If you remember this is one commandment I could never understand. When my father would beat me and my mother would tell me things. But what God is telling Fathers is not to hit the children but to bring them up in the way God intended. In the same way the children should respect the parents who do this. This way it is a win/win situation and no one is hurt.

Romans 13:3

3 Those who do right do not have to fear the rulers; only those who do wrong fear them. Do you want to be unafraid of the rulers? Then do what is right, and they will praise you.

Note: Paul is referring to people who don't do things to help people. Or as a government tries to cover up something. Like the school trying to cover up my rape. Parents who don't get help when they abuse kids and so on. They would rather pretend it isn't there. In my case I was the victim in each circumstance. The kids bullying me, etc. So I shouldn't have to fear them. I did what was right. If I don't get rewarded for helping report the problem here on earth I will be rewarded later. The sooner you report it, the sooner you get rewarded for stopping the cycle of abuse.

Faith

1 Thessalonians 2:10-17

10 When we were you, we lived in a holy and honest way, without fault. You know this is true, and so does God. 11 You know that we treated each of you as a father treats his children. 12 We encouraged you, we urged you, and we insisted you live good lives for God, who calls you to his glorious kingdom. 13 Also, we always thank God because when you heard his message from us, you accepted it as the word of God, not the words of humans. And it really is God's message which works in you who believe. 14 Brothers and sisters, your experiences have been like those of God's churches in Christ that are in Judea. You suffered from the people of your own country, as they suffered from the Jews, 15 who killed both the Lord Jesus and the prophets and forced us to leave the country. They do not please God and are against all people. 16 They try to stop us from teaching those who are not Jews so they may be saved. By doing this, they are increasing their sins to the limit. The anger of God has come to them at last. 17 Brothers and sisters, though we were separated from you for a short time, our thoughts were still with you. We wanted very much to see you and tried hard to do so.

Note: This helped me a lot in trying to understand that God has gone through the same things I have. He has an understanding heart. He knows your needs. He has saved people. You can be saved too from all of this. Everyone is a brother and sister in Christ. You are a family now. Just like the spiritual family I have been mentioning. You are not separated again.

False Teachers

2 Peter 2:1-10

1 There used to be false prophets among God's people, just as you will have some false teachers in your group. They will secretly teach things that are wrong – teachings that will cause people that will be

lost. They will even refuse to accept the Master, Jesus, who bought their freedom. So they will bring quick ruin on themselves. 2 Many will follow their evil ways and say evil things about the evil truth. 3 Those false teachers only want your money, so they will use you by telling you lies. Their judgment spoken against them long ago is still coming, and their ruin is certain.

4 When angels sinned, God did not let them go free without punishment. He sent them to hell and put them in caves of darkness where they are being held for judgment. 5 And God punished the world long ago when he brought a flood to the world that was full of people who were against him. But God saved Noah, who preached about being right, and seven other people with him. 6 And God also destroyed the evil cities of Sodom and Gomorrah by burning them until they were ashes. He made those cities an example of what will happen to those who are against God.

7 But he saved Lot from those cities. Lot, a good man, was troubled because of the filthy lives of evil people. 8 (Lot was a good man, but because he lived with evil people every day, his good heart was hurt by the evil things he saw and heard.) 9 So the Lord knows how to save those who serve him when troubles come. He will hold evil people and punish them, while waiting for the Judgment Day. 10 That punishment is especially for those who live by doing the evil things their sinful selves want and who hate authority. These false teachers are bold and do anything they want. They are not afraid to speak against the angels.

Note: In Hebrew Prophets are referred to as Teachers. False teachers would definitely fit what kind of people who led the test church I had in Maryland. Just as people who controlled the church in Texas. I'm sure people can remember "cult" leaders who made their members do things like kill themselves and made news. This would be another example. The stores of Sodom and Gomorrah is used also to show that churches who are false teachers will eventually be punished. If not here on Earth then when they meet God. After reading this I felt so much like Lot. The good Lord help rescued me from all of this. Bringing me from the test church, to the church of refuge and now to a church of sanctuary.

Jude 1:10 - 13

10 But these people speak against things they do not understand. And what they do not know, by feeling, as dumb as animals know things, are the very things that destroy them. 11 It will be terrible for them. They have followed the way of Cain, and for money they have given themselves to doing the wrong that Balaam did. They have fought against God as Korah did, and like Korah, they surely will be destroyed. 12 They are like dirty spots in your special Christian meals you share. They eat with you and have no fear, caring only for themselves. They are clouds without rain, which the winds blow around. They are autumn trees without fruit that are pulled out of the ground. So they are twice dead. 13 They are like waves of the sea, tossing up their own shameful actions like foam. They are like stars that wander in the sky. A place like the blackest darkness has been kept them forever.

Note: Again showing how the test church was using us for their purpose. I mentioned how they collected all that money and it never went into their building like they said. They got paid by us for service they never gave us. God paid by other churches to preach and they did there. So where is all that money? Never bought new office space. The Texas church never grew. When I left they didn't have a pastor and was being led by several people taking over. No mediator so to speak to keep them together.

Mathew 7:15-16

Jesus saying: "Be careful of false prophets. They come to you looking like sheep, but are really dangerous like wolves. 16 You will know these people by what they do. Grapes don't come from thornbushes, and figs don't come from thorny weeds."

Note: Again Jesus is talking about prophets being false teachers. Just like the ones I had at the test church. They were ministers, elders, and all the way down to a worship team leader. So they looked like sheep. The same as us. But when you saw what they did to the congregation and their members. They in reality were like wolves and attacked me. Even when I tried to leave nicely.

Jeremiah 23:30-32

30 "So I am against the false prophets," says the LORD. "They keep stealing words from each other and say they are from me. 31 I am against the false prophets," says the LORD. They use their own words and pretend it is a message from me. 32 I am against the prophets who prophesy false dreams," says the LORD. "They mislead my people with their lies and false teachings! I did not send them or command them to do anything for me. They cannot help the people of Judah at all," says the LORD.

Note: Now God is saying what he thinks about false teachers. If it wasn't so important why would he mention it three times in this paragraph. This again refers to the test church I went to in Maryland. They said they were teaching what God says. But in reality they were changing God's word to what they wanted us to hear. I have never heard the scripture read the same before I went to the test church or after I left. Makes me wonder how many other "test" churches are out there and how many people are being preyed upon.

Mission Work

2 Kings 17:27-28

27 Then the king of Assyria commanded, "Send back one of the priests you took away. Let him live there and teach the people what the god wants." 28 So one of the priests who had been carried away from Samaria returned to live in Bethel. And he taught the people how to honor the LORD.

Note: This is why people go on mission trips. They go to remote areas where the bible is not preached. Or areas where devastation has been affected and show them that people do care. There are people who want to help. No matter what religion, race or wealth you have.

Luke 24:45-48

45 Then Jesus opened their minds so they could understand the Scriptures. 46 He said to them, "It is written that the Christ would suffer and rise from the dead on the third day 47 and that a change of hearts and lives and forgiveness of sins would be preached in his name to all nations, starting at Jerusalem. 48 You are witnesses to these things.

Note: Jerusalem is usually referred to your home town or city. You start locally and then work outside. Such as city, state, nation and then to another country. Mission work is usually spreading the word of the gospel from one place to another. Through one method or another. Like some you see on TV. Listen to radio. Giving our brochures or just talking. Most people find out. The best way is just talking to other people. Even if you have to do it in another language.

Performing

Psalm 150:3-6

3 Praise him with trumpet blasts; praise him with harps and lyres. 4 Praise him with tambourines and dancing; praise him with stringed instruments and flutes. 5 Praise him with loud cymbals; praise him with crashing cymbals. 6 Let everything that has breathes praise to LORD. Praise the LORD!

2 Samuel 6:15-16

15 David and all the Israelites shouted with joy and blew the trumpets as they brought the Ark of the Lord to the city. 16 As the Ark of the Lord came into the city, Saul's daughter Michal looked out the window. When she saw David jumping and dancing in the presence of the Lord, she hated him.

Ephesians 5: 19-20

19 Speak to each other with psalms, hymns and spiritual songs, singing and making music in your hearts to the Lord. 20 Always give thanks to God the Father for everything, in the name of our Lord Jesus Christ.

Note: In each of these books it refers to performing (no matter which way) that it is in praise for and to the Lord. Plus it is rejoicing to the glory of God. If he didn't like it, I'm sure he would have struck people ages like he did with Sodom and Gomorrah. Each way is how you rejoice and celebrate the Lord. Some people are against one way or another. How can it be if you praising him? I've also have been told that it is only in heaven that they do that. All the ones I've been posting are here on earth.

Persecution: Suffering for Doing Right

1st Peter 3:13-18

13 If you are trying hard to do good, no one can really hurt you. 14 But even if you suffer for doing right, you are blessed. "Don't be afraid of what they fear; do not dread those things." 15 But respect Christ as the holy Lord in your hearts. Always be ready to answer everyone who asks you to explain about the hope you have, 16 but answer in a gentle way and with respect. Keep a clear conscience so those who speak evil of your good life in Christ will be made ashamed. 17 It is better to suffer for doing good than for doing wrong if that is what God wants. 18 Christ himself suffered for sins once. He was not guilty, but he suffered for those who are guilty to bring you to God. His body was killed, but he was made alive in the spirit.

Note: In one way you will be expected to answer for your faith. Sooner or later people will question you. You should be prepared to answer them. Speak the truth. If someone doesn't like it or agree with you they will hurt you. It is better to get hurt here on earth for something you have done for God. He will reward you a lot more in heaven than man will ever reward you here on earth. Just like an innocent child being punished nothing they did wrong.

Daniel 6:7-23

7 The supervisors, the people who advise you, and the captains of the soldiers have all agreed that you should make a new law for everyone to obey: "For the next thirty days no one should pray to any god or human to you, O king. Anyone who doesn't obey will be thrown into the lions' den. 8 Now, O king, make the law and sign your name to it so that it cannot be changed, because then it will be a law of the Medes and Persians and cannot be cancelled." So King Darius signed the law.

10 Even though Daniel knew that the new law had been written, he went to pray in an upstairs room in his house, which that had windows that opened toward Jerusalem. Three times each day Daniel would kneel down to pray and thank God, just as he always done. 11 Then those men went as a group and found Daniel praying and asking God for help. 12 So they went to the king and talked to him about the law he had made. They said, "Didn't you sign a law that says no one can pray to any god or human except you, O king? Doesn't it say that anyone disobeys during the next thirty days will be thrown into the lions' den?" The king answered "Yes, that is the law, and the laws of Medes and Persians cannot be cancelled."

13 Then they said to the king, "Daniel, one of the captives from Judah, is not paying attention to you, O king, or to the law you signed. Daniel still prays to his God three times a day." 14 The king became very upset when he heard this. He wanted to save Daniel, and he worked hard until sunset trying to think of a way to save him. 15 Then those men went as a group to the king. They said, "Remember, O king, the law of Medes and Persians says that no law or command given by the king cannot be changed."

16 So King Darius gave the order, and Daniel was brought in and thrown into the lions' den. The king said to Daniel, "May the God you serve all the time save you!" 17 A big stone was brought and placed over the opening of the lions' den. Then the king used his signet ring

and the ring of his royal officers to put special seals on the rock. This ensured that no one would move the rock and bring Daniel out. 18 Then King Darius went back to his palace. He did not eat that night, he did not have any entertainment brought to him, and he could not sleep.

19 The next morning King Darius got up at dawn and hurried to the lions' den. 20 As he came near the den, he was worried. He called out to Daniel, "Daniel, servant of the living God! Has your God that you always worship been able to save you from the lions?" 21 Daniel answered, "O king, live forever! My God has sent his angel to close the lions' mouths. They have not hurt me, because my God knows I am innocent. I never did anything wrong, to you O king."

23 King Darius was very happy and told his servants to lift Daniel out of the lions' den. So they lifted him out and did not find any injury on him, because Daniel had trusted his God.

Note: After what happened to me at the vet clinic. I kept feeling like I was Daniel being yelled at. Those two that were calling me names. Were the kings men. When I watched what happened to two employees that were calling me names. I felt like I was in the lions' den watching everything. I can relate to this story so much. Just like God protected Daniel when he was innocent. I feel like God has protected me so much from being innocent on more than one occasion throughout my whole life.

Rape

Deuteronomy 22: 25-27

25 But if a man meets an engaged girl out in the country and forces her to have sexual relations with him, only the man who had sexual relations with her must be put to death. 26 Don't do anything to the girl, because she has not done a sin worthy of death. This is like the person who attacks and murders a neighbor; 27 the man found the engaged girl in the country and she screamed, but no one was there to save her.

Note: In others words man doesn't see you as a virgin anymore, but in God's eyes you still are. Because you didn't decide to have the sex. You were forced to. The definition of rape. Whether it be a man or woman. You are God's creation you should be seen different. If you are saved you now a son or daughter of God and sister or brother of Christ. You can't be judged by man's standards.

Spiritual Abuse (Recovery)

Romans 12:2-3

2 Do not change yourselves to be like the people of this world, but be changed within by a new way of thinking. Then you will be to decide what God wants for you; you will know what is good and pleasing to him and what is perfect. 3 Because God has given me a special gift, I have something to say to everyone among you. Do not think you are better than you are. You must decide what you really are but the amount of faith God has given you.

Note: If you remember earlier, my test church wanted me to act a certain way. Do what they wanted and not be my normal self. The same thing happened with my dad and me. Even my sisters were complaining I didn't act a certain way. They still do. I have gotten phone calls, voice mails and ordered to act the way they want me to. Not the way God wants me to.

If you pray and ask God he will let you know.

Jeremiah 23:16-18

16 This is what the LORD All-Powerful says: "Don't pay attention to what those prophets are saying to you. They are trying to fool you. They talk about visions their own minds have made up, not about visions from me. They say to those who hate me: 'The LORD says: You will have peace.' They say to all those who are stubborn and do as they please: 'Nothing bad will happen to you.' But none of these prophets has stood in the meeting of angels to see or hear the message of the LORD. None of them has paid close attention to his message.

Note: In other words God is against false teachers. Like the ones I had at the test church. They wanted us to conform to their ways. They told us if we spoke out or questioned them. That we or I was at fault. Like a voter complaining about the government. I was supposed to keep my mouth shut and not say anything. Like they were superb. Plus this place was fine till you showed up. As if this was a peaceful setting till Betty came and asked questions. They were even hurting me when I did do something wrong. Dumped me outside my apartment as if that was the end of it. And they say it is a peaceful setting. Just like God just said. They are doing this in his own temple/church. It is not right with God, it shouldn't be what you are going through. Get out and find a refuge. Don't try to punish them. Believe me anything you do won't be as harsh as what God can do to them.

## Romans 13:4

4 The ruler is God's servant to help you. But if you do wrong, then be afraid. He has the power to punish, he is God's servant to punish those who do wrong.

Note: This is why we have social services. To protect kids from abusive people. They are like God's legal people to help those who need it. If they don't do right they will be punished. Remember rulers in the bible who ended up not doing what God wanted? They were removed from their position. The same thing here. The teacher was removed from his job. I wouldn't be surprised if the churches I left are not there. I haven't been brave enough to find out. The church in another state I heard had a fire. So you can visualize why that happened.

## Spiritual Attacks (Warfare)

Note: This is sometimes referred to as persecution also. It can be mild or strong. It can come in any form. From having trouble remembering your bible verse (for example) or as severe as getting cancer to keep you from finishing a spiritual book.

1 Peter 5:8-9

8 Control yourselves and be careful! The devil, your enemy, goes around like a roaring lion looking for someone to eat. 9 Refuse to give in to him, by standing strong in your faith. You know that your Christian family all over the world is having the same kinds of suffering.

Note: The devil's temptation is referred to as a roaring lion. Being devoured or eat is him taking over you spirit and winning through your faith. Here is the rest of the verses 10-11. 10 And after you suffer for a short time, God, who gives all grace, will make everything right. He will make you strong and support you and keep you from falling. He called you into share in his glory in Christ, a glory that will continue forever. 11 All power is his forever and ever. Amen. Here it shows that it is temporary and God is in control. I could write a whole book on all the things I have been going through, because someone doesn't want me to finish this book.

Job 2:6-10

6 The LORD said to Satan, "All right, then. Job is in your power, but you may not take his life. 7 So Satan left the LORD'S presence. He put painful sores on Job's body, from the top of his head, to the soles of his feet. 8 Job took a piece of broken pottery to scrape himself, and he sat in ashes in misery. 9 Job's wife said to him, "Why are you trying to stay innocent? Curse God and die!"

10 Job answered, "You are talking like a foolish woman. Should we only take good things from God and not trouble?" In spite of all of this Job did not sin in what he said.

Note: Okay. Here is a good example of Satan attacking someone to see them loose their faith in God. In other words a spiritual attack. Using one method of making someone sick to where you would want to give up. According to verse nine, Job's wife already gave up, while Job kept his faith. If you do become stronger from one spiritual attack. Satan will do something stronger to get you to give in. He has even used my seizures to get me to stop doing something. (for example playing in a concert) Because he doesn't want me doing that. It will help someone spiritually and he doesn't like that. If you read the whole book of Job you will see constant examples of spiritual warfare.

### Lifetime Verse

### Romans 8:28

28 We know that in everything God works for the good of those who love him. They are the people he called, because that was his plan.

Note: People have a particular verse out of the bible. This is what is already memorized and they feel it explains what is going on in their life. Right now or maybe they just have gotten over something. This one is mine right now. Ask me later and I bet it will be different. Ask someone you know what theirs is and I bet they can recite it for you.

### Abused All Over Again

Even today it is very hard to handle all of this abuse. Some have been so repressed that even when I've been working on this book it seems like it didn't hurt me so hard. It did, I just repressed it to the point that even though I am reliving it again that it is like nothing compared to the others I went through.

On the other hand some of the abuse is so traumatic that I was suffering from Posttraumatic Stress Disorder and today I still am. I am finding myself on the floor, rolled up into a ball and crying my eyes out. I've gotten to the point where I don't even want to leave the house or go to church where I feel most comfortable at. I have to take breaks and practice my signing or something else to take my mind off of it. People keep telling me you should just be putting it behind you.

Believe me it is easier said than done. I agree it is in the past, but if you don't do something about it, it will just fester and grow. Plus repressed memories have a way of coming back to haunt you even if you know it is in the past. The best thing for it is to bring it out and deal with it so that it doesn't bother you anymore. This also helps you to overcome it and forgive the person or people who have hurt you. This is also the same method people use to become "survivors" of whatever they are dealing with. No matter what the situation is.

Out of all the "abuses" that I have gone through, the worst for me is or was the spiritual abuse. Some can say it is because you trust these people. Didn't you trust your parents? Your teachers? Anyone in authority? If the answer is yes than you were abused by someone you can trust too.

The difference with the spiritual abuse is that they are abusing you not just with the area that affects you here on earth but your own area of trust with what happens you after death and with God personally. That is something bigger than you can even imagine. Losing your trust in God and faith is too big to imagine and is harder to get back. When I was in counseling I could get through the abuses in no time. The counselors told me this one we would have to work on slower, because it is something greater that you want to take a longer time to work on. It is too big to lose and it is definitely too important that you want to get back. It affects you here on earth, after death and is harder to get back compared to the other abuses.

One thing about being a survivor is not only being able to tell someone that you are one and that you have dealt with the situation, but now you have forgiven the person/people who have done this to you and now that you are really "free" from all of this and any future situations. You are not only free physically, emotionally, but mostly spiritually. It is really hard to explain until you have gone through it yourself. It is an awesome experience.

Explanation?

I think part of the reason could be that my dad was an only child. My mom told me ages ago "If you think you're father was mean to you, you should have seen how his father was to him."

"If you think your father beat you up, you should have seen how badly his father beat him up." I've seen my dad's back, because we would give him back rubs. He would have his shirt off. There weren't welts or markings or scars on him, unless they were where no one could see them, such on his head.

I remember when we got our family home reels converted to VHS tapes I would see my dad smoking. I don't remember him smoking. He would have a cigarette in one hand and a mixed drink in the other.

Doctors will tell you that the bipolar disorder that runs in the family can be the cause. Others might say it is the alcoholism – and two of my sisters ended up becoming alcoholics. Some will even say the depression.

I'm not a medical doctor, counselor, psychologist or any other kind of specialist. I'm not doing this to even give you a reason to say, "Oh that is why this happened", or "That is why she's acting like this". If you this is what all you are thinking after you have read all of this, I suggest you re-read this-- you have probably missed a lot, or skimmed over it.

My mom would complain about her mother-in-law to me at times. She couldn't get over how much more drinking she did compared to my dad. "If you think he drinks a lot, you should see your grandmother." She would always tell me, when my grandmother came to stay with us in Vegas before she died. Since I was so young then, I don't remember her not doing much of anything and of being scared of her even I just had to go into her room to tell her dinner was ready.

When I researched my family's genealogy, I found, sure enough, that alcoholism and depression and bipolar disorder run on my dad's side of the family. I have a picture of my dad's grandfather on the wall in my living room. He had bipolar disorder, and ended killed himself after his wife died by putting his head into an oven and succumbing from the fumes. My grandmother wasn't even sixteen yet and was forced to raise her two young brothers by herself. Since they didn't even know what might happen to them, I'm surprised they were able to stick together. My grandmother pretended she was the mother and took care of her two bothers. Maybe that is why I've been a fighter through all of this. I never did have any kids myself. That could be hereditary also if you believe everything is hereditary can account for everything.

One thing I noticed about writing this book is that our family is very different when compared to others. One of the first things we learned right away was to not help each other and to pretty much fend for ourselves -- if you could leave the room, for instance, you did it as soon as possible. This was almost like a wild animal trying to survive on its own.

When I try to explain this to people they look at me almost like I'm from another planet. "How can a family do that?" is something similar I've heard a lot. You could live on the same street that my kind of family lived on, and never even be aware of it. How well do you know your family, friends, and neighbors? Believe me, the guy walking down the street could be having the same problems I encountered and you would never know it.

People can be really good at fooling you. On the outside they look like normal people living normal lives, but once you step inside their lives or homes, you realize they are nothing like what you thought. It is like a 180 degree opposite of the one you just took.

The Bible, says to start out in your own Jerusalem, meaning in your own neighborhood -- you never know ho or what you will encounter. I would encourage everyone reading this book to make a friend of the guy next door, learn who they are and try to help them. Even just listening could be enough. You will never know until you at least try and...

...learn how BEING RAISED UP really makes a difference in every type of abuse, especially physical, emotional and SPIRITUAL situations.

# Would you like to see your manuscript become a book?

If you are interested in becoming a PublishAmerica author, please submit your manuscript for possible publication to us at:

**acquisitions@publishamerica.com**

You may also mail in your manuscript to:

**PublishAmerica
PO Box 151
Frederick, MD 21705**

# www.publishamerica.com

CPSIA information can be obtained at www.ICGtesting.com
Printed in the USA
238290LV00002B/8/P